Fit to Eat

Wholesome, Nutritious & Economical Recipes for Active People

Ann Budge

Hurtig Publishers
Edmonton

Copyright © 1986 by Ann Budge

Hurtig Publishers Ltd.
10560-105 Street
Edmonton, Alberta
Canada T5H 2W7

Canadian Cataloguing in Publication Data

Main entry under title:

Fit to Eat

Originally published: Vanier, Ont. : Canadian
 Orienteering Federation, 1983.
Includes index.
ISBN 0-88830-291-6

1. Cookery.   I. Budge, Ann, 1937-
TX715.F57 1986   641.5   C85-091514-7

I dedicate this book to my daughter
Susan, a member of the Canadian
Orienteering team from 1976 to 1984, who
was my inspiration in putting together *Fit
To Eat*, and to active people everywhere
who care about what
they eat.

Edited by Nancy Marcotte
Designed by David Shaw/Bookends East
Composed by Accurate Typesetting Ltd.
Printed and bound in Canada
by Friesen Printers

Contents

Thanks & Appreciation

Many people have helped to make *Fit To Eat* a reality, and I would like to thank every one of them.

The production costs of the first edition in 1983 were funded entirely by a generous donation from Nabisco Brands Ltd to the Canadian Orienteering Federation. Proceeds from the sale of that edition went into the Nabisco Brands Fund for Elite Orienteers for special medical and coaching needs. This trust fund is administered by the Canadian Orienteering Federation. We are grateful to Nabisco Brands for this contribution to orienteering.

A number of people assisted in one way or another with the first edition. Special thanks are owed to John Denison of The Boston Mills Press, who gave invaluable professional advice and assistance with the preparation of *Fit To Eat*. I am grateful to my daughter Susan, who designed the illustrations in the original edition. The support, assistance, and interest of Barb Pearson, Steve Pearson, Lynda Sidney, Sheila Smith, Julie DePass, Colin Kirk, and Susan Budge made production much easier for me.

The first edition of *Fit To Eat* was well reviewed and received and we felt it should continue to be available to active Canadians who care about what they eat. We approached Hurtig Publishers, and they enthusiastically agreed to publish this revised and enlarged edition. Hurtig Publishers' editor-in-chief, Elizabeth Munroe, was always willing to answer my queries no matter how basic and to give supportive advice. Nancy Marcotte edited the book beautifully and her enthusiasm was much appreciated.

Margot Videki typed the revised manuscript in a most expert manner. Frank Farfan advised me on many matters. Margaret Hedley was enthusiastic about *Fit To Eat* and we were pleased to have her write the valuable "Nutritional Notes." Mark Smith and Colin Kirk added information on orienteering. For their assistance, I thank them all.

I must not forget my husband, Don; our daughters, Heather and Susan; our son-in-law, Ian; and numerous house guests who endured many culinary experiments.

Sincere thanks go to those who took time to submit recipes and, to those who have purchased *Fit To Eat*.

Putting together *Fit To Eat* will always be a most memorable and rewarding experience for me — a labour of love, most definitely. I sincerely hope you enjoy it!

Ann Budge

About This Book

Fit To Eat is a collection of wholesome recipes from the author's kitchen, as well as from the recipe boxes of a number of Canadian orienteers of all ages from coast to coast. Like most physically active people, orienteers are nutrition-conscious because of their strong desire to be healthy in order to maintain their energetic lifestyles. This book gives other active people a chance to try some orienteers' delicious and nutritious favourites.

Fit To Eat provides a *moderate* approach to good nutrition. The recipes are wholesome, inspiring, economical, and generally easy to prepare; they appeal to both novice and experienced cooks, whether they are preparing food for growing children, athletes in training, or "armchair" athletes. The first edition of *Fit To Eat* was especially popular with university students and other young people cooking for themselves for the first time.

Many family favourites can be found in the meat and other main-dish sections. These have a special appeal for those looking for a new approach to tonight's dinner, and they could become *your* family's favourites!

Hikers and cross-country skiers are attracted to the "Trail Foods" section for suggestions for good sustaining foods to go into their backpacks. These and other recipes throughout the book are ideal for family picnic baskets on those weekend outings.

Athletes on intensive training programmes will enjoy the hearty recipes in the sections containing breads, muffins, and desserts. These foods help to provide that extra spurt of energy so necessary for top performance. Less active people who are watching their weight may focus more on the sections containing soups and salads.

The "Day Starters" section will help to eliminate the "breakfast blahs" and get you off to a quick start in the morning even if you think you "don't have time." The "Light Lunches and Snacks" section has nutritious ideas for light meals and between-meal treats for children as well as for adults.

Fit To Eat contains recipes for some of those newly-popular foods such as tofu, bulgur, legumes, and yogurt. Try making your own pita bread, crackers, soft pretzels, falafels, pizza dough, muffin mix, and sour dough starter from these home-tested recipes. We dare you to try such unusual recipes as Creamed Stinging Nettles, Carrot Marmalade, Spaghetti Squash au Gratin, and Raspberry Vinegar!

The Story of *Fit to Eat*

Fit to Eat was born during the summer of 1981. One rainy day my daughter Susan and I were sitting at our old pine kitchen table in our home in the Caledon Hills of Ontario. I was sharing with her a number of nutritious recipes I had tried while she was in Europe training for the upcoming World Orienteering Championships in Switzerland. As a young woman of twenty years competing in what is said to be one of the most physically demanding sports in the world, she needed a highly nutritious diet.

Realizing how difficult it is to keep all these recipes in good order, we looked at each other and said, "Why don't we put together a cookbook? Great idea! It can be a fund-raiser for the National Team!"

That was four and a half years ago, and *Fit to Eat* has been an on-going project ever since. We collected recipes, raised money through the kindness of Nabisco Brands Ltd, and with the help of a number of people, particularly John Denison of The Boston Mills Press, the first edition of *Fit to Eat* became a reality in August 1983. The Nabisco Brands Fund for Elite Orienteers was born and has helped finance important medical and coaching needs for Canada's top orienteers.

That first edition was published by the Canadian Orienteering Federation with Nabisco Brands Ltd's donation. The two thousand copies sold within the first year. Another one thousand copies were printed because there were unfilled orders. Instead of withdrawing money from the interest-making Nabisco Brands Fund for yet another printing, we decided to approach a publisher. Mel Hurtig, the first publisher we approached because of his interest in things Canadian and his appreciation of the out-of-doors, agreed immediately to publish *Fit to Eat*. We are most grateful for his support. The book has been revised and enlarged with a great many new recipes.

While this second edition of *Fit to Eat* is not a fund-raiser for the orienteering team, we hope it is helping to spread the word about this excellent outdoor sport and to provide assistance to active people in planning what they will eat today and every day!

Nutritional Notes

The recipes in this cookbook reflect many of the food and nutritional interests of orienteers, who are active and busy people. The foods are quick and easy to prepare; nourishing and flavourful to eat; yet include foods which are readily available and relatively inexpensive. These characteristics appeal to all people who enjoy eating good foods and are concerned about their health, yet too busy to spend a great deal of time in the kitchen.

Many of the recipes contain whole grains, dried legumes, and fresh fruits and vegetables. Ingredients such as sugar, salt, and fat are minimized. These follow the Nutrition Recommendations for Canadians that were developed by Health and Welfare Canada to help us maintain and improve our health. The recommendations apply to athletes in training as well as to less active Canadians. Recipes also contain lean meats, fish, and poultry and milk products to include a balance from all four of the food groups in Canada's Food Guide (see next page). Selecting a variety of foods from each of the food groups will help you and your family to meet all of your nutritional needs.

Although physically active people have nutritional requirements similar to the average person, they do have an increased need for food energy, or calories, and several of the B complex vitamins that are involved in producing energy. The amount of energy you or any member of your family need depends on body size, stage of growth, and daily physical activity. Your energy requirement can best be assessed by whether there is a change in your weight or amount of body fat. If you are gaining fat, your energy intake is higher than you need. Weight loss occurs when energy intake is below your requirement. That means that you are using some of your fat to provide energy for your activity. Too rapid weight loss (more than 2 pounds or 1 kilogram per week) usually includes loss of muscle with the fat. This could lead to decreased athletic performance or just feeling tired.

With most active people, including children, the appetite increases with increased activity to help meet the increased energy requirement. The extra foods eaten also provide the extra needed B vitamins if they are wholesome foods containing complex carbohydrates, such as breads, pastas, legumes, and cereal products. These foods provide energy and some protein without extra fat — a desirable combination for active people.

Fluids are particularly important to people taking part in physical activities such as orienteering, hiking, jogging, and even

Variety

Choose different kinds of foods from within each group in appropriate numbers of servings and portion sizes.

Energy Balance

Needs vary with age, sex and activity. Balance energy intake from foods with energy output from physical activity to control weight. Foods selected according to the Guide can supply 4000 – 6000 kJ

(kilojoules) (1000 – 1400 kilocalories). For additional energy, increase the number and size of servings from the various food groups and/or add other foods.

Moderation

Select and prepare foods with limited amounts of fat, sugar and salt. If alcohol is consumed, use limited amounts.

milk and milk products

Children up to 11 years	2-3 servings
Adolescents	3-4 servings
Pregnant and nursing women	3-4 servings
Adults	2 servings

Skim, 2%, whole, buttermilk, reconstituted dry or evaporated milk may be used as a beverage or as the main ingredient in other foods. Cheese may also be chosen.

Some examples of one serving
250 mL (1 cup) milk
175 mL (¾ cup) yoghurt
45 g (1½ ounces) cheddar or process cheese

In addition, a supplement of vitamin D is recommended when milk is consumed which does not contain added vitamin D.

meat, fish, poultry and alternates
2 servings

Some examples of one serving
60 to 90 g (2–3 ounces) cooked lean meat, fish, poultry or liver
60 mL (4 tablespoons) peanut butter
250 mL (1 cup) cooked dried peas, beans or lentils
125 mL (½ cup) nuts or seeds
60 g (2 ounces) cheddar cheese
125 mL (½ cup) cottage cheese
2 eggs

breads and cereals
3-5 servings

whole grain or enriched. Whole grain products are recommended.

Some examples of one serving
1 slice bread
125 mL (½ cup) cooked cereal
175 mL (¾ cup) ready-to-eat cereal
1 roll or muffin
125 to 175 mL (½ – ¾ cup) cooked rice, macaroni, spaghetti or noodles
½ hamburger or wiener bun

fruits and vegetables
4-5 servings

Include at least two vegetables.

Choose a variety of both vegetables and fruits — cooked, raw or their juices. Include yellow, green or green leafy vegetables.

Some examples of one serving
125 mL (½ cup) vegetables or fruits – fresh, frozen or canned
125 mL (½ cup) juice – fresh, frozen or canned
1 medium-sized potato, carrot, tomato, peach, apple, orange or banana

swimming. Drinking cold tap water or more interesting beverages will prevent tiredness due to dehydration. The "Drinks" section of this cookbook has some new ideas for providing those much-needed fluids.

Less active people can eat most of the same foods as athletes, but in smaller amounts to prevent gaining fat. People trying to lose weight will want to limit their choices from the high energy "Trail Foods," "Cookies and Squares," "Cakes," and "Puddings and Other Desserts" Sections. They should choose recipes that are lower in energy or calories. These recipes contain smaller amounts of fat and sugar. If you can't resist some of those richer recipes, try a smaller serving size. Many of the soups and main dishes are high in nutrients without extra calories and thus are ideally suited to a weight-loss program.

Canada's Food Guide is an excellent basis for selecting foods for all ages, whatever your activity level. The more active people can make more selections from the food groups, especially the bread and cereal group, or have larger servings. Many physically active people find that three large meals are not suitable for their lifestyles. More frequent lighter meals or snacks, chosen wisely from Canada's Food Guide, seem to satisfy appetites better without that "stuffed" feeling that can occur after a large meal.

Everyone hears about special diet plans and nutritional products. Athletes are especially receptive to these ideas so they can gain an advantage over their competitors. For many of these schemes and products, the advantage is psychological rather than physical. There is often no sound scientific research to support the claims of the products. Some may even have negative effects on your performance. If you require further nutrition advice on this or related issues, consult a qualified nutrition professional. Qualified nutrition professionals can be located through your local or provincial public health department or your provincial dietetic association.

Margaret Hedley, M.Sc., R.P.Dt.
Nutrition Education Consultant

Baking Hints

During many years of cooking for a family and in compiling *Fit to Eat*, I have come across a number of helpful hints that I would like to pass along.

- To make butter or margarine cream more easily, first rinse your bowl and beaters with hot water.
- Roast nuts for a few minutes before adding to a recipe. Roasted nuts have more flavour.
- Daphne Tomblin says she substitutes soy nuts for the nuts called for in most recipes. They are tasty, nutritious, and so much less expensive.
- Remember to grease the *tops* of muffin pans; the muffins will be easier to remove should they run over the top.
- Yeast dough rises well in the oven of an electric stove with the inside oven light on. The bulb provides just the right amount of heat (85°F). If you feel it is not warm enough, switch the oven element on for 30 seconds or so every once in a while, particularly to warm the oven at the beginning.
- The addition of cornmeal is said to enhance the texture of breads, muffins, and cookies. The rule of thumb is 1 part cornmeal to 3 parts all-purpose flour.
- To eliminate many empty (non-nutritional) calories in muffins and fruit breads, cut the amount of sugar down drastically. This has some effect on the texture and appearance of the final product, but not significantly enough to eliminate the practice, if you don't mind the change in texture.
- Researchers in the United States have concluded that the addition of the followng ingredients, *in the proportions given,* will greatly enhance the nutritional value of bread. It is called the *Cornell Triple Rich Mixture,* and is courtesy of Jeanette and Clive McCay's *Cornell Bread Book.*

    Per cup of flour, add 1 tbsp. soy flour, 1 tbsp. skim milk powder, and 1 tsp. wheat germ.

- In *yeast bread* baking, to enhance flavour and nutrition, specialty flours may be substituted for part of the all-purpose flour. The substitution ratios are given below:

    whole-wheat flour 1:1 all-purpose flour
    oat flour 1:3 all-purpose flour
    medium rye flour 2:1 all-purpose flour
    dark rye flour 1:1 all-purpose flour
    soy flour 1:5 all-purpose flour

    Example: For a recipe calling for 6 cups of all-purpose flour, use 1 cup of soy flour and 5 cups of all-purpose flour (a 1:5 ratio); or use 3 cups of dark rye flour and 3 cups of all-purpose flour (a 1:1 ratio).

Add the specialty flours first when mixing the dough. Then incorporate the all-purpose flour gradually.

- In muffin and quick-bread (non-yeast) recipes, the following more nutritious substitutions may be made. The taste and texture will change somewhat, but experimenting can be interesting. For 1 cup of all-purpose flour, substitute the following:

  $^7/_8$ **cup whole-wheat flour**
  $^3/_4$ **cup whole-wheat flour and** $^1/_4$ **cup bran**
  $^2/_3$ **cup whole-wheat flour and** $^1/_3$ **cup wheat germ**
  1 cup unbleached flour
  $^7/_8$ **cup cracked wheat flour**
  $1^1/_4$ **cups light rye flour**

- Cookies, muffins, squares, and cakes are less likely to stick to the pan if it is greased with vegetable shortening instead of butter or vegetable oil.
- When freezing casseroles, remember that the flavours of garlic and green pepper intensify, while the flavour of onion becomes less strong.
- Take advantage of reduced prices on overripe bananas at the grocery store; they may be mashed and frozen in portions to fit your favourite recipes, or they may be frozen whole in their skins. When thawed, the bananas will be very mushy, but they will be just fine for adding to recipes.

What Is Orienteering?

Orienteering, or more simply *map-running*, is an exhilarating outdoor sport. It combines the physical challenge of cross-country running or hiking with the mental challenge of map-reading.

Imagine yourself jogging along a well-worn trail in the midst of a large, leafy forest. You are looking for a small knoll just to the west of a pond. After passing a stream junction and heading downhill for a short while, you spot the two boulders in the clearing that indicate that you are getting close. Checking the map carefully now, you slow down and look for the little-used path on the right that leads to the knoll. Another twenty metres and . . . there it is — the marker you've been looking for! Quickly you punch in, look at your map, and head off for the next marker. You are orienteering!

The ideal playing field for such orienteering adventures is rolling hills in open, hardwood forests with little undergrowth.

Placed throughout the area are small orange and white markers with which courses of varying length and difficulty are designated. For example, a typical beginner's course might involve visiting eight to twelve markers on a two- to three-kilometre course. The advanced orienteer has twice as many points to locate during a six- to eleven-kilometre course.

The locations of the markers for the chosen course are indicated on a specially-produced, rather detailed topographic map carried by the participant. By reading terrain features such as hills, valleys, fields, streams, and boulders, as well as paths and fences, the orienteer is able to choose and follow a route from one marker to the next.

The route chosen by the orienteer is the one he or she thinks will be the fastest, least tiring, and/or surest. For example, a physically strong orienteer may choose the most direct route, which might lead up and over a hill. A particularly swift runner, however, may decide on a longer round-about trail that avoids the climb. On the other hand, an experienced navigator may decide on an intricate route that avoids the difficult climb up the hill, and is shorter than a run on the trail. *The choice of routes belongs to the orienteer; this is the appeal and uniqueness of the sport.* Finding the balance between one's map-reading skill and one's speed through the terrain is the key to success. On occasion a slow jog and careful map-reading will produce a winning time!

Orienteering appeals to active, outdoor people of all ages. Courses for beginners and children allow them to follow paths, fences, and other "handrails" to get from point to point. Intermediate level participants leave the obvious pathways from time to time and rely on an understanding of natural features such as clearings, forest boundaries, and general terrain relief indicated on the map by contour lines to locate their markers. Advanced level orienteers have challenging route choice problems to solve while moving through all sorts of terrain. Courses for all levels are generally completed in times ranging from forty to ninety minutes.

If you enjoy challenging outdoor activities and have not tried orienteering, why not contact an orienteering club or association in your area? Orienteering may be the sport for you! Try it! Be in it for LIFE!

Mark Smith, B.P.E., B.Ed.
Orienteering Consultant
President
Chrismar Mapping Services

Development of Orienteering in Canada

Although for centuries Canadians have been concerned with finding their way through wilderness terrain, orienteering was first introduced to Canada as an organized sport in the mid-1960s. The Canadian Orienteering Federation was formed by orienteers from Nova Scotia, Ontario, and Quebec in 1968. By 1974, there were provincial associations across the land and in the Yukon, each with many enthusiastic and active members.

The young Federation wasted little time in arranging its first Canadian Championships in August 1968 in the Gatineau Park near Ottawa. One hundred and sixty participated. The championships, held each year since, now move from province to province, with as many as five hundred competitors in recent years.

On the international scene, a Canadian National men's team first competed in the 1972 World Orienteering Championships in Czechoslovakia. Denmark hosted the 1974 event and four-member Canadian teams competed in both the men's and women's events. Full representation has continued at all biennial World Championships. Canada's best international results are yet to come as we are a relatively new nation in the orienteering world and have yet to break the dominance of Norway, Sweden, and Finland in this challenging sport.

World Championships were held for the first time in 1983 in Finland for Masters orienteers, those aged thirty-five years and older. While there is not yet a World Junior Championship, Canada is represented by Junior teams each year in the top international meets in Europe, giving promising youngsters valuable international experience.

Ski-Orienteering (on cross-country skis) is now growing in popularity in Canada, and the first Canadian Championships were held in February 1985 in Alberta with 180 competitors. Canada was represented at the second biennial World Ski-Orienteering Championships in 1984 in Italy. Watch for Ski-Orienteering to be included in the 1992 Winter Olympics if they are awarded to a Ski-Orienteering Nation.

In Scandinavia, orienteering is a very popular sport on equal footing with hockey, soccer, and cross-country skiing. The annual Swedish *5-day O-Ringen* event attracts as many as twenty-five thousand daily participants, and from a participation standpoint is the largest sporting event in the world. By comparison, North America's largest event was the Quebec *O-Ringen* with eleven hundred competitors!

As more and more Canadians search for a rewarding outdoor activity, we are confident orienteering will continue to grow here. With an abundance of beautiful wilderness to enjoy in this country, few sports are more suited to Canada than orienteering. Today, the Canadian Orienteering Federation has fifteen hundred full-fleged, active members from coast to coast, ranging in age from eight to eighty years. There are also hundreds of non-member participants enjoying orienteering events and thousands of school children participating in school programmes developed in several provinces.

In 1975 the Canadian Orienteering Federation was accepted into the National Sport and Recreation Centre in Ottawa where, in 1985, we have three full-time staff to serve our membership. If you would like any information about orienteering, or if we can be of other assistance, please contact the Canadian Orienteering Federation, 333 River Road, Vanier City, Ontario, K1L 8H9.

Colin Kirk
Executive Director
Canadian Orienteering Federation

Soups

Homemade Chicken Stock

A good stock is necessary for a great soup!

2 lb. chicken pieces (backs, necks, wings)
3 stalks celery with leaves, chopped
2 medium carrots, chopped
1 tsp. salt
¹/₄ tsp. pepper
6 cups water
1 large onion, cut into thirds
3 whole cloves

Insert a clove in each piece of onion. In a very large soup pot combine chicken, vegetables, seasonings, and water. Bring to a boil over high heat. Reduce heat, cover, and simmer about 1 hour, or until chicken is tender. Lift out chicken pieces. When cool, remove meat from bones and refrigerate or freeze for use later in chicken soup. Drain stock through a sieve. Refrigerate stock, then skim off fat when it has solidified. Use within a day or two, or freeze in 1-cup portions for later use.

Makes about 4¹/₂ cups of stock.

Homemade Beef Stock

A thrifty cook's trademark and the base of a good beef soup!

4 lb. meaty beef bones
3 onions, quartered
1½ cups celery leaves
4 sprigs parsley
1 tsp. salt
5 peppercorns
1 clove garlic, cup up
2 or 3 bay leaves
2 tsp. crushed dried thyme *or* basil
2½ qt. water

Making sure vegetables are well washed or scrubbed and using cut up vegetables if tops and peelings are not available, add two or three of the following:

1½ cups potato peelings
1½ cups carrot peelings
1½ cups turnip tops or peelings (Remove any wax coating.)
1½ cups parsnip tops or peelings
4 or 5 outer leaves of cabbage
¾ cup chopped green onion tops

Put all ingredients into a very large soup pot and bring to a boil. Cover and simmer over low heat 2½ to 3 hours. Remove bones and set aside. Strain stock and discard vegetables and herbs. Refrigerate stock, then skim off fat when it has solidified. Use stock within a few days or freeze in 1-cup portions. When bones are cool, remove meat from them. Discard bones and reserve meat for soups.

Makes 7 to 8 cups of stock.

Basic Vegetable Soup

Add just about any cooked vegetable to a seasoned white sauce. Some of our favourites are puréed cauliflower or broccoli, or mashed potatoes.

3 tbsp. margarine
3 tbsp. whole-wheat flour
$^1/_2$ onion, chopped
1 cup milk
salt, pepper, thyme, *or* other herbs
$^1/_2$ to $^3/_4$ cup mashed *or* puréed vegetables
grated cheese (optional)

Melt margarine, sauté onion, stir in flour, and cook 3 to 4 minutes over medium heat, stirring constantly. Slowly add milk while continuing to stir. Bring almost to the boiling point. Grated cheese may be added to make a cheese sauce base for the soup. Add cooked mashed or puréed vegetable(s) of your choice, heat through, and serve.

Makes 1 large or 2 small servings.

Terry Knight, Cambridge, Ont

Vegetable-Beef Soup

6 cups water
1 lb. *lean* ground beef
$^1/_3$ cup pot barley *or* rice
3 medium carrots, sliced
2 cups diced turnip
4 medium onions, diced
3 stalks celery, sliced
4 to 6 cups tomato juice *or* stewed tomatoes
$^1/_4$ tsp. salt
dash of ground pepper

Bring water to a boil. Add ground beef and barley or rice. Simmer 10 minutes.

Add vegetables. Bring back to a boil, cover, and simmer 20 minutes.

Add tomato juice or stewed tomatoes (the quantity depends on how thick you like your soup) and seasonings. Heat thoroughly.

Makes 10 servings.

Nancy Roy, Pierrefonds, Qué

3

Chicken Mulligatawny Soup

5 cups water
2 to 3 lb. chicken
½ cup diced onion
½ cup diced carrot
½ cup diced celery
1 apple, peeled and chopped
⅓ cup all-purpose flour

2 cloves garlic
1 tbsp. curry powder
½ tsp. freshly-ground nutmeg
2 cups stewed tomatoes
butter
vegetable oil

Cut chicken into 6 to 8 pieces. Bring water to a boil in a large saucepan. Add chicken and simmer for 1½ hours. Remove chicken pieces from saucepan and add tomatoes. Allow to cool.

Sauté vegetables, garlic, and apple in a mixture of butter and oil until tender. Sprinkle the curry powder and nutmeg into the vegetable mixture and cook gently for 3 to 4 minutes. Add flour and cook again for 2 to 3 minutes. Add vegetable mixture to chicken broth and tomatoes, then simmer gently for one hour.

Put mixture through a blender or food processor and return to pot. Remove chicken from bones and cut meat into bite-sized pieces. Add chicken to puréed vegetable mixture and reheat.

Makes 6 servings.

Mike Day, Ottawa, Ont

Egg Drop Soup

This recipe comes with kind permission from an excellent book, *The Athlete's Kitchen*, which is loaded with sound nutritional advice and excellent recipes. The author is Nancy Clark, M.S., R.D., a nutritionist from Boston, Massachusetts.

This is so easy . . . and low in calories. It makes a nice lunch, or an appetizer to a light dinner. By adding spinach leaves, broccoli, bean sprouts, or other vegetables, you can increase the nutritional value. Increase the portions according to how many you wish to feed.

1 cup chicken stock, homemade, canned, *or* from bouillon
1 egg
2 tsp. cornstarch mixed with a little cold water
dash of soy sauce

4

spinach leaves, chopped broccoli, chopped green pepper, bean
    sprouts, shredded Chinese cabbage, chopped scallions,
    and/or cooked rice (all optional)

Bring broth to a boil. Stir in cornstarch to slightly thicken the
broth. Meanwhile slightly beat the egg with soy sauce.

    Stir the boiling soup quickly. While it swirls, slowly add the
beaten egg. Remove from heat. Do not stir. Add the vegetables.
They will cook from the heat of the soup just enough to be
crunchy but warmed. Serve immediately.

Makes 1 serving.

Newfoundland Chowder

1 medium onion, chopped
2 cups boiling water
2 or 3 medium potatoes, diced
salt and pepper
2 cups whole milk
¼ lb. scallops
½ lb. fresh *or* frozen cod
¼ lb. fresh, canned *or* frozen shellfish: crab, lobster, *or* shrimp
1 small tin clams
1 or 2 oz. smoked cod *or* eel
cayenne pepper
Scrunchions (recipe follows)

In a large soup pot, melt 2 tbsp. salt pork fat. In the melted fat, sauté
the onion until soft but not brown. Add boiling water, salt, and
pepper, then diced potatoes. Cook until tender.

    Cut all the fish into 1-inch pieces and add to the pot. Simmer
until the cod and shrimp are opaque (not more than 7 minutes). Add
milk and bring to the boiling point. Serve with a very light sprinkling
of cayenne pepper, and top with scrunchions.

Serves 4.

Scrunchions: Cut ¼ lb. salt pork into very small bits, sauté until
crisp, and set aside to drain on paper towels. It's these scrunchions
that give the chowder the Newfoundland touch!

Peanut Butter Soup

3 cups chicken stock
¼ cup finely-chopped celery
¼ tsp. salt
1 small onion, finely chopped
2 tbsp. butter
½ cup peanut butter, smooth *or* chunky, salted *or* unsalted
1 cup milk
¼ cup all-purpose flour
¼ cup water
¼ cup finely chopped unsalted peanuts, for garnish

Combine stock, celery, salt, onion, butter, and peanut butter in an electric slow-cooking pot. Cover and cook on high for 2 to 3 hours. Add milk, then flour mixed with ¼ cup water. Cook on high for 15 minutes or until slightly thickened, stirring several times. Sprinkle peanuts over each serving.

Makes 4 servings.

Terry Knight, Cambridge, Ont

Three-Legume Soup

5 cups water
¼ cup green split peas
¼ cup yellow split peas
¼ cup baby lima beans
¼ cup pot barley
1 large onion, chopped finely
1 large potato, grated
2 large carrots, chopped
¼ cup chopped celery with leaves
celery salt and garlic salt

Wash and rinse well peas, beans, and barley. Bring 5 cups of water to a boil. Add peas, beans, and barley, and cook until soft. Leave to sit overnight. The next day add onion, potato, carrots, and celery. Simmer until vegetables are tender. Sprinkle with a little celery salt and garlic salt.

Serves 6.

Barb Pearson, Hamilton, Ont

French Onion Soup

This Québec favourite brings back to our family memories of St. Sauveur des Monts, the Laurentian mountain village near where we used to live. French Onion Soup is perfect after a day of skiing.

¹/₃ **cup butter**
5 large onions, thinly sliced
¹/₂ **tsp. pepper**
1 cup grated Swiss cheese (or more if you wish)
3 cans beef consommé, diluted, *or* 3 bouillon cubes and 6 cups
    hot water
4 to 6 thick slices of French bread

Melt butter, add onions, and stir well. Cover the pot and simmer for 20 minutes. Edges of the onions should be browned *lightly.*

Add consommé or bouillon. Cover and simmer for half an hour. Taste for seasoning. This soup is best if allowed to sit for a day in the refrigerator at this point. Alternatively, it may be simmered all day in an electric slow crock cooker.

Put some grated cheese in the bottom of 4 to 6 ovenproof onion soup bowls. Ladle the soup on top, then put the bowls in 350°F oven to heat. When heated, toast the bread and lay a piece on top of each soup bowl. Sprinkle *generously* with grated Swiss cheese and allow it to melt and brown under the broiler.

Makes 4 to 6 servings.

Heather Budge, London, Ont

Lentil Soup

2 slices bacon, chopped
1 celery stalk
1 large carrot
½ medium onion
1 clove garlic, minced
8 cups ham, beef, *or* chicken stock
1 lb. dried red lentils
1 tomato, diced
1 bay leaf
1 tbsp. steak sauce
½ tsp. pepper
¼ tsp. salt
dried sausage *or* cooked ham, diced *or* sliced (optional)

Soak lentils overnight. Rinse and drain in the morning. Chop carrots, celery, and onion.

Fry bacon in a large pot until almost crisp. Add celery, carrots, onion, and garlic. Sauté until onion is transparent. Stir in stock, lentils, tomatoes, and bay leaf. Bring to a boil over high heat. Reduce heat and simmer about 1 hour.

Stir in remaining ingredients and heat through. For a thicker soup, increase the amount of vegetables.

Makes 6 to 8 servings.

Lentil and Lamb Soup

This soup is high in fibre and protein, hearty, and nutritious!

1 tbsp. vegetable oil
½ lb. lean lamb *or* leftover roast lamb
1 large onion
2 carrots
2 celery stalks
1 clove garlic, minced (optional)
1 tsp. to 1 tbsp. curry powder
¼ cup brown rice
1½ cups dried red lentils
8 cups lamb *or* chicken stock
1 bay leaf
salt and pepper

Dice onion, carrots, and celery. Chop lamb into very small cubes and sauté in oil in soup pot until lightly browned. Stir in curry powder. Add onion, carrot, celery, and optional garlic. Stir and cook until onion is transparent.

Rinse rice and add to vegetable mixture along with lentils, stock, bay leaf, salt, and pepper. Bring to a boil; simmer uncovered for 40 minutes. Remove bay leaf. Thin soup if necessary with additional stock or water.

Makes 8 servings.

Old-Time Pea Soup

A most satisfying, hearty winter soup. Wonderful after skiing, skating, or other outdoor activity.

12 cups water
2 cups dried split peas
1 ham bone (with a little meat)
1 small turnip
3 medium carrots
1 medium potato
1 medium onion
$^1/_3$ cup chopped celery leaves
$^1/_2$ to 1 tsp. salt
$^1/_4$ tsp. freshly-ground pepper

Dice turnip, carrots, potato, and onion. Combine peas and 10 cups of water in a large soup pot. Bring quickly to a boil. Boil 2 minutes, then turn heat off and let sit for 1 hour. Meanwhile, place ham bone in 2 cups of water in another pot. Cover, bring to a boil, lower heat, and simmer 30 minutes. Remove bone and refrigerate liquid until fat forms on top. Skim off the fat, then add liquid and any bits of ham to the peas.

Now add vegetables and seasonings. Bring to a boil, reduce heat, and simmer 1 to $1^1/_2$ hours, until vegetables are tender. If a creamy texture is preferred, the soup may be puréed in a blender or food processor at this point.

Makes 10 servings.

Pasta E Fagioli

This is a hearty pasta and bean soup.

¹/₄ cup vegetable oil	¹/₄ cup chopped parsley
1 large onion	1 tsp. dried basil
2 cloves garlic, minced	5 cups beef stock
1 small green pepper	1 cup uncooked small pasta
2 stalks celery	(elbow macaroni *or* shells)
1 large carrot	1 15-oz. can kidney beans
1 15-oz. can Italian tomatoes	salt and pepper

Chop vegetables finely. In a large saucepan, heat oil, add vegetables and garlic, and cook 10 minutes over medium heat. Add tomatoes, parsley, basil, and stock. Simmer 15 minutes. Bring to a full boil, then add pasta. Cook until tender. Add beans, then salt and pepper to taste, and heat.

Makes 8 large servings.

Jenny Birchell, Hamilton, Ont

So-Simple Soup

This simple-to-make soup may be prepared with many different vegetables or combinations thereof. It may be served hot or cold (although you may prefer it hot with certain vegetables). The recipe here calls for broccoli, but it is equally good with cauliflower, potatoes, leeks (white part only), asparagus or spinach. The yogurt garnish gives a tangy taste.

1 bunch fresh broccoli	pinch of thyme *or* dill weed
2 cups homemade chicken stock	salt and pepper
1 small onion	plain yogurt, for garnish
milk	

Wash and cut up broccoli. Place in a saucepan and add enough chicken stock to cover the broccoli. Slice and add the onion. Bring to a boil, reduce heat, and simmer until broccoli is tender.

Purée in blender, food mill, or food processor. Return mixture to pot and thin with milk to desired consistency. Add thyme or dill and salt and pepper. Heat, but *do not boil*, for about 10 minutes, stirring occasionally. Ladle into bowls (or chill) and top with a spoonful of yogurt.

Makes 2 to 3 servings.

Carrot Soup

A nutritious soup that's a change from the ordinary.

¹/₄ **cup butter**
¹/₂ **cup chopped onion**
2 cups thinly-sliced carrots
3 cups vegetable *or* **chicken stock**
¹/₄ **cup white** *or* **brown long-grain rice**
¹/₂ **tsp. salt**
2 cups milk

In a medium saucepan, sauté onions in butter until golden. Add carrots and toss until coated with butter. Add stock and rice. Cover and simmer until carrots and rice are cooked. Add salt. Put one-third of soup at a time into a blender or food processor and blend until smooth. Return to saucepan, add milk, and heat.

Makes six 9-oz. servings

Terry Knight, Cambridge, Ont

Parsnip Soup

This easily-prepared soup is delicate in colour but full in flavour.

6 cups chicken stock
1 stalk celery with strings removed
2 medium onions
8 medium parsnips
salt and freshly-ground pepper
$\frac{1}{4}$ tsp. grated nutmeg
$\frac{1}{2}$ tsp. coarsely-grated orange rind
6 tbsp. chopped fresh parsley
6 tbsp. yogurt

Slice celery and onions coarsely and add to stock in a large saucepan. Peel and chop parsnips, then add to stock. Cover and bring to a boil; reduce heat and simmer about 30 minutes or until vegetables are soft.

Purée soup in a blender, food mill, or food processor and add to saucepan. Thin with a little milk if necessary. Add seasonings and bring to a simmer.

Serve in soup bowls. Sprinkle 1 tbsp. of parsley over each bowl and add one tbsp. of yogurt.

Makes 6 servings.

Corn Chowder

Great after a winter's day outdoors!

6 slices of bacon
2 tbsp. finely-chopped onion
2 cups fresh *or* frozen corn kernels
2 tbsp. butter

2 tbsp. flour
4 cups milk
$\frac{1}{2}$ tsp. salt
$\frac{1}{2}$ tsp. pepper
dash of curry powder

Dice bacon and fry until crisp. Add onions along with curry powder, then sauté until onions are soft. Put corn through a food chopper or chop finely in a food processor and add to bacon pieces and onions, then cook until corn begins to brown. Add butter, then flour. Stir well. Cook slowly 3 minutes. Stir in 2 cups milk, salt, and pepper, then cook until thickened. Add 2 additional cups of milk and heat until smooth.

Serves 6.

Hearty Potato Chowder

4 cups diced potatoes	½ cup all-purpose flour
½ cup chopped onion	½ tsp. salt
1 tbsp. vegetable oil	dash of black pepper
4 tsp. butter	4 cups milk

Boil potatoes until tender in just enough water to cover them. Set aside. Meanwhile sauté onions in vegetable oil. Melt butter over low heat. Blend in flour, salt, and pepper, then slowly add milk. Stir constantly until mixture thickens. When it bubbles, remove from heat and add undrained potatoes. Add sautéed onions. Simmer a few more minutes.

Serves 6.

Variation: 2 cups cooked corn, 3 cans minced clams, or 2 cups cooked mixed vegetables may be substituted for potatoes.

Barb Pearson, Hamilton, Ont

Irish Soup

A delicately-flavoured green soup.

4 tbsp. butter
1 large onion
2 leeks (white part only)
2 large potatoes
3 to 4 cups chopped fresh spinach, well washed
5 to 6 cups chicken stock
salt and pepper
grated Parmesan cheese

Chop onion, leeks, and potatoes. Gently sauté onions and leeks in butter in a heavy saucepan about 10 minutes. Add potatoes and cook 5 more minutes. Add spinach and stock. Cook uncovered until potatoes are tender. Allow to cool.

Purée soup in a food mill, food processor, or blender. Add salt and pepper. Thin with milk if soup is too thick. Heat gently. Ladle into bowls and sprinkle with grated Parmesan cheese.

Makes 6 servings.

Nippy Cheese Soup

Hearty and delicious!

3 tbsp. butter
1 onion, diced
2 cloves garlic, minced
1 cup chicken stock
2 cups skim milk
1 cup mashed potatoes, without lumps
1 cup extra old Cheddar cheese, grated
1 tsp. Dijon mustard
$^1/_8$ to $^1/_4$ tsp. Tabasco sauce

In a heavy-bottomed pot, melt butter and sauté onions until soft. Add garlic and sauté for several minutes. Add chicken stock, milk, and mashed potatoes, then stir over medium heat until very smooth. Simmer for about 5 minutes. Reduce heat, then while stirring gradually add the grated cheese, Tabasco sauce, and Dijon mustard. Continue to stir gently until the cheese has melted.

Serves 4

Turnip Soup

This hearty soup is sensational. A favourite at our house!

$1^1/_4$ cups water
1 large potato
3 cups diced yellow turnip
2 medium onions
2 tbsp. butter
salt and freshly-ground black pepper
2 to 3 cups milk
1 cup shredded extra old white Cheddar cheese
1 cup fresh *or* frozen peas
dill weed, for garnish

Peel potatoes and dice. Chop onions finely. Simmer potato and turnip in 1¼ cups of water for about 5 minutes. Drain, reserving liquid. Cook peas and set aside.

Heat butter in a heavy saucepan. Add onion, then salt and pepper to taste, and cook over medium heat until onion is soft, about 4 minutes. Add potato and turnip along with 1 cup of reserved cooking water. Simmer, covered, until vegetables are very tender, about 10 minutes.

Pour into a blender or food processor and process until smooth. Thin with milk. Return to saucepan and add cheese and peas. Heat over low heat and season to taste. Garnish with a sprinkling of dill and grated cheese.

Makes 6 servings.

Ann Budge, Belfountain, Ont

Low-Cal Cauliflower Soup

The recipe for this delicious, low-calorie cauliflower soup was given to us by Angela Hohban of Mississauga, Ontario. It was served to the organizing committee of the North American Orienteering Championships in 1982. They loved it!

¼ **cup chopped onion**
½ **cup diced celery**
1 small clove garlic, minced
1 tbsp. butter *or* **margarine**
2 chicken *or* **vegetable bouillon cubes, broken up**
4 cups chopped cooked cauliflower
4 cups unsalted water drained from cooked cauliflower
salt and pepper
dash of cayenne pepper

Sauté onion, celery, and garlic in butter for 5 minutes. Add water and bouillon cubes. Mix well. Bring to a boil. Cover and simmer over low heat for 30 minutes. Add cauliflower and heat thoroughly. Purée half of the soup in a blender or food processor, and add purée to remainder of soup. Add salt, pepper, and cayenne.

Serves 6. Only 38 calories to a 1-cup bowl.

Borscht

This soup may be served warm or chilled.

6 medium beets	2 tbsp. butter
1 medium onion	6 to 8 cups beef stock *or*
1 medium potato	boiling water
1 medium apple	1/2 cup lemon juice
2 medium carrots	1 tsp. dill weed
1/2 small cabbage	salt and pepper
3/4 lb. lean, tender beef	yogurt *or* sour cream,
1 tbsp. vegetable oil	for garnish

Peel all vegetables and apple, then grate medium coarsely. Slice beef *very* thinly.

Brown meat in vegetable oil in a large soup pot; remove meat and set aside on a paper towel to drain. Add butter, allow it to melt, then add beets, onion, potato, carrots, and apple. Cover pot and cook over low heat for 1 hour. Give it a good stir occasionally. Now add boiling stock or water, as well as cabbage, beef, lemon juice, and seasonings. Simmer soup for about 15 minutes. Test for seasonings. Serve warm with a dollop of yogurt or sour cream on each serving.

To serve chilled, refrigerate and skim off any solid fat which forms on the surface. Spoon into bowls and top with yogurt or sour cream.

Serves 8

Cantaloupe Soup

This cold soup makes a refreshing lunch on a hot summer's day.

1 cantaloupe (very ripe)
3 tbsp. lemon juice (preferably fresh)
1/2 tsp. grated fresh ginger root *or* a pinch of powdered ginger
1 cup unflavoured yogurt (skim milk yogurt is fine)
2 to 3 fresh mint leaves, for garnish

Remove seeds from cantaloupe and spoon the pulp from the rind. Place pulp in a blender or food processor and process to a purée. Add lemon juice, yogurt, and ginger, processing to combine well. Refrigerate until serving time. Sprinkle each bowl with chopped fresh mint.

Serves 4.

Meat/Beef

American Beef Pot Roast

Miles ahead of the usual pot roast! This recipe is adapted from a recipe that appeared in Helen Gougeon's *Original Canadian Cookbook*. Helen is a journalist and an authority on Canadian food.

4 to 5 lb. beef pot roast
½ tsp. salt
¼ tsp. pepper
1 clove garlic, cut in half
2 to 3 tbsp. vegetable oil
¾ cup water
1½ cups tomato juice *or* stewed tomatoes
4 tbsp. catsup
1 tbsp. Worcestershire sauce
3 small onions, diced
2 to 3 tbsp. brown sugar
½ tsp. dry mustard
3 tbsp. lemon juice
hot cooked noodles

Rub roast with salt, pepper, and garlic, then brown in hot vegetable oil. Add water, tomato juice or stewed tomatoes, catsup, Worcestershire sauce, onions, and garlic. Cover and cook over low heat for 1½ hours.

Combine remaining ingredients and pour over meat. Cover and continue cooking for 1 hour or until meat is tender.

Skim off fat from gravy, then slowly stir in 2 tbsp. flour mixed with 2 tbsp. of water. Simmer gently until slightly thickened. Serve with hot cooked noodles.

Serves 4 to 6.

From *Original Canadian Cookbook* © 1975 Helen Gougeon Schull, published by Tundra Books.

Grandma's Beef Stew with Dumplings

Long, slow cooking is the secret to a perfect stew. Grandma left it to simmer slowly all day on the back of the old wood stove. Dumplings add an old-time country touch. Stew is a practical dish as it can be prepared well ahead, even the day before; reheating it improves the flavour.

2 lb. lean beef
1 onion, sliced
4 cups hot liquid (any combination of water, beef stock, tomato
juice, *and/or* red wine)
6 large carrots, cut up
12 very small onions, peeled
12 very small potatoes, peeled
peas, green beans, cauliflower, diced turnip, *or* mushrooms
(optional)
thyme, Worcestershire sauce, *or* parsley (optional)

Cut beef into 1½-inch chunks. Sprinkle with salt and pepper, then dredge with flour. Pour 2 tbsp. vegetable oil into a deep heavy stew pot. Add the sliced onion and the beef. Brown beef well on all sides over high heat.

Reduce heat and pour hot liquid over meat. Bring to a boil. Cover and reduce heat to allow pot to barely simmer. Cook in this manner for 1½ hours. Skim off any fat that collects on the surface.

Add carrots and onions. Simmer slowly for ½ hour. Add potatoes and any other vegetables. Continue to simmer for another hour. Add any seasonings you wish, such as a pinch of thyme, a little Worcestershire sauce, or chopped parsley.

At this point there are 3 choices: serve as is, thicken the gravy, or top with dumplings! To thicken gravy, mix 2 tbsp. flour with ¼ cup cold water until smooth, and stir slowly into stew. Bring stew to boil and simmer for 3 minutes.

Serves 4 or 5.

Dumplings

1½ cups all-purpose flour   **¾ cup milk**
1 tbsp. baking powder   **½ tsp. salt**

Sift dry ingredients together. Slowly stir in milk. Mix until just blended. With stew simmering, drop batter by heaping tablespoons on top of bubbling stew. (There should not be too much gravy; it should cover the meat and vegetables but still allow the dumplings to rest on the meat and vegetables as they cook.) Cover the pot immediately and cook *without lifting cover* for 12 to 15 minutes or until dumplings are firm. A glass lid will let you peek through!

Makes about 8 dumplings.

Autumn Stew

This tasty stew cooks itself while you go off on a long autumn bike ride in the country! Serve it with cornbread and add a side helping of Brussels sprouts or green beans.

2½ lbs. stewing beef, cubed
1 tbsp. vegetable oil
1 large onion, chopped
2 cloves garlic, minced
5 tbsp. flour
½ tsp. *each* salt and pepper
2 cups apple cider *or* apple juice

2 tsp. rosemary
1 tbsp. cider vinegar
2 tsp. Dijon mustard
1 small turnip, diced
4 to 5 apples, peeled, cored, and thickly sliced

Place 1 tablespoon of oil in a heavy cast-iron oven-proof frying pan or casserole and place over medium heat. Add onions and garlic and sauté about 5 minutes, then remove with a slotted spoon and set aside.

Dredge beef in flour that has been mixed with salt and pepper. Add more oil to the frying pan if necessary and brown meat, half at a time, over medium-high heat. Remove beef and set aside with onions.

Pour apple cider or juice into pan and carefully scrape browned bits off the bottom of the pan. Mix mustard and vinegar, then add rosemary. Stir into liquid in pan, then add onions and beef. Add apples and turnip and mix well. Cover pan and bring to a boil. Now place pan in preheated 300°F oven and cook for at least 2 hours. If you are nearby, give it a stir now and then. Make sure beef is well cooked; it must be tender to a fork.

Makes 6 generous servings.

Beer Stew

A favourite recipe from a longtime friend, Lee Lindsay. This a wonderful make-ahead dish if you are entertaining after a day of orienteering, skiing, hiking, or whatever. Everybody loves this simple yet hearty casserole.

$3^{1}/_{2}$ lbs. lean stewing beef, cubed
3 tbsp. butter *or* vegetable oil
6 onions
1 cup well-seasoned beef bouillon
4 cups beer
2 tbsp. brown sugar
1 or 2 bay leaves
garlic powder
salt and pepper
thyme

Brown beef in $1^{1}/_{2}$ tbsp. oil or butter and set aside. Brown sliced onions in the same pan in remaining $1^{1}/_{2}$ tbsp. oil or butter. Add salt, pepper, and garlic powder to taste.

Arrange beef and onions in alternate layers in a casserole dish. Season every second layer with salt and pepper.

Heat bouillon in the same frying pan while scraping up the juices and browned bits. Add brown sugar and 1 or 2 bay leaves. Pour over meat and onions, then add enough beer to just cover. Sprinkle with thyme. Cook 2 to 3 hours in a slow oven (275°F to 300°F) until meat is tender.

This dish may be prepared in advance and refrigerated. Before reheating, remove any solidified fat from the top.

The gravy may be thickened with cornstarch or flour after cooking, but this is usually unnecessary. Serve with boiled or mashed potatoes or broad noodles. Mashed turnips are particularly delicious with this dish.

Serves 6.

Vegetable-Beef Stir Fry

This is best cooked in a wok, but a large covered frying pan will do.

1 lb. lean ground beef
3 tbsp. vegetable oil
$1/2$ cup finely-chopped onion
$1/2$ cup diagonally-sliced celery
1 medium carrot, as carrot curls
$1/4$ lb. fresh green beans, sliced lengthwise
1 small turnip, sliced as apples for a pie
6 large fresh mushrooms
$1/2$ cup chicken broth
1 tbsp. honey
$1/4$ cup soy sauce
1 tbsp. cornstarch
1 pkg. fresh spinach
3 cups hot cooked rice

To prepare carrot curls, peel carrot and cut into paper-thin strips with a potato peeler. Allow strips to curl and secure each with a toothpick until serving time. Place in a plastic bag in refrigerator.

Heat 1 tbsp. oil in a wok and brown beef. Remove beef and set aside on a paper towel to drain.

Pour remaining 2 tbsp. oil into wok. When hot, add onion, celery, carrot, beans, turnip, and mushrooms. Stir-fry for 2 minutes. Pour in broth and reduce heat. Cover and steam for 2 to 3 minutes. Stir occasionally.

Stir in honey, soy sauce, and cornstarch dissolved in 2 tbsp. water. Return meat to wok. Place spinach on top of meat and vegetables. Cover and steam for 1 minute. Uncover and stir spinach into sauce. Serve over hot rice.

Makes 4 to 6 servings.

Susan Budge, Waterloo, Ont

Herbed Meat and Spinach Loaf

This unique meat loaf, which is good served cold or hot, is an excellent picnic accompaniment; or pop a slice into your day-pack for lunch on the trail. The recipe comes from Betty Aldridge's Farm House Kitchen Cooking School in Tottenham, Ontario, and appeared in her weekly column in the *Caledon Citizen*. We appreciate permission to print it here.

3 lb. lean ground beef, pork, *and/or* veal
6 slices bacon, finely chopped
2 tbsp. butter
1 cup chopped onions
1 clove garlic, minced
2 cups packed chopped fresh spinach
1 tsp. dried basil
1 tsp. dried rosemary
1 tsp. fennel seeds

1 tsp. salt
$1/2$ tsp. pepper
$1/4$ cup chopped fresh parsley
2 eggs
1 cup soft bread-crumbs
$3/4$ cup milk
4 slices bacon
6 hard-cooked eggs
6 to 8 slices partially-cooked lean bacon

In a large bowl, combine ground meats and chopped bacon.

In large frying pan, melt butter and sauté onions and garlic until soft. Add spinach, basil, rosemary, and fennel; cook, stirring, 1 minute. Blend into meat mixture along with salt, pepper, parsley, eggs, bread-crumbs, and milk.

Arrange partially-cooked bacon slices on bottom of two 9 x 5-inch loaf pans. Pack one quarter of the meat mixture into each pan. Peel hard-cooked eggs and arrange whole eggs down centre of the meat. Cover with remaining meat mixture, pressing down lightly to seal eggs. Cover pans with foil and set in large deep baking pans. Fill pans with hot water to reach halfway up sides of loaf pans.

Bake at 350°F for $1 1/4$ hours. Pour off any accumulated fat. Let meat loaf sit for 5 minutes, then turn out onto serving plate. Slice and serve hot, or refrigerate and serve cold the following day, or take it along in a picnic basket! Nice with Dijon mustard or homemade chili sauce.

Should you wish to freeze this meat loaf, omit the hard-cooked eggs.

Makes 8 to 10 servings.

Green Pepper Steak

1 lb. sirloin tip steak
1 clove garlic (optional)
a little margarine
2 onions, sliced
2 green peppers, chopped
fresh mushrooms, sliced
Worcestershire sauce
pinch of salt

Slice steak into thin strips. Melt margarine in a frying pan.
Crush garlic and sauté in pan. Quickly fry meat until brown.
Add Worcestershire sauce and a little salt. Add onions and
peppers, and cook until soft. Add mushrooms and heat through.
Serve on a bed of hot white or brown rice.

Makes 3 servings.

Barb Pearson, Hamilton, Ont

Stir-Fried Rice

This recipe calls for fresh meat, but you could also use leftover
roast beef, pork, or chicken.

3 cups cooked rice
4 tbsp. vegetable oil
1½ cups beef, pork, *or* chicken, cut into thin strips
1 large onion, chopped
2 cloves garlic, minced
1 tsp. sugar
1 tsp. pepper
2 tbsp. soy sauce
1 cup leftover *or* frozen vegetables, such as corn, peas, *or* carrots
2 eggs, beaten

Heat 4 tbsp. vegetable oil in a large pot. Add meat, onion, garlic,
sugar, pepper, and soy sauce. Stir-fry until meat is tender, about
3 minutes. Add vegetables and rice and stir-fry about 5 minutes.
Just before serving, add beaten eggs. Stir eggs into rice mixture
until eggs are cooked. Serve hot.

Serves 4 or 5.

Jennifer Hamilton, Winnipeg, Man

Hawaiian Meat Loaf

Pineapple in meat loaf? Give it a try! This is a nice
subtly-flavoured loaf. The recipe makes one large or two small
loaves.

2 lbs. medium ground beef
2 eggs
1 14-oz. can crushed pineapple
¼ cup catsup *or* tomato sauce
2 tbsp. brown sugar
1½ tbsp. soy sauce
2 tsp. prepared mustard
¼ tsp. garlic salt
black pepper
1 onion
1 cup dry whole-wheat bread-crumbs
slices of pineapple and sprigs of parsley, for garnish

In a large bowl, whisk eggs. Drain pineapple well and add, along
with catsup, sugar, soy sauce, mustard, garlic salt, chopped
onion, and bread-crumbs. Work in meat with a fork or your
hands. Press into 1 large or 2 small greased loaf pans. Cover
loosely with foil and bake at 350°F for 1 hour. Remove foil and
pour off any accumulated fat. Continue baking for 30 to 40
minutes longer (less time if you have used 2 small pans). Let sit
5 minutes before turning out onto serving platter. Garnish with
slices of pineapple and sprigs of parsley.

Serves 6.

Gehoppeltes-Gepoppeltes

1 medium-sized cabbage	2 bay leaves
1 lb. lean ground beef	pepper and salt
5 to 6 potatoes	1 cup beef bouillon

Shred the cabbage and combine all ingredients in a pressure cooker.
Cook 8 to 10 minutes. Remove bay leaves. Mash together.
Serve with a fresh salad.

Serves 4 to 5.

Rena Weiler, Morin Heights, Qué

Stuffed Green Peppers

An excellent simple supper when green peppers are plentiful at harvest time.

6 medium-sized firm green peppers
1 lb. lean ground beef
1 small onion
2 cloves garlic
salt and pepper
2 cups stewed tomatoes
$\frac{1}{2}$ cup water
$\frac{1}{2}$ cup uncooked rice
2 tsp. Worcestershire sauce
$\frac{1}{2}$ tsp. dried thyme, marjoram, *or* chili powder
6 small round slices of cheese, for garnish

Slice stem end off each pepper, then remove seeds and membrane from inside, being careful not to cut through the pepper. Fill a large saucepan three-quarters full of water; bring to boil, then add peppers. Cook 4 to 5 minutes until peppers are bright green. Be careful not to overcook. Drain upside-down in a colander.

Brown meat in a large frying pan over medium heat. Meanwhile cut onions and garlic cloves into small pieces and add to meat. Continue to cook until onion is tender. When meat is brown, tip pan to one side. Spoon off any accumulated fat so the stuffed peppers will not be greasy. Season with salt and pepper. Add tomatoes, water, rice, Worcestershire sauce, and spice. Cover and cook over low heat for about 15 minutes or until rice is tender. Remove rice mixture from heat.

Stand peppers up in a greased baking dish that just holds all the peppers. Spoon rice mixture carefully into the peppers. Bake, uncovered, in a 350°F oven for 20 minutes. Top each pepper with a slice of cheese and heat 5 minutes longer.

Makes 6 servings.

Sweet and Sour Meatballs

This oven meatball preparation method is much simpler than the usual frying pan method.

2 lb. lean ground beef
1 cup fresh bread-crumbs
$1/4$ cup milk
1 egg, slightly beaten
1 medium onion, chopped finely
$1/2$ green pepper, chopped finely
1 clove garlic, minced
$1/2$ tsp. salt
$1/4$ tsp. pepper
$1^1/2$ tsp. soy sauce

Combine all ingredients. Shape into 1-inch balls and place in a shallow roasting pan. Bake at 375°F for about 40 minutes. Drain off fat.

Sauce

2 tbsp. cornstarch
$1/4$ cup cider vinegar
$1/2$ tsp. ginger
1 cup sliced celery
$1/2$ green pepper, sliced
$1/2$ cup soy sauce
$1/2$ cup water
$1/4$ cup firmly-packed brown sugar
1 $13^1/2$-oz. can pineapple tidbits with juice
$1/2$ cup canned water chestnuts, thinly sliced

In a large saucepan, blend cornstarch with vinegar until smooth. Add ginger, soy sauce, water, and brown sugar. Cook, stirring occasionally, until thickened.

Stir in pineapple (including juice), celery, water chestnuts, and green pepper. Add meatballs; simmer, stirring occasionally, for about 20 minutes. Serve with hot cooked rice.

Serves 6 to 8.

Shepherd's Pie

A family favourite for generations! There are many variations; this tasty one is a meal in one casserole. It can be prepared in the morning, refrigerated, and cooked at dinnertime. You may even go for a run or ride your exercise bicycle while it is in the oven!

2 cups cut-up peeled uncooked potatoes *or* leftover mashed
    potatoes
3 tbsp. potato cooking water *or* warm milk
2 tbsp. grated Parmesan cheese
2 eggs
1 lb. lean ground beef *or* 2 cups ground leftover roast beef
2 cups water
2 tbsp. all-purpose flour
2 tsp. Worcestershire sauce
1 beef bouillon cube, broken up
$^1/_2$ tsp. celery salt
2 tbsp. chopped onion
1$^1/_2$ cups frozen mixed vegetables *or* frozen corn kernels
1 cup sliced mushrooms (optional)
paprika

Cook potatoes until tender in lightly salted water, then drain, reserving 3 tbsp. cooking water. Mash with cooking water or warm milk. Beat eggs and Parmesan cheese into potatoes until fluffy. If using leftover mashed potatoes, add warm milk if potatoes are stiff, then beat in eggs and Parmesan cheese. Set potatoes aside.

Brown uncooked meat in a frying pan. Remove any fat, and set meat aside on paper towel to drain well.

Combine water, flour, Worcestershire sauce, bouillon cube (broken up), and celery salt; whisk until smooth. Pour mixture into frying pan. Add onions and cook over medium heat for 3 minutes. Add vegetables, bring to a boil, and cook 2 minutes. Add mushrooms and browned meat or ground leftover roast beef. Heat through.

Grease a 6-cup casserole and spoon in beef mixture. Top with potatoes and spread smoothly. Sprinkle with paprika. At this point casserole may be refrigerated. Bake at 375°F for 30 minutes (longer if casserole has been refrigerated) until potatoes are puffy and lightly browned and casserole is bubbly.

Makes 4 servings.

Tamale Supper Dish

A hearty supper dish for after a day in the out-of-doors.

1 cup cornmeal	1 green pepper
3 cups water	1 lb. lean ground beef
¹/₂ tsp. salt	¹/₂ tsp. chili powder
2 to 3 tbsp. vegetable oil	4 tomatoes
1 onion	

Bring water to a boil in a medium saucepan. Stir in salt. With water boiling, slowly but steadily add cornmeal while stirring constantly. Turn heat to low and cook for 10 minutes, stirring frequently. Set aside.

Heat vegetable oil in skillet. Chop onion and green pepper, and add to hot oil. Sauté until soft but not browned. Add beef and cook until all pink colour has disappeared. Stir in chili powder, then remove skillet from heat.

Grease a medium casserole and spread half the cornmeal mixture evenly over the bottom. Cover with two of the tomatoes, sliced. Add the meat mixture, then the remaining cornmeal, spreading evenly. Top with the remaining tomatoes, sliced. Bake at 375°F for about 25 minutes.

Makes 4 servings.

Beans, Beans, Beans, and Beef

This dish is particularly great for a crowd of teenagers after a cold-weather outdoor activity. It can be put together well ahead of time and "stretches" easily at the last minute with additional beans and tomatoes should more people than expected turn up!

This versatile recipe can also be made with dried beans that have been soaked and cooked.

1 lb. lean ground beef	¹/₃ cup vinegar (white *or* cider)
8 slices of bacon	2¹/₂ cups stewed tomatoes
2 onions, chopped	1 medium can kidney beans
1 green pepper, chopped	1 small can lima beans
1 clove garlic, halved	1 medium can baked beans
2 tbsp. molasses	1 tsp. Worcestershire sauce
2 tbsp. brown sugar	salt, pepper, and Tabasco sauce
1 tsp. dry mustard	

Fry bacon until crisp, remove from pan, and crumble. Brown beef and onion in bacon fat, then drain well.

Drain beans and mix together. Combine remaining ingredients and add to beans. Add beef, onion, and bacon. Bake uncovered in a large casserole 2 to 2½ hours at 300°F.

Delicious with coleslaw and corn bread.

Serves 8 to 10.

Ann Budge, Belfountain, Ont

Easy Deep Pizza

The biscuit-mix crust makes this simple to prepare — even for the novice cook!

3 cups commercially-prepared biscuit mix
¾ cup water
1 lb. ground beef
½ cup chopped onion
¼ tsp. salt
2 cloves garlic, minced
2 cups Quick Tomato Sauce (See page 41.)
1 tsp. oregano
½ cup sliced mushrooms
½ cup chopped green pepper
2 cups shredded Mozzarella cheese

Lightly grease a 15½ x 10½ x 1-inch jellyroll pan. Mix biscuit mix and water until soft dough forms. Gently form dough into a ball on a floured board. Knead 20 times. With floured hands, press and stretch dough over bottom and up sides of pan.

Cook and stir ground beef, onion, salt, and garlic until beef is brown; drain.

Mix tomato sauce and oregano. Spread evenly over dough.

Spoon beef mixture evenly over sauce. Top with mushrooms, green pepper, and cheese. Bake in a 425°F oven until crust is lightly brown, about 20 minutes.

Makes 8 servings.

Ron's Spaghetti Sauce (With or Without Meat)

Ron is well-known for the mound of spaghetti he can consume at one sitting! It provided him with lots of carbohydrates while he was a member of Canada's Orienteering Team from 1974 to 1985.

2 Spanish onions
1 or 2 cloves garlic
vegetable oil
2 28-oz. cans tomatoes
1 10-oz. can tomato soup
1 13-oz. can tomato paste
6 green peppers

¹/₂ celery stalk
salt, pepper, oregano, and
    Italian seasonings (optional)
ground beef (optional)
soya grits (optional)
carrots (optional)

Take a big pot and pour in a little vegetable oil to cover the bottom. Add water — about 3 cm deep. Cut up 2 Spanish onions, or equivalent of the little guys, into small pieces (dicing, optional). Fire up the old stove. (I send Denise out to get more wood!) Cut up one or two cloves of garlic. Toss the onions and garlic in and let the onions cook until they're soft.

Open two 28-oz. cans of tomatoes with a can opener or tomahawk, whichever is closest at hand. Dump in the tomatoes and chop into pieces with a big knife. Open a small can of tomato soup and one 13-oz. can of tomato paste. Mix these into the sauce. You might need a little H_2O. (That's technical talk for water.)

Now, chop up about 6 good-sized green peppers and half a celery stalk. Add these to the pot. I usually add a bunch of seasonings such as salt, pepper, oregano, and Italian seasonings. I don't put too much in because I don't like it tasting like a Mexican taco. Add the seasonings as to how *you* like it.

You can add whatever else you might like, such as ground beef (browned), soya grits, an old sautéed orienteering shoe, or whatever suits your fancy. You can even toss in carrots. Continue to cook this stuff for a couple of hours over low heat. (You can eat it whenever you're hungry, but the longer it cooks, the better it tastes.)

You can freeze this sauce; I make sure the iceman has just filled up the ice box before. Then when unexpected guests drop in, just thaw the sauce and serve on a mess of spaghetti. While this sauce may not arouse the palate of a Parisian chef, it may tickle your fancy.

Makes enough sauce for 4 heaping plates of spaghetti.

Ron Lowry, Hamilton, Ont

Lasagna

1 pkg. lasagna (8 to 10 noodles)
1 lb. lean ground beef
1 tbsp. minced onion
¼ cup chopped green pepper
3 7½-oz. cans tomato sauce
1 tsp. sugar
1 tsp. garlic salt
⅛ tsp. pepper

1 egg, beaten
½ tsp. oregano
2 cups cottage cheese
2 tsp. salt
1 tbsp. parsley
½ cup grated Parmesan cheese
½ lb. Mozzarella cheese

Cook noodles and drain well. Brown beef and pour off fat. Add tomato sauce, onion, green peppers, garlic, oregano, sugar, salt, and pepper. Simmer 10 minutes, stirring occasionally.

In a separate bowl mix cottage cheese, egg, parsley, and Parmesan cheese. Place a layer of noodles in the bottom of a greased 9 x 13-inch pan. Add layers of meat mixture, cheese mixture, and noodles, ending with meat mixture. Top with grated Mozzarella cheese. Bake at 350°F for 45 minutes. Let sit 5 minutes before cutting into squares.

Serves 6.

Sue Waddington, Hamilton, Ont

Macaroni-Beef Casserole

This is equally good with the spinach served separately.

1 lb. lean ground beef
1 large onion
1 19-oz. can tomatoes
1 5½-oz. can tomato paste
1 tsp. oregano

salt and pepper
3 to 4 cups cooked macaroni
½ pkg. fresh spinach
Parmesan cheese

Cook spinach, drain well, and chop. Chop onion. Sauté onion in a little oil. Add ground beef and brown. Drain off fat. Stir in tomato paste, tomatoes and juice, oregano, salt, and pepper. Simmer for 1 hour. Combine macaroni and spinach with the above sauce. Spoon into a casserole, sprinkle with Parmesan cheese, and bake for 30 minutes at 350°F.

Serves 5 or 6.

Barb Pearson, Hamilton, Ont

Ski-O Chili

Served traditionally following our annual New Year's
ski-orienteering competition for neighbours, friends, and family.

1 lb. lean bacon
1 large onion
½ cup chopped green pepper
1½ lb. lean ground beef
2 14-oz. cans kidney beans
1¼ cups stewed tomatoes
1 5½-oz. can tomato paste

4½ tsp. chili powder
½ tsp. salt
¼ tsp. cumin seeds
¼ tsp. oregano
⅛ tsp. sage
1 14-oz. can pineapple tidbits,
    drained (optional)

Chop bacon and slice onion. Fry bacon in a deep pan until pan is
well greased. Add onion and green pepper; cook and stir over
moderate heat for 5 minutes.

Remove pan from heat and cool 2 minutes. Add beef and
return to heat. Cook, stirring, until beef is lightly browned. Stir
in kidney beans, tomatoes, and tomato paste. Mix spices and add
along with optional pineapple. Pour into a greased 2½-quart
casserole. Cover casserole and bake at 250°F for 1 hour. Uncover
and bake 1 hour more.

Serves 6, but is easily doubled, tripled, quadrupled, and so on!

Nancy Roy, Pierrefonds, Qué

Moussaka

4 medium eggplants
salt
¾ cup butter, divided
2 large onions, chopped
2 cloves garlic, minced
1½ lb. ground beef *or* lamb
½ cup tomato sauce

salt and pepper
dash of nutmeg
½ cup all-purpose flour
4½ cups hot milk
3 egg yolks, well beaten
1¼ cups grated Parmesan cheese

Slice eggplants into ¼-inch slices. Sprinkle eggplant generously
with salt and let stand while preparing meat and milk sauce.
Sauté onion and garlic in 3 tbsp. butter; add beef and brown;
drain off some fat. Add tomato sauce, salt, and pepper; simmer
for 5 to 10 minutes. Set aside.

In a saucepan, melt remaining butter, then blend in flour.
Gradually add milk, stirring constantly; cook over low heat until
smooth and thickened. Add salt, pepper, and nutmeg to taste.

Add a small amount of the milk sauce to egg yolks and whisk into milk sauce. Cook an additional 2 minutes, stirring constantly; reserve.

Rinse eggplant and pat dry. Brown eggplant slices on both sides under broiler. Place 1/3 of the eggplant slices in a greased 9 x 13-inch baking pan; cover with half the beef mixture and sprinkle with 1/2 cup cheese. Repeat layering. Top with eggplant. Cover with milk sauce, sprinkle with the remaining cheese, and bake at 350°F for 1 hour.

Makes 6 to 8 servings.

Courtesy of The Ontario Milk Marketing Board

Keith's Tacos

Those of you who orienteer and who know Keith French have no doubt seen him tearing through the woods at break-neck speed! Could these tacos be his fuel? Or is it his other favourite, Oji San?

1 to 1 1/2 lb. lean ground beef
3 onions
2 cups tomato juice
1 cup catsup
1 to 2 tbsp. firmly-packed brown sugar
2 tbsp. vinegar
2 tbsp. Worcestershire sauce
1/2 tsp. salt
8 to 10 taco shells

Slice onions. Brown ground beef in a heavy pan with a cover. Stir in remaining ingredients and mix well. Cover and cook over low heat, stirring occasionally, for 2 1/2 hours or until mixture is thick. Long slow cooking is the secret.

Spoon mixture into heated taco shells. Add condiments such as shredded lettuce, chopped tomatoes, grated cheese, yogurt, or sour cream.

Makes enough to fill 8 to 10 taco shells generously.

Gwenn French, Hannon, Ont

Beef and Liver Loaf

This is a tricky way to serve liver to a liver-hating family!

¾ **lb. beef liver**
1¼ **lb. lean ground beef**
1 **cup oatmeal** *or* **bread-crumbs**
⅔ **cup liquid (milk, beef** *or* **chicken stock** *or* **vegetable cooking liquid)**
2 **eggs**
4 **tbsp. chopped onions**
¼ **tsp. salt**
⅛ **tsp. pepper**
2 **tsp. Worcestershire sauce**
¼ **cup chopped parsley**
¼ **cup chopped celery with leaves**
½ **tsp. savory, sage, thyme,** *or* **marjoram (optional)**

Pour boiling water over liver and let sit for 5 minutes. Drain, then grind in food chopper. Beat liquid and eggs together. Add oatmeal, beef, and liver. Add remaining ingredients and mix thoroughly. Press into 9 x 5 x 3-inch loaf pan. Bake at 350°F for 1½ to 1¾ hours. Serves 8. Provides 10 mg of iron per average serving.

Ann Budge, Belfountain, Ont

Liver in Creamy Yogurt Sauce

1 **tbsp. vegetable oil**
6 **oz. beef liver**
1 **tbsp. all-purpose flour**
1 **tsp. paprika**
salt and pepper

1 **tbsp. red wine vinegar**
1 **small onion, thinly sliced**
½ **tsp. chopped fresh dill**
4 **tbsp. plain yogurt**

Slice liver crosswise (with sharp scissors) into ½-inch strips. Mix flour, paprika, salt, and pepper. Coat liver thoroughly with this mixture. Sauté liver in oil for 3 to 5 minutes until brown outside. Drain on a paper towel and set aside in a warm oven.

Lower heat under skillet and add vinegar. Add onions and sauté until soft. Sprinkle dill over the onions. Add yogurt and mix together well. Heat sauce but do *not* boil. Quickly pour it over liver. Serve immediately.

Makes 2 servings.

Meat/Pork & Lamb

Oji San (Pork Curry)

Gwenn obtained this recipe from a Japanese lady while she and Keith were living in Nairobi. If it isn't his tacos, then it must be this curry that gives Keith his great speed through the woods while orienteering!

$2^1/_2$ to 3 lb. pork *or* beef
1 lb. onions
4 tsp. curry powder
2 tbsp. tomato paste
1 small chili pepper, chopped
1 sweet red pepper, chopped
6 to 8 cloves garlic, minced

4 to 5 tbsp. vinegar
$1^1/_2$ tsp. salt
1 beef bouillon cube
fresh ginger root, sliced thinly
hot cooked rice
curry condiments

Cube pork or beef, removing all fat and gristle. Brown meat in a little butter, then remove from pan and set aside. Sauté onions in pan, then add curry powder and tomato paste. Return meat to pan and stir. Add peppers, garlic, vinegar, salt, and bouillon cube. Add enough water to cover and stir well. Cover and simmer $2^1/_2$ to 3 hours or until tender. Add more water as needed. Add ginger root just before serving. Serve with rice and curry condiments.

Suggested condiments: sliced bananas, grated fresh coconut, peanuts, raisins, chopped cucumber, and chutney.

Serves 6

Gwenn French, Hannon, Ont

Braised Pork with Ginger

A friend and neighbour in St. Sauveur des Monts, Québec, gave us this favourite of hers.

1 lb. lean pork
1½ tbsp. vegetable oil
1 cup chicken stock
2 tbsp. soy sauce
1 tbsp. sherry

2 tbsp. chopped onion
½ clove garlic, minced
1 tsp. white *or* brown sugar
1 tsp. ground ginger
dash of pepper

Cut pork into 1-inch cubes and coat with flour. Brown quickly in oil. Remove from pan and pour out fat.

Add stock, soy sauce, and sherry to the frying pan. Stir well. Add onions and remaining ingredients. Return pork to pan.

Bring to a boil, lower heat, cover, and simmer 15 minutes or so, until pork is tender. Serve with hot fluffy rice.

Makes 3 servings.

Chops 'n' Cabbage

A tasty supper dish with autumn flair. Serve with rice or mashed potatoes and a green vegetable.

4 pork chops (not too thick)
½ medium cabbage, red *or* green
1 or 2 medium apples, peeled
1 medium onion
3 tbsp. lemon juice
1½ tsp. ground cumin
salt and pepper

Slice cabbage, apples, and onion thinly.

Brown chops in a heavy frying pan over medium-high heat. When browned on both sides, remove chops and set aside. Mix apples, onions, and cabbage in pan. Combine lemon juice, cumin, salt, and pepper, then add to cabbage mixture and stir well. Return chops to pan with cabbage mixture. Cover pan and cook over medium-low heat until chops are tender, about 25 to 30 minutes. Stir occasionally.

Makes 4 servings.

Gingered Pork Chops with Fruit

12 pitted prunes *or* dried apricots
1/4 cup orange juice *or* pineapple juice
4 thick pork chops (remove fat)
freshly ground black pepper
2 tbsp. vegetable oil
2 cloves garlic, minced
1/2 tsp. grated lemon rind
2 slices fresh ginger, finely diced
1 large apple, thickly sliced
1 cup apple juice *or* cider
1 cup plain yogurt
1 tbsp. cornstarch

Mix cornstarch into yogurt and set aside. Cut prunes or apricots in half and soak in orange juice or pineapple juice while proceeding.

Sprinkle chops with black pepper. Heat oil in a large frying pan; add ginger, lemon rind, and garlic. Brown chops on both sides. Pour off any remaining oil. Add apples, prunes or apricots, orange or pineapple juice, and apple juice. Cover and cook 20 to 30 minutes, until chops are tender.

Reduce heat and add yogurt to frying pan; stir well. Cook until sauce is slightly thickened and heated through, but do not simmer.

Makes 4 servings.

Spiced Orange Pork Chops

My long-time friend, Janey McNab Hotton of Stittville, New York, served us this dish years ago when we visited her. It's been a favourite at our house ever since.

4 pork chops,	2 tbsp. water
trimmed of excess fat	3 to 5 tbsp. sugar
1 tsp. seasoned salt	1/4 tsp. cinnamon
1/2 tsp. paprika	10 whole cloves
1/4 tsp. black pepper	1/2 cup orange juice

Mix seasoned salt, paprika, and pepper. Coat the chops on both sides with this mixture. Brown well in a heavy frying pan, then transfer to a low casserole dish. Mix the remaining ingredients and pour over chops. Cover and bake 1 hour at 350°F. If sauce is not thick enough, remove cover for last few minutes. Serve with rice.

Makes 4 servings.

Ann Budge, Belfountain, Ont

Sweet and Sour Pork Tenderloin

1/2 lb. pork tenderloin	1 14-oz. can pineapple tidbits
1/4 cup vegetable oil	2 tbsp. vinegar
1 green pepper	1 tbsp. soy sauce
1 medium onion, chopped	1/2 tsp. ground ginger
2 tbsp. cornstarch	

Cut meat into small pieces. Sauté onions in oil gently for 5 to 10 minutes. Add tenderloin pieces and brown lightly.

In a small bowl, mix cornstarch with 2 tbsp. pineapple juice and then add the following ingredients: pineapple tidbits, remainder of juice, vinegar, soy sauce, and ground ginger.

Pour mixture into a pot and heat to boiling, stirring constantly. You may need to add water as the sauce thickens. Reduce heat, cover, and simmer for about 1/2 hour. Slice pepper into rings and add to mixture. Cook another 1/2 hour, stirring occasionally while cooking. Serve over white or brown rice.

Serves 3.

Barb Pearson, Hamilton, Ont

Ham and Sesame Pasta

1 lb. spaghetti *or* fettucine
2 tbsp. vegetable oil
4 green onions
$^1/_2$ cup ground cooked ham
$^1/_4$ cup unsalted peanuts
$^1/_3$ cup sesame seeds
$^1/_3$ cup soy sauce (a less salty variety)
1 tbsp. cider vinegar
1 tsp. honey *or* Demerara sugar
2 drops Tabasco sauce
2 tbsp. tomato catsup *or* tomato paste
1 small cucumber *or* zucchini *or* 2 stalks celery

Cook pasta according to package directions, drain, toss with
1 tbsp. vegetable oil, and set aside. Slice green onions, chop
peanuts, toast sesame seeds, and dice cucumber, zucchini, or
celery.

Sauté green onions in 1 tbsp. vegetable oil for 1 minute. Add
ham, peanuts, sesame seeds, soy sauce, vinegar, honey or sugar,
Tabasco sauce, and catsup or tomato paste. Bring to the simmer
point and simmer 2 to 3 minutes, stirring occasionally. Stir in the
cucumber, zucchini, or celery, then cook a little longer until the
vegetables are tender.

Stir in the pasta and heat through.

Makes 3 or 4 servings.

Lasagna Roll-Ups

This dish resembles cannelloni, but is much easier to prepare. Try the variations below!

1 tbsp. vegetable oil
8 lasagna noodles
8 slices of cooked ham
2 tbsp. prepared mustard
1 cup grated strong Cheddar cheese
salt and pepper
2 cups Mushroom Sauce, Quick Tomato Sauce *or* Tomato Sauce (Italian Style) (recipes follow)
2 large tomatoes
parsley sprigs, for garnish

Cook lasagna noodles carefully without breaking them, according to package instructions, for 5 minutes. Drain well and place the noodles on a baking sheet. Lay a slice of ham on each noodle, spread with mustard, sprinkle with cheese, and season to taste. Roll up each noodle, enclosing the ham and cheese filling.

Place the rolls in a greased shallow baking dish. Pour **Mushroom Sauce, Tomato Sauce (Italian Style)** or **Quick Tomato Sauce** over all. Slice tomatoes and arrange on top. Bake at 375°F for 30 minutes. Garnish with parsley.

Makes 4 hearty servings.

Variation: Noodles, with ham and cheese, may be rolled around spears of pineapple, cooked broccoli, or cooked asparagus.

Mushroom Sauce

2 cups milk
4 tbsp. butter
2 tbsp. all-purpose flour
salt and pepper
1 tbsp. Tamari sauce
½ tsp. thyme
4 tbsp. butter
1 cup chopped mushrooms

In a heavy saucepan, melt 4 tbsp. butter and stir in flour. Cook over low heat for 3 to 4 minutes, stirring constantly. Slowly stir in milk. Sprinkle with salt and pepper. Cook, stirring, until sauce has thickened.

Sauté mushrooms in 4 tbsp. butter for 2 minutes over moderate heat. Add to sauce along with Tamari sauce and thyme. Stir and heat through.

Quick Tomato Sauce

4 tbsp. butter
4 tbsp. all-purpose flour
2 cups tomato juice *or* finely-chopped stewed tomatoes
seasonings (optional)

In a heavy saucepan melt butter and heat until light brown; stir in flour. Slowly add tomato juice or stewed tomatoes. Cook, stirring, over low heat until thickened. Add seasonings, if you wish, such as a pinch of nutmeg, oregano, tarragon, salt, or pepper.

Tomato Sauce (Italian-Style)

¹/₄ cup vegetable *or* olive oil
1 clove garlic
2 onions
4 cups chopped stewed tomatoes
¹/₂ cup tomato paste
¹/₂ cup water
¹/₂ tsp. salt
1 tsp. *each* basil, oregano, and parsley
¹/₄ tsp. ground pepper
1 bay leaf
¹/₂ cup sliced mushrooms

Heat oil in a heavy saucepan. Mince garlic and dice onion. Add to oil and sauté for 3 minutes. Stir in tomatoes, tomato paste, water, spices, parsley, and bay leaf. Without actually boiling the sauce, simmer it, uncovered, for 1 to 6 hours — the longer the better! Add mushrooms for the last 15 minutes. Add a little water if sauce becomes too thick.

Autumn Ham Bake

We always have in our garden a great many tomatoes that do not ripen before frost, so we are always on the lookout for recipes that call for green tomatoes. This is a favourite.

1 ham steak ($\frac{1}{2}$ to $\frac{3}{4}$ inch thick)
1 tbsp. vegetable oil
4 to 6 green tomatoes
2 onions
2 tbsp. lemon juice
$\frac{1}{4}$ cup firmly-packed brown sugar
$\frac{1}{4}$ tsp. cinnamon

Slice tomatoes thickly and onion thinly.

Brown the ham on both sides in 1 tbsp. vegetable oil over medium heat. (This step may be eliminated.) Place ham in a baking dish and cover with onions and green tomatoes. Combine the rest of the ingredients and spread over the onions and tomatoes. Cover. Bake in a 350°F oven for 40 minutes. Serve with mashed potatoes.

Serves 4.

Ann Budge, Belfountain, Ont

Ham Soufflé with Broccoli Sauce

$2\frac{1}{2}$ tbsp. butter
$2\frac{1}{2}$ tbsp. flour
$\frac{3}{4}$ cup finely-ground cooked ham
2 or 3 drops Tabasco sauce
cream of tartar
1 cup milk
salt and pepper
pinch of nutmeg
3 egg yolks
6 egg whites
$\frac{1}{4}$ cup grated Parmesan cheese
Broccoli Sauce (recipe follows)

Bring milk to a boil. Melt butter, stir in flour, and cook over medium heat for 2 minutes. While stirring with a wire whisk, gradually add the boiling milk. Add salt and pepper and a pinch of nutmeg. Cook over low heat for 5 minutes. Set sauce aside.

Grease soufflé dish or casserole and sprinkle with 1 tbsp. of the grated Parmesan cheese.

Season the ham with salt, pepper, and Tabasco sauce, then stir in the hot sauce. Add the egg yolks one at a time. Mix well.

Beat egg whites until stiff. Start on low speed. Add a pinch of cream of tartar after 2 minutes of beating, then gradually increase speed. Egg whites are ready when they do not fall out of the bowl if it is turned up-side down.

Add 3 tbsp. of the beaten egg whites to the ham mixture along with the remaining grated Parmesan cheese. Mix well.

Pour ham mixture over the egg whites and fold together very gently with a spatula.

Pour into prepared soufflé dish. (If dish is more than ¾ full, add a collar of waxed paper tied with string.) Put dish in centre of a preheated 425°F oven and reduce heat to 400°F. Bake 30 minutes, or until well set in the middle. Serve immediately with **Broccoli Sauce.**

Makes 4 servings.

Broccoli Sauce

¼ **cup chopped onion**
2 **tbsp. butter**
2 **tbsp. all-purpose flour**
½ **cup hot chicken stock** *or* **1 chicken bouillon cube dissolved in**
    ½ **cup boiling water**
1 **cup milk**
1 **cup chopped cooked broccoli**

Sauté onion in butter until tender. Blend in flour. Add hot chicken stock or bouillon cube in boiling water to onion and flour along with milk. Cook and stir until thick and bubbly. Stir in the chopped, well-drained broccoli. Heat through.

Makes enough sauce for 8 servings of soufflé. Delicious on plain cheese soufflé too.

Raisin Sauce — Ski Inn Style

Vermont hospitality abounds at the Ski Inn on the lower slopes of Mt. Mansfield in Stowe, Vermont, where dinner is served family-style around one long table. Innkeepers Harriet and Larry Heyer serve this delicious Raisin Sauce with ham to their ravenous skiing guests.

$^1\!/_2$ **cup brown sugar**
3 tbsp. cornstarch
$^1\!/_4$ **tsp. salt**
2 cups apple juice
$^1\!/_2$ **cup raisins**
dash *each* of cloves and cinnamon
2 tbsp. butter
1 to 2 tsp. lemon juice *or* vinegar (optional)

In a saucepan combine brown sugar, cornstarch, and salt. Slowly stir in apple juice. Cut raisins in half and add along with cloves and cinnamon. Cook over medium heat, stirring, for about 10 minutes, until thick and clear. Stir in 2 tbsp. butter. For a little more tang, add 1 to 2 tsp. lemon juice or vinegar.

Serve warm in a sauce boat and let folks help themselves!

Lamb and Barley Fry-Pan Casserole

A hearty casserole cooked on top of the stove. A crisp salad and home-made bread make this a complete main course.

$2^1\!/_2$ **lb. lean lamb**
$^1\!/_2$ **cup flour seasoned with** $^1\!/_4$ **tsp. salt,** $^1\!/_2$ **tsp. oregano, and**
$^1\!/_4$ **tsp. pepper**
2 to 4 tsp. vegetable oil
2 large onions
3 cloves garlic, sliced
10 to 12 large mushrooms
$^3\!/_4$ **cup pearl barley**
2 cups lamb *or* chicken stock
2 tsp. lemon juice
$^1\!/_4$ **tsp. rosemary**

Cut lamb into small cubes, trimming off fat. Slice onions and mushrooms. Coat lamb with seasoned flour and sauté in hot oil in a heavy covered frying pan. Remove lamb pieces as they brown and set aside to drain on paper towels. Sauté onions, garlic, and mushrooms in remaining oil in pan. Stir in barley, stock, lemon juice, and rosemary. Return lamb to pan. Cover and simmer 1 hour, until lamb is tender. Add additional stock or water if needed.

Serves 6.

Roast Lamb with Rosemary

My mother roasts lamb this way. It's one of my favourite dinners.

6 to 8 lb. leg of lamb (preferably boned and rolled)
2 cloves garlic, thinly sliced
salt and pepper
1 tsp. rosemary
8 potatoes, unpeeled and sliced
butter
2 large onions, sliced
1 to 2 cups chicken stock

With the point of a small sharp knife, make small slits in the lamb at 2-inch intervals. Insert the slices of garlic. Rub lamb well with rosemary, salt, and pepper. Into a greased roasting pan, place a layer of potatoes dotted with butter. Add a second layer of potatoes and the onions, then pour the chicken stock over top. Place leg of lamb on top and roast at 350°F for 2 to 3 hours.

Serves 6 to 8.

Heather Budge, London, Ont

Lamb Curry

1½ lb. boneless lamb
seasoned flour
2 tbsp. vegetable oil *or* unsalted butter
2 to 3 tbsp. curry powder
¼ tsp. ground ginger
1 large onion, chopped
1 clove garlic, crushed
1 large apple, peeled and chopped
1 cup chicken stock
1 tbsp. tomato paste *or* catsup
salt and pepper
2 tbsp. yogurt *or* sour cream
condiments

If you open a tin of tomato paste for just 1 tablespoon, freeze remainder.

Cut lamb into 1½-inch cubes and toss in seasoned flour. In a skillet, heat oil; add curry, ginger, onion, and garlic, then cook lightly. Add meat; cook and stir until lightly browned. Add chopped apple, stock, and tomato paste. Simmer covered about 1 hour or until tender, adding a little extra liquid if needed. Salt and pepper to taste. Stir in yogurt. Heat but *do not simmer.*

Serve with rice and, if desired, small bowls of condiments: chutney, raisins, coconut, chopped cucumber, peanuts, and sliced bananas.

Serves 4 to 6.

Meat/Poultry

Low-Fat Crunchy Chicken

Crispy and delicious, with all the fat removed!

2 lb. chicken pieces
¹/₄ tsp. salt
¹/₄ tsp. lemon pepper
¹/₂ tsp. sage *or* savory
¹/₂ cup plain low-fat yogurt
bread-crumbs, wheat germ, cornflakes, cornmeal, *or*
   quick-cooking oatmeal

Remove skin and any fat from chicken pieces. Blend seasonings with yogurt. Dip chicken pieces in yogurt mixture; then roll in bread-crumbs, wheat germ, crushed cornflakes, cornmeal, or quick-cooking oatmeal.

Place on an ungreased baking sheet and bake at 400°F for 40 to 45 minutes or until brown, crispy, and tender.

Serves 4. About 230 calories per serving.

Chicken with Grapes and Almonds

A delicious and different sauce for chicken.

4 boned chicken breasts
¼ cup all-purpose flour
salt and pepper
3 tbsp. butter *or* margarine
⅓ cup flaked almonds
1 cup seedless green grapes, halved
2 tsp. lemon juice

Dip chicken into flour seasoned with salt and pepper. Sauté gently in butter or margarine until golden brown and cooked. Drain on paper towels and place chicken in a warm oven.

Add almonds to the pan and stir around until beginning to turn pale golden brown. Add grapes to pan. Stir in lemon juice. Heat through. Pour over chicken breasts and serve.

Makes 4 servings.

Barb Pearson, Hamilton, Ont

Baked Turkey Salad

This is just as tasty made with chicken. It is a nice simple luncheon dish.

½ cup grated old Cheddar cheese
1½ cups toasted oat flakes *or* bread-crumbs
1 tbsp. butter
½ cup chopped walnuts *or* almonds
2 cups diced cooked turkey
2 cups thinly-sliced celery
2 tbsp. grated onion
¼ tsp. salt
2 tbsp. lemon juice
2 tbsp. parsley
½ cup mayonnaise
paprika

Grease a 10 x 6-inch low baking dish. Mix cheese with flakes or crumbs, then spread a little more than half the mixture in the bottom of the dish.

Heat butter in a small skillet and add nuts. Cook gently, stirring, until nuts are lightly browned.

Combine turkey, nuts, celery, and onions. Mix salt, lemon juice, parsley, and mayonnaise. Stir into turkey mixture, then spread over cheese mixture in baking dish. Top with remaining cheese mixture. Sprinkle with paprika. Bake in a 450°F oven 15 to 20 minutes or until well heated through. Serve immediately.

Makes 4 or 5 servings.

Chicken-Corn Supper Pie

A super version of the ever-popular main-course pie. Add a pinch of herbs if you wish, but this pie is equally good without.

thin slices of cooked chicken *or* lean bacon
¹/₂ cup soft bread-crumbs
3 eggs
1¹/₂ cups fresh *or* frozen corn kernels
³/₄ cup milk
pinch *each* of salt and pepper
2 tbsp. butter, melted
pinch of tarragon, basil, *or* curry (optional)

Spread bread-crumbs on the bottom of a well-greased pie plate. Cover crumbs with thin slices of chicken or partially-cooked and drained bacon.

Steam corn kernels for 3 to 4 minutes, then drain if necessary. Beat eggs lightly with a whisk and stir in corn, milk, melted butter, salt, pepper, and herbs, if you wish.

Add egg-corn mixture to pie plate. Bake in 325°F oven about one hour or until a knife inserted in the centre comes out clean.

Allow pie to sit several minutes before cutting into wedges.

Serves 4 to 6.

Chicken-Cheddar Layers

This is a good make-ahead one-dish dinner! Ham or tuna fish may be substituted for chicken.

1½ cups chopped cooked chicken
5 cups fresh whole-wheat bread cubes
½ cup sliced mushrooms
1 300-g pkg. frozen chopped broccoli *or* cauliflower
2 cups grated medium or old Cheddar cheese
6 eggs
3 cups skim milk
1 small onion, finely chopped
¼ tsp. salt
dash of pepper
1 tsp. dry mustard

Thaw broccoli or cauliflower and drain well.

Grease a 2-quart, deep, straight-sided baking dish or soufflé dish.

Layer 1/3 of bread, meat, mushrooms, vegetables, and cheese. Add 2 more layers of each.

Beat eggs with milk, onion, salt, pepper, and mustard until well blended. Pour over layers. Cover and refrigerate at least 3 hours or overnight.

Bake uncovered at 350°F for 1¼ hours or until puffy and golden.

Serves 6.

Pineapple Chicken

This is a stir-fry recipe and is best made in a wok.

2 cups chopped uncooked chicken
1 egg
2 tbsp. soy sauce
2 tbsp. wine vinegar
2 tbsp. cornstarch
1/2 fresh very ripe pineapple
1/4 cup slivered almonds, lightly toasted
2 inches fresh ginger root, peeled
1 tsp. liquid honey
1/2 cup chicken stock
2 tsp. cornstarch
2 tbsp. water
1/4 cup vegetable oil (Peanut oil is preferred as it withstands higher temperatures.)

Using a wire whisk, beat together the egg, soy sauce, vinegar, and 2 tbsp. cornstarch. Marinate chicken in this sauce in the refrigerator for an hour or so.

Remove skin from pineapple and cut pineapple into small cubes, making about 2 cups. Save all the juice and add enough water to it to make 1/2 cup of liquid. Place this liquid into a heavy medium saucepan. Grate or finely chop ginger. Add ginger, stock, and honey to liquid in saucepan. Dissolve 2 tsp. cornstarch in 2 tbsp. water and stir into sauce in saucepan. Stir constantly while cooking over medium heat until thickened. Add pineapple cubes and lightly-toasted almonds. Season with salt and pepper, if desired.

Remove chicken pieces from marinade. Heat oil in large heavy frying pan or wok. When oil is very hot, add chicken pieces and stir-fry for about 5 minutes, or until chicken pieces appear cooked. Pour pineapple sauce over chicken and heat through. Serve over hot fluffy rice. Add a green salad and crusty roll for a delicious dinner.

Serves 4.

Chicken Teriyaki

4 chicken breasts
$^1/_4$ cup teriyaki sauce
$^1/_4$ cup cooking sherry *or* water
1 tsp. sesame oil *or* other vegetable oil
$^1/_4$ tsp. grated fresh ginger *or* 1 tsp. ground ginger
1 clove garlic *or* $^1/_2$ tsp. garlic salt
1 scallion *or* green onion, finely chopped
2 tsp. sugar

Bone and remove skin from chicken breasts. Prick both sides of chicken with a fork. Combine teriyaki sauce, sherry or water, oil, ginger, garlic, onion, and sugar to make marinade. Rub marinade into chicken to ensure that it is covered. Marinate for 3 hours. Remove chicken with slotted spoon.

Broil the chicken 3 to 4 minutes per side or until done. Heat remaining marinade in a small saucepan; simmer for several minutes. Cut chicken across the grain into $^1/_2$-inch pieces. Spoon heated sauce over chicken. Serve with rice.

Makes 4 servings.

Judy Andrew, Fredericton, NB

Sticky Chicken Wings

Easy, economical, and tasty!

30 to 36 chicken wings
$^1/_3$ cup white *or* brown sugar
2 tbsp. finely-chopped onions
1 clove garlic, minced
$^1/_2$ tsp. ground ginger *or* 1 tsp. grated fresh ginger root
1 cup beer
1 cup unsweetened orange *or* pineapple juice
$^1/_4$ cup vegetable oil

Cut off wing tips and discard. Snip off as much of the fatty excess skin as possible. Wash wings well and dry. Mix remaining ingredients and marinate wings in the sauce overnight in the refrigerator, turning occasionally. Place wings in a baking dish and pour marinade over them. Bake uncovered for 2 hours at 325°F. Baste wings occasionally during the first hour.

Serves 6 or 7 people, depending on their appetites!

Meat/Fish

Poached Fish Parmesan

1¼ lb. fillets of sole, turbot, *or* haddock
2 cups milk
3 tbsp. butter
3 tbsp. flour
½ cup dry white wine
½ cup grated Parmesan cheese
2 tbsp. chopped chives *or* green onions
salt and pepper
1 sweet red *or* green pepper, thinly sliced
1 lb. fettucine *or* broad egg noodles

Cut fillets into serving portions. In a large covered frying pan, simmer fillets gently in milk for 5 to 10 minutes or until fish flakes easily with a fork. Carefully transfer fish to a platter and keep warm; reserve milk.

Melt butter in a medium saucepan; add flour and cook for 2 minutes. Gradually add reserved hot milk; cook over low heat, stirring constantly, until thickened. Add wine, Parmesan cheese, chives, salt, pepper, and red or green pepper. Heat an additional 10 minutes.

Meanwhile cook fettucine or noodles in boiling, salted water until tender; drain. Place pasta on a serving plate and arrange fish and sauce over top.

Serves 4.

Courtesy of The Ontario Milk Marketing Board

Quick and Easy Fish Bake

Two couldn't-be-easier options are offered here. Both are low in calories, if that's important.

1 lb. fish fillets, such as cod, haddock, *or* Boston bluefish
$1/2$ cup or more grated cheese
pinches of basil, garlic powder, salt, and pepper (optional)
2 ripe tomatoes, thinly sliced (optional)
3 to 4 tbsp. lemon juice (optional)

Preheat oven to 400°F. Place fillets in a greased low baking dish just large enough to arrange them in a single layer. Either sprinkle with spices and arrange tomatoes on top, or sprinkle with lemon juice. Top either with grated cheese. Bake 8 to 10 minutes until fish flakes easily.

Serves 3 or 4.

Susan's Broiled Fish Fillets

Great-tasting and so easy. Add a green vegetable and boiled potatoes topped with butter and parsley.

2 lb. fresh *or* frozen fish fillets
$1/3$ cup vegetable oil
$1/4$ cup fresh lemon juice
1 tsp. grated lemon rind (optional)
$1/4$ cup Worcestershire sauce
1 clove garlic, minced
$1/4$ tsp. salt
$1/3$ tsp. rosemary
$1/4$ tsp. pepper

Thaw fish fillets, if frozen. Combine the remaining ingredients in a deep bowl and whisk well. Marinate fillets in this sauce for 1 to 4 hours in the refrigerator.

Place fillets on a greased broiler pan, baste with marinade frequently, and broil 4 inches from heat for 5 to 8 minutes, depending on thickness. When browned on one side, turn and baste with the sauce and continue broiling until fish flakes with a fork.

Serves 6.

Susan Budge, Waterloo, Ont

Kedgeree

A garnish of fresh parsley and sliced tomatoes makes this nutritious dish more attractive.

1 lb. white fish
3 hard-cooked eggs, chopped
2 cups Cheese Sauce (recipe follows)
3 cups cooked white rice
sliced tomatoes
parsley

Bake fish in a covered dish with a little water for 20 minutes at 325°F. Flake fish when cooked.

In a large bowl combine cooked rice, chopped eggs, and fish. Bind with cheese sauce. Turn into a casserole dish and decorate with sliced tomatoes and parsley. Heat 20 minutes in oven at 325°F.

Serves 4.

Cheese Sauce

½ cup butter *or* margarine
¼ cup all-purpose flour
2 cups milk
1 cup grated sharp Cheddar cheese
salt and pepper

Melt butter in a small pan, stir in flour, and cook for 4 minutes. Remove from heat and gradually beat in the milk. Return to medium heat and bring to a boil, stirring all the time. When thickened, add grated cheese, and salt and pepper to taste.

Barb Pearson, Hamilton, Ont

Baked (Barbecued) Salmon

This form of salmon has been served to orienteers visiting Vancouver who have been entertained by the North Shore Orienteers. This is Bruce Rennie's recipe!

whole salmon, cleaned
basil, tarragon, *or* **other herbs**
onions
1 lemon
butter
lemon wedges (optional)
tartar sauce (optional)

Expensive salmon is not needed as this is a very moist method of preparation.

Liberally place pats of butter in cavity of salmon along with thinly sliced onions. Season with herbs of your choice; basil and tarragon are favourites. Finally, insert 4 to 6 lemon slices. As you wrap salmon in foil, dot sides with butter. Wrap the fish in several layers of foil and in a manner that will allow for a sneak preview!

Bake on a grate approximately 2 inches above coals. Usually 7 to 10 minutes per inch of thickness is a good guide. Serve with lemon wedges and/or tartar sauce.

Susan Foster, Vancouver, BC

Baked Salmon in a Blanket

1¹/₂ **lb. piece of salmon**
³/₄ **cup all-purpose flour**
¹/₄ **tsp. salt**
¹/₄ **cup margarine**
¹/₄ **tsp. dry mustard**
few grains of pepper

Scale and wash salmon. Put cut side down in a greased baking dish. Cream margarine. Sift dry ingredients and blend with margarine. Spread this mixture over salmon. Bake at 350°F for 50 minutes.

Serves 4 or 5.

Barb Taylor, St. John's, Nfld

Super Salmon Supper Pie

Good hot or cold! The rice crust may be used as a base for many other main-course pies.

1 7-oz. can salmon, drained and flaked
2 eggs
$^1/_2$ cup uncooked long-grain rice
1$^1/_2$ cups water
1 tsp. vegetable shortening
2 tsp. butter
1 cup thinly-sliced celery
1 onion, chopped
$^1/_2$ cup grated Swiss *or* mild Cheddar cheese
$^1/_2$ cup milk
$^1/_2$ tsp. salt
pepper
pinch *each* of nutmeg, curry powder, and cinnamon

Add a pinch of salt to water and bring to a boil. Add rice and return to the boil. Cover, reduce heat, and simmer until all the water is absorbed, about 15 to 20 minutes. Set aside to cool.

Grease a 9-inch pie plate well with 1 tsp. of shortening. Melt 2 tsp. butter in a frying pan. Sauté celery and onion for about 4 minutes and set aside.

Beat 1 egg and add to rice. Season with pepper. Press rice mixture onto bottom and sides of pie plate. Sprinkle half the cheese over top. Spread half the onion-celery mixture over the cheese, then cover with salmon. Top with the remaining onion-celery mixture and cover with the rest of the cheese.

Lightly beat together the remaining egg, milk, and spices. Pour this over the ingredients in the pie plate. Bake at 375°F for 30 to 35 minutes or until a knife inserted in the centre comes out clean (very important). Cool 5 minutes before serving. Serve with a salad or green vegetable.

Serves 4.

Variation: Add a layer of cooked peas or French-cut green beans over the salmon for a meal in one dish.

Salmon Loaf

2 8-oz. cans salmon
1 egg, beaten
$^1\!/_2$ cup low-fat cottage cheese
1 cup cracker crumbs, wheat germ, *and/or* rolled oats
3 green onions, chopped
$^3\!/_4$ cup fresh *or* frozen green peas
1 tsp. Worcestershire sauce
1 tbsp. lemon juice
$^1\!/_4$ tsp. dill weed *or* seed
$^1\!/_2$ tsp. paprika
salt and pepper
$^1\!/_4$ cup milk

Cook and drain green peas. Drain salmon and mash, including bones. Add the remaining ingredients and mix well. Pack lightly into a greased loaf pan or baking dish. Bake at 350°F for 30 minutes.

Serves 4.

Tuna, Cottage Cheese, and Rice Casserole

A simple supper casserole.

3 cups cooked brown rice
2 6$^1\!/_2$-oz. cans tuna fish
1 cup cream-style low-fat cottage cheese
1 cup thinly-sliced celery *or* chopped cooked broccoli
1 small onion, diced
$^1\!/_2$ cup yogurt
2 tsp. Worcestershire sauce
salt and pepper
$^3\!/_4$ cup grated cheese of your choice

Drain tuna and break apart with a fork. Carefully mix together rice, tuna, cottage cheese, celery or broccoli, and onion. In another bowl combine yogurt, Worcestershire sauce, salt, and pepper. Stir the two mixtures together. Spoon into a greased 2-quart casserole. Sprinkle grated cheese over the top. Bake in 350°F oven for 25 to 30 minutes. Serve with a crisp salad and country-style whole-wheat bread.

Serves 5 or 6.

Tuna Casserole with Brown Rice

Brown rice gives a chewy texture and a nutty flavour to this simple casserole.

1¼ **cups uncooked brown rice**
3 **cups water**
1 **tbsp. butter**
3 **stalks celery**
½ **green pepper**
1 **small onion**
1 **cup grated sharp Cheddar cheese**
½ **cup low-fat plain yogurt**
1 **cup milk**
¼ **tsp. salt**
½ **tsp. tarragon**
¼ **tsp. black pepper**
2 **7-oz. cans tuna, drained**
1 **cup cooked peas** *or* **thawed frozen peas**

Chop celery, green pepper, and onion, then set aside. Add rice to water in a large saucepan. Bring to a boil, reduce heat, cover, and cook until rice is tender and water has been absorbed. Remove from heat and stir in butter. Add celery, green pepper, onion, ½ cup of cheese, yogurt, and milk. Toss gently, then add salt, pepper, and tarragon. Mix well, then add flaked tuna and peas. Mix once more. Turn into a 2-quart greased casserole, top with remaining ½ cup of cheese, and bake at 325°F for 30 minutes.

Serves 6.

Variation: Top with a mixture of ground walnuts, whole-wheat bread-crumbs, wheat germ, and enough mayonnaise to make it spreadable. Spread over casserole before baking.

Tuna Casserole Florentine

³/₄ **pkg. fresh spinach**
2 7-oz. cans tuna, drained
¹/₄ **lb. mushrooms**
1 tbsp. lemon juice
salt and pepper
3 tbsp. butter

1¹/₂ **tbsp. all-purpose flour**
1 tbsp. minced onion
1 cup milk
1 egg, lightly beaten
grated Cheddar cheese

Arrange well-washed, drained, and trimmed spinach in a greased 1¹/₂-quart casserole. Flake tuna and spread over spinach. Sprinkle with lemon juice. Slice mushrooms and sauté in 1 tbsp. butter. Spread over tuna.

Melt 2 tbsp. butter over low heat and blend in flour. Add onion, then stir in milk. Continue to stir until mixture thickens and comes to a boil. Season to taste. Stir sauce slowly into lightly-beaten egg and pour over tuna and mushrooms.

Sprinkle with grated Cheddar cheese. Bake at 350°F for about 30 minutes, until hot and bubbling.

Makes 4 servings.

Tomatoes Stuffed with Sardines

This is a very economical lunch or light supper dish, especially if you are lucky enough to be able to pick the tomatoes off the vine.

4 large firm ripe tomatoes
1 can sardines
2 tsp. soft butter
1 small onion, finely chopped

4 to 6 soda crackers
1 tsp. Worcestershire sauce
dash of cayenne pepper
butter *or* **grated cheese**

Cut a thin slice off the top of each tomato and carefully scoop out the pulp. Set tomato shells aside. Drain sardines. Crumble crackers.

Mash sardines, cracker crumbs, and remaining ingredients with some of the tomato pulp. Fill tomato shells with sardine mixture. Top each tomato with ¹/₂ tsp. butter or a little grated cheese. Bake at 325°F until warmed through, 20 to 25 minutes. Cover the baking dish for more moist tomatoes.

Serves 2.

Meatless/Eggs

Egg Islands

A colourful, nutritious, and quick lunch or supper dish with great child appeal!

2 tbsp. butter
2 green onions, sliced
2¼ cups stewed tomatoes, chopped
2 tbsp. fresh parsley, chopped
¼ tsp. salt
freshly-ground pepper
1 large green pepper
4 eggs
4 slices whole-wheat toast
grated Parmesan cheese (optional)

Slice green pepper carefully into 4 large rings.

In a large skillet, heat butter and sauté onions until transparent. Stir in tomatoes, parsley, salt, and pepper, and simmer for 5 minutes.

Place green pepper rings on top of tomato sauce. Break 1 egg into each pepper ring. Cover skillet. Simmer over low heat for a few minutes until eggs are set. To serve, lift out each pepper ring with egg and some sauce and place on toast. Sprinkle with a little Parmesan cheese if you wish.

Makes 4 servings.

Eggs 'n' Onions

An interesting brunch or lunch! The quantities are easily increased.

3 medium onions
salt, pepper, and tarragon
6 eggs
3 tbsp. dry bread-crumbs
3 tsp. butter
³/₄ cup grated Cheddar cheese

Grease 3 individual baking dishes. Heat butter in a skillet. Add very thinly-sliced onions and cook, stirring, for about 5 minutes. Divide amongst baking dishes. Sprinkle with seasonings.

Break 2 eggs into each baking dish. Combine bread-crumbs with melted butter and sprinkle over eggs. Bake at 350°F for 10 minutes. Top with cheese and bake about 5 minutes longer, until cheese is melted and eggs are cooked to your liking. Serve immediately.

Serves 3.

Pannesuffle

This is a recipe that Sue picked up while living in Norway. The name translates to "skillet soufflé."

4 eggs, separated   **¹/₂ tsp. white pepper**
100 ml flour   **100 g cheese, grated**
200 ml milk   **200 g cooked bacon pieces**
¹/₂ tsp. salt   **dill (optional)**

Mix egg yolks with all other ingredients except egg whites. Beat whites and fold into mixture. Heat in a greased heavy skillet until cooked through. Shake a little to avoid burning.

Serves 2.

Sue Waddington, Hamilton, Ont

Fiddlehead Omelette

Fiddleheads are the tightly-furled tops of ostrich ferns and are picked before the ferns open in the early spring. These ferns grow in deep mysterious moist woodlands and are often passed by orienteers on the run! Fiddleheads are considered to be Canada's national vegetable.

6 large eggs	**$^1/_4$ lb. fiddleheads**
$^1/_4$ cup water	**pinch of salt**
2 tbsp. melted butter	**2 tbsp. butter**

Wash fiddleheads and remove brown papery scale. Boil fiddleheads for 1 to 2 minutes in just enough salted water to cover, then drain. Beat together eggs, water, melted butter, and salt until lightly foamed. Sauté fiddleheads in butter in a frying pan and add beaten egg mixture. Reduce to medium heat and cook until texture is still slightly moist.

Serve with baked, boiled, or French fried New Brunswick potatoes!

Serves 3.

Tim Andrew, Fredericton, NB

Potato-Carrot Pancakes

These are great topped with cheese, or made into a "sandwich" with cheese in the middle, for a quick and easy supper.

4 eggs	**2 tbsp. whole-wheat flour**
2 cups grated potatoes	**$^1/_2$ tsp. salt**
2 cups grated carrots	**$^1/_4$ tsp. baking powder**
1 tbsp. chopped onion	

Mix baking powder and salt with whole-wheat flour.
Beat eggs. Combine all ingredients and mix thoroughly. For each pancake, pour $^1/_4$ cup of batter into a moderately hot, well-greased frying pan. Flatten with a pancake lifter. Fry until golden brown and crisp.

Makes 4 servings.

Terry Knight, Cambridge, Ont

Vegetable Patties

Serve these patties in pita breads and garnish with fresh vegetables and yogurt.

3 eggs
$\frac{1}{2}$ tsp. seasoned salt
1 tsp. cumin
$\frac{1}{4}$ tsp. pepper
3 tbsp. sesame seeds
3 tbsp. whole-wheat flour
3 tbsp. wheat germ
2 carrots
2 cups cooked spinach
$1\frac{1}{2}$ cups green beans
6 to 8 pita breads
tomatoes, cucumbers, *and/or* onions, for garnish
yogurt (optional)

Grate carrots. Cook green beans, drain, and cut up finely. Chop cooked spinach. Lightly toast sesame seeds. Mix vegetables with sesame seeds and set aside. Meanwhile beat eggs lightly and add dry ingredients and seasonings. Combine egg mixture with carrots, spinach, and beans. Drop by spoonfuls onto a greased cookie sheet and bake at 450°F for 10 minutes. Makes 6 to 8 patties.

Cut slices off the tops of pita breads and fill with patties. Add slices of tomatoes, cucumbers, and onions. Carefully spoon a little yogurt into each pocket, if desired. Serve immediately and munch away!

Serves 6 to 8.

Cabbage Pie

A wonderful dish for a special brunch or supper. It's like a deep quiche but with a crunchy topping. All you need with it is a colourful tomato or a green salad. This recipe is adapted from *Canadian Living* magazine with their kind permission.

Crust

³/₄ **cup shredded Mozzarella cheese**
1 cup whole-wheat flour
1 cup rolled oats
¹/₄ **cup grated Parmesan cheese**
¹/₂ **cup butter**

In a bowl, mix together cheese, flour, oats, and Parmesan cheese. With a pastry blender or your fingers, cut in butter until evenly mixed. Remove 1 cup and set aside. Press remaining crumbs over bottom and up sides of a greased 9-inch springform pan. Set aside.

Filling

2 tbsp. butter
4 cups shredded cabbage
1 onion, chopped
1 small sweet red *or* green pepper, diced

In a skillet, melt butter; sauté cabbage, onion, and pepper just until limp, about 5 minutes. Spoon into prepared crust.

Custard

4 eggs
1 cup sour cream *or* ¹/₂ cup yogurt and ¹/₂ cup sour cream
¹/₂ **cup shredded Mozzarella cheese**
2 tbsp. grated Parmesan cheese
¹/₂ **tsp. dried basil**
¹/₂ **tsp. dried oregano**

Beat eggs. Blend in remaining ingredients, pour over filling, and sprinkle with reserved crumbs.

Bake in a 375°F oven until puffy and set in centre, about 45 minutes. Let cool for 20 minutes. Remove pan sides and cut pie into wedges. Serve warm or cool.

Makes 8 servings.

Zucchini-Cheese Frittata

A wonderful brunch dish!

2 or 3 small zucchini	½ cup grated old Cheddar cheese
1 medium onion	2 tbsp. additional grated cheese
1 small garlic clove	salt, pepper, and tarragon
8 fresh eggs	1 tbsp. butter

Slice zucchini, onion, and garlic. Melt butter in frying pan. (A non-stick frying pan works best; cover the handle with foil when broiling later on.) Add garlic and onion. Sauté for 1 minute. Add zucchini and sauté, stirring, 1 more minute. Cover frying pan, lower heat, and cook 4 minutes. Remove cover and cook 1 to 2 minutes to evaporate some of the moisture. Preheat broiler.

In a large bowl combine eggs, cheese, and seasonings. Beat with a whisk until well blended. Pour over vegetable mixture in frying pan. Cook over medium heat 4 to 6 minutes until bottom is well browned and top is still a little bit runny. Sprinkle 2 tbsp. grated cheese on top. Broil 6 inches from broiler for 5 minutes or until frittata is well-browned and cooked.

Serves 4.

Egg and Potato Dinner

This is another recipe from an excellent book, *The Athlete's Kitchen*. We appreciate permission to include it here.

This meal is designed for those who hate to wash dishes! It is also good for those who like to exercise after work. Simply put the potato in the oven to bake while you go for an hour's workout.

1 large baking potato	1 oz. Swiss cheese, shredded
1 to 2 tsp. margarine (optional)	pepper
1 egg	salt

Pierce potato in several places with a fork. Bake in 350°F oven for one hour, or until done. The potato will be soft. You will be able to pierce it easily with a fork.

Make a cross in the top. Fluff up the potato with a fork and make a well. Add margarine, if desired, and break the egg into the well. Top with salt, pepper, and cheese. Return to the oven until egg is cooked, about 15 minutes.

Makes 1 serving.

Meatless/Cheese

Country Vegetable Casserole

A make-ahead, easily-stretched-to-feed-a-crowd recipe from Betty Aldridge of Tottenham, Ontario. Betty is the author of *The Best of the Farmhouse Kitchen*, from which this recipe comes. Thank you, Betty.

4 tbsp. butter
2 large onions, thinly sliced
4 carrots, thinly sliced
1 small rutabaga, chopped
2 potatoes, thinly sliced
1 cup frozen corn
$^1/_2$ green pepper, diced
$1^1/_4$ cups chicken stock
$^1/_2$ cup grated cheese

Melt butter in an ovenproof casserole, add onions, and sauté until soft. Add vegetables in layers with salt and pepper on each. Pour stock over vegetables. Cover casserole and cook in a 350°F oven for 45 minutes or until tender and stock is absorbed. Sprinkle with cheese and brown under broiler.

Makes 6 to 8 servings.

Noodle Casserole

Served with a tossed salad, this makes a nice light summer meal.

8 oz. broad noodles, cooked and well drained
1¼ cups plain yogurt *or* sour cream
1 cup low-fat cottage cheese
¼ cup butter *or* margarine
4 tbsp. chopped fresh parsley *or* 1 tbsp. dried parsley
3 green onions, sliced
1 egg, lightly beaten
salt and pepper

Combine all ingredients and pour into 1½-quart greased casserole. Bake uncovered at 300°F for 40 minutes.

Serves 4.

Lynda Sidney, Sudbury, Ont

Vegetarian Lasagna

A very interesting version of a classic dish. This freezes well.

1 8-oz. package lasagna noodles
1 package fresh spinach
1 clove garlic, minced
1 large onion
3 stalks celery
1 green pepper
½ tsp. *each* of oregano, basil, and marjoram
1 medium zucchini, unpeeled
1½ cups thinly-sliced mushrooms
1½ cups Tomato Sauce (Italian Style) (See page 41.)
1 5½-oz. can tomato paste
½ cup freshly-grated Parmesan cheese
2 cups cottage *or* ricotta cheese
1 egg
2 cups grated Mozzarella cheese

Cook noodles according to package directions, rinse, and drain. Toss with a couple of drops of vegetable oil to keep noodles from sticking together, then set aside. Tear spinach into small pieces. Chop onion, celery, and green pepper.

Sauté minced garlic in 2 tbsp. vegetable oil for 1 minute. Add onion, celery, green pepper, and spices. Cook, stirring occasionally, for 5 minutes. Grate zucchini coarsely, squeeze out excess liquid, and add to pan. Cook and stir for about 5 minutes. Add mushrooms, tomato sauce, and tomato paste. Simmer gently for 20 minutes. While sauce is simmering, beat egg into cottage cheese with a fork or wire whisk. Remove sauce from heat and stir in Parmesan cheese.

Grease a 2-quart lasagna baking dish and spread a little sauce on the bottom. Add a layer of half of each of the following in this order: noodles, sauce, cottage cheese, spinach, and Mozzarella cheese. Repeat layers. Cover dish and bake at 350°F for about 1 hour. Allow to stand for 10 minutes before cutting into large squares to serve.

Serves 6 to 8

Triple-Cheese Spaghetti

An easy, tasty way to serve spaghetti.

8 oz. spaghetti
1 tsp. vegetable oil
1 cup ricotta *or* cottage cheese
1 cup diced old Cheddar cheese
1 cup plain yogurt
6 green onions, sliced
¹/₄ cup chopped parsley
¹/₂ cup freshly-grated Parmesan cheese, for topping

Cook spaghetti according to package directions. Drain well and toss with 1 tsp. vegetable oil.

Reserving Parmesan cheese, mix remaining ingredients and combine with spaghetti. Spoon into a greased 2-quart casserole and sprinkle with Parmesan cheese. Bake at 350°F for about 25 minutes, until heated through and slightly browned on top. Serve with a crisp green salad and country-style whole-wheat bread.

Serves 4.

Baked Ziti

This dish is often on the menu at suppers following orienteering meets in the Northeastern United States. Ziti is a tubular-shaped noodle, larger than macaroni.

1 16-oz. pkg. ziti, cooked 10 minutes and drained well
8 ounces Mozzarella cheese, cubed, *or* 2 cups cottage cheese
4 cups Tomato Sauce (Italian Style) (See page 41.)
1 tsp. oregano
salt and pepper

Mix the ziti, three-quarters of the cheese, and the remaining ingredients. Spread in 2 greased 12 x 8 x 2-inch baking pans. Sprinkle with remaining cheese.

At this point, the ziti may be either baked or frozen for future use. Bake at 350°F for 30 to 45 minutes or until casserole is bubbly around the edges and cheese is melted.

Each pan serves about 6 people.

Fettucini with Cheese, Raisin, and Walnut Sauce

Fettucini is a perennial favourite and is excellent with this mild cheese sauce. The raisins and walnuts are an interesting addition. Just be sure the Gruyère cheese is aged; young cheese tends to be springy.

1 lb. uncooked fettucini   **2 tbsp. flour**
5 qt. water   **¹/₂ cup grated Gruyère cheese**
1 tsp. salt   **¹/₂ cup grated Gouda cheese**
1 tbsp. vegetable oil   **¹/₃ cup golden raisins**
2 cups milk   **¹/₃ cup chopped walnuts**
4 tbsp. butter   **grated Parmesan cheese**

Combine water, salt, and vegetable oil, and bring to a full boil in a very large pot. Slowly add fettucini, making sure water doesn't stop boiling. Cook, uncovered, until fettucini is tender but still firm. Stir occasionally. Drain well, toss with 1 tsp. of vegetable oil, and place in a large warmed serving dish.

Meanwhile prepare sauce. Melt butter in a medium saucepan, stir in flour, and allow to cook over medium heat for several minutes. Lower heat and slowly add milk, stirring constantly, and cook until sauce has thickened. Remove pan from heat and stir in Gruyère and Gouda cheese, raisins, and walnuts. Return to low heat; heat through and pour over fettucini. Toss gently but thoroughly. Sprinkle with Parmesan cheese.

Makes 8 small or 6 large servings.

Creamy Macaroni and Cheese

An always-popular old-timer!

1½ **cups uncooked macaroni**
4 **tbsp. butter**
¼ **cup all-purpose flour**
3 **cups milk**
1¾ **cups grated old Cheddar cheese**
1 **tbsp. minced onion**
½ **tsp. prepared mustard**
¼ **tsp. pepper**
¾ **tsp. Worcestershire sauce**
½ **tsp. salt**
1 **cup bread-crumbs**
¼ **cup grated Cheddar cheese, for topping**
chopped tomato *and/or* **green pepper (optional)**

Cook macaroni according to package directions and drain well. Melt butter in a medium saucepan over low heat. Blend in flour, onion, and seasonings. Add milk slowly, stirring constantly, and cook until thickened.

Layer the macaroni, cheese, tomato or pepper if used, and sauce twice in a greased 6 to 8-cup casserole. Mix bread-crumbs with 1 to 2 tbsp. melted butter and ¼ cup grated Cheddar. Spread over top. Bake at 350°F for 30 to 40 minutes, or until hot and bubbly.

Serves 4.

Triple-Cheese Macaroni

If you like your macaroni loaded with cheese, then this three-cheese recipe is for you! It is adapted from *Canadian Living* magazine and appears here with their permission.

2 cups uncooked macaroni

Cook macaroni in boiling salted water until just tender, then drain.

Sauce

2 tbsp. butter
2 tbsp. all-purpose flour
2¹/₂ cups hot milk
¹/₂ tsp. salt
¹/₈ tsp. *each* pepper and nutmeg
dash of Worcestershire sauce
dash of cayenne pepper
1¹/₂ cups shredded Cheddar cheese
1 cup shredded Swiss cheese
2 tbsp. grated Parmesan cheese

In a heavy saucepan, melt butter and stir in flour; cook, stirring, for 2 to 3 minutes. Whisk in milk and seasonings; bring to a boil, stirring constantly. Reduce heat and add cheeses, stirring just until melted. Taste and adjust seasoning.

Place macaroni in a buttered casserole and pour sauce over; toss gently but thoroughly.

Topping

1 cup coarse bread-crumbs
2 tbsp. melted butter
1 cup shredded Cheddar cheese
¹/₂ cup shredded Swiss cheese
2 tbsp. grated Parmesan cheese

Combine topping ingredients and sprinkle on top.

Bake casserole in a 375°F oven for 20 to 30 minutes, until bubbling.

Makes about 6 servings.

Macaroni and Cheese Puff

An elegant way to serve macaroni and cheese!

¹/₃ cup dry bread-crumbs
1 tbsp. butter
³/₄ cup uncooked regular macaroni
¹/₄ cup butter
1 medium onion
2 tbsp. flour
¹/₄ tsp. dry mustard *or* 1 tsp. Dijon-style mustard
sprinkle of cayenne pepper
¹/₂ tsp. salt
¹/₄ tsp. ground black pepper
1 cup milk
1 cup soft bread cubes
2 tbsp. chopped pimiento
1 tbsp. chopped parsley
1 cup grated old Cheddar cheese
4 eggs, separated

Cook macaroni according to package directions until just tender, about 6 minutes. Rinse in cold water and drain well. While macaroni is cooking, grease a 6-cup soufflé dish with 1 tbsp. butter. Sprinkle dry bread-crumbs on bottom and sides of dish. Turn dish upside down to remove excess crumbs.

Heat ¹/₄ cup butter in a heavy saucepan, add chopped onion, and stir over medium heat for about 3 minutes, until onion is transparent. Sprinkle on the flour, mustard, cayenne, salt, and pepper, and stir to combine. Remove pan from burner and add milk all at once, return pan to heat, and stir constantly until sauce comes to a boil and is thick and smooth. Turn heat to low and add bread cubes, pimiento, parsley, and Cheddar cheese, stirring until cheese melts.

Beat egg yolks. Gradually stir a little of the hot sauce into the beaten egg yolks, then stir it all back into the pan. Stir in the well-drained macaroni.

Beat egg whites until stiff but not dry. Carefully fold in the macaroni mixture. Spoon into prepared soufflé dish. Bake at 375°F until set in the middle and golden brown on top, about 1 hour.

Makes 4 to 6 servings.

Nut, Cheese, and Grain Loaf

2 cups uncooked Red River Cereal®
1 cup boiling water
1 cup milk
1 onion
1 cup diced medium *or* old Cheddar cheese
1 cup coarsely-chopped walnuts
2 to 3 tbsp. Worcestershire sauce
1 tsp. sage *or* savory
1 egg
Cheese Sauce (see page 55), Mushroom Sauce (see page 40), *or*
    Quick Tomato Sauce (see page 41)

Add boiling water to the cereal and stir. Add the milk, stir well, and let stand. Chop onion. Combine the remaining ingredients and add to cereal. Stir well. Grease a loaf pan well and place 2 tbsp. vegetable oil in the bottom. Firmly press cereal mixture into loaf pan. Bake at 350°F for about 1 hour. Serve with **Cheese Sauce, Mushroom Sauce, Quick Tomato Sauce,** or your favourite home-made pickles.

Serves 4.

Nutty Cheese Loaf

Serve this nutritious, meatless "meat loaf" with a tomato sauce, and accompany it with several tender-crisp colourful vegetables and crusty rolls.

1 cup shredded medium *or* old Cheddar cheese
1 cup ground walnuts
¹/₂ cup wheat germ
¹/₄ cup rolled oats
¹/₂ cup chicken *or* beef stock *or* vegetable cooking water
2 green onions
2 tbsp. lemon juice
2 eggs, lightly beaten
1 tsp. sage *or* savory
1 tsp. basil *or* thyme
¹/₄ tsp. salt
Quick Tomato Sauce (see page 41)

Red River Cereal® is a registered trademark of Maple Leaf Mills Limited.

Add oats to broth and let sit 10 minutes. Meanwhile mix walnuts, cheese, and wheat germ in a large bowl. Add oats to walnut, cheese, and wheat germ mixture and stir well. Chop green onions and stir in, along with the beaten eggs. Finally, stir in lemon juice and seasonings. Blend thoroughly.

Grease an 8 x 4-inch loaf pan and press mixture into pan. Bake at 350°F for 30 to 40 minutes, until top of loaf is browned. Top with **Quick Tomato Sauce.**

Serves 4.

Cheese 'n' Leek 'n' Potato Supper Dish

Vary the amount of the ingredients and the casserole size according to the number of people to be fed.

mashed potatoes
milk
leeks
sunflower seeds
Gruyère *or* **Mozzarella cheese**
butter
paprika
bacon (optional)

Grease a casserole and coat with bread crumbs.

Mash boiled potatoes with a little warm milk and place a layer in the casserole.

Cook a few leeks (white part only) in simmering water for 20 minutes. Slice and place on top of potatoes. Add a layer of toasted sunflower seeds, and crumbled crisp bacon if desired. Add a layer of grated Gruyère or Mozzarella cheese.

Cover with another layer of mashed potatoes. Dot with butter and sprinkle with paprika, and perhaps a little grated cheese. Bake at 350°F until heated through.

Carrot-Cheese Bake

This is a good recipe for using up leftover rice. Brown rice will give a nuttier flavour.

2 cups cooked white *or* brown rice
3 cups shredded carrots
2 cups grated medium *or* old Cheddar cheese
¹/₂ cup sliced fresh mushrooms
¹/₂ cup milk
2 eggs, beaten
2 tbsp. grated onion
¹/₂ tsp. salt
¹/₄ tsp. pepper
6 thick tomato slices

Mix rice, carrots, mushrooms, and 1¹/₂ cups cheese. Combine milk, beaten eggs, onion, and seasonings, then stir into rice mixture. Pour into a greased 9 x 9-inch baking dish. Top with tomato slices and sprinkle with remaining cheese. Bake at 350°F for 1 hour.

Serves 6.

Cheese Curd Bake

People are acquiring a taste for these delightful mild nuggets of newly-formed cheese. They are readily available from cheese factories in cheese-making regions and are now making their appearance in supermarkets. Serve this casserole as a light supper or lunch accompanied by a crisp green salad with a tangy dressing.

4 medium potatoes
2 tbsp. butter
2 large onions, chopped
¹/₂ lb. mushrooms, sliced
2 tbsp. all-purpose flour
1¹/₄ cups milk
salt and freshly-ground pepper
¹/₂ tsp. dry mustard
2 cups cheese curds
2 tbsp. chopped chives *or* green onion tops
¹/₂ sweet red pepper, diced

Wash potatoes but do not peel. Boil for 20 minutes or until tender. When cool, slice thinly.

Melt butter in a heavy saucepan. Add chopped onions and sauté over medium heat until soft. Add sliced mushrooms and sauté for 5 minutes more. All moisture should have evaporated. Stir in flour and cook for 2 minutes. Gradually add milk, stirring constantly to prevent lumps. Stir in salt, pepper, and mustard. Cook, stirring, for 5 minutes. Remove from heat, then add curds, chives, and red pepper.

Grease a 6-cup baking dish. Place half the potato slices over the bottom. Cover with half the creamed curd sauce. Repeat layers.

Topping

3 tbsp. butter
¹/₂ cup bread-crumbs *or* crushed cereal flakes
¹/₂ cup grated Parmesan cheese.

Prepare topping by melting butter and stirring in crumbs and cheese. If topping is too dry, add 1 additional tablespoon of melted butter. Sprinkle topping over casserole.

Bake at 350°F for 30 minutes or so. Crumbs should be lightly browned and sauce should be bubbling around the edges.

Makes 6 servings.

Cheese and Spinach Bake

1 12-oz. pkg. chopped frozen spinach *or* equivalent amount of fresh spinach
3 eggs
6 tbsp. whole-wheat flour
2 cups low-fat cottage cheese
2 cups grated medium *or* old Cheddar cheese
¹/₄ cup wheat germ

Cook spinach, drain well, and chop.

Mix all ingredients except wheat germ. Pour into 8 x 8-inch or 9 x 9-inch baking pan.

Top with wheat germ. Bake uncovered at 350°F about 30 to 45 minutes.

Serves 4 to 6.

Gloria Charlow, Montreal, Qué

Spinach Squares

Quick to prepare, these squares freeze well for convenience.

4 tbsp. butter
3 eggs, beaten
1 cup flour
1 cup milk
¹/₂ tsp. salt
1 tsp. baking powder
2 to 3 cups grated old Cheddar cheese
2 12-oz. pkg. frozen chopped spinach, thawed

Melt butter and pour into a 9 x 13-inch pan. Squeeze water out of spinach. Mix flour, baking powder, and salt. Add to eggs along with milk. Now add cheese and well-drained spinach cut into bite-sized pieces. Turn into baking dish with melted butter and bake at 350°F for 35 minutes. Cut into 6 or 8 squares and serve or freeze.

To freeze, place squares on a cookie sheet and place in freezer. After 45 minutes or so, bag or wrap squares separately in freezer paper. To serve, reheat at 350°F for about 12 minutes.

Gillian Bailey, West Hill, Ont

Swiss Cheese Flan

A rich but delicious dish that tastes a bit like cheese fondue. It's a favourite of the Hollensteins, a keen orienteering family living in Switzerland.

pastry for 10-inch pie or flan
³/₄ cup grated Gruyère cheese
³/₄ cup grated Emmenthal cheese
6 tbsp. whole-wheat flour
²/₃ cup milk
²/₃ cup table cream
salt and pepper
paprika and nutmeg
additional grated cheese for top of flan

Toppings

Choose one of the following or invent your own!

8 tomatoes, sliced

8 oz. lean bacon, chopped and sautéed with 1 chopped onion
  or leek (white part only)

8 oz. prawns (large shrimps)

1½ cups sliced mushrooms, sautéed in ¼ cup butter and mixed
  with ½ cup raw sliced mushrooms (my favourite!)

Line a 10-inch pie plate or flan pan with pastry, fill with dried beans, and bake for 15 minutes at 400°F. Discard beans.

Prepare filling by mixing remaining ingredients together well. Spoon into pastry and add topping of your choice. Sprinkle with a little additional grated cheese.

Bake at 350°F until firm, about 40 minutes. Superb!

Serves 4.

Susan Budge, Waterloo, Ont

Gouda Cutlets

1¼ lb. Gouda cheese

¼ cup all-purpose flour

1½ cups dry bread-crumbs

1¼ tsp. seasoned salt

¼ tsp. nutmeg

⅛ tsp. black pepper

2 eggs, beaten

3 to 4 tbsp. vegetable oil

Cut cheese into ½-inch slices. Roll in flour. Mix bread-crumbs with seasoned salt, nutmeg, and pepper. Dip floured cheese slices into beaten egg, then into crumb mixture, being careful to coat completely.

Heat oil in a heavy frying pan over *low* heat. Cook breaded Gouda slices for about 3 minutes on each side until lightly browned. Watch carefully as they may brown quickly. Serve immediately.

Makes 6 servings.

Welsh Rarebit

1½ tbsp. butter
3 cups grated old Cheddar cheese
1 tsp. Worcestershire sauce
½ tsp. dry mustard
¼ tsp. salt
dash of cayenne pepper
2 egg yolks
½ cup beer
4 slices of dried whole-wheat toast, buttered

Place cheese and butter in the top of a double boiler over hot but *not* boiling water. Stir constantly until both are melted. Then add Worcestershire sauce, mustard, salt, and cayenne, stirring as you add. Add the egg yolks, one at a time, stirring hard with each addition. Then slowly add the beer. Be sure to keep stirring constantly until the sauce is very smooth. Spoon over the hot toast and serve with a green salad.

Makes 4 servings.

Authentic Swiss Fondue

This recipe comes from the kitchen of Lorna Hollenstein, who lives near Zurich, Switzerland. Susan lived with the Hollensteins, who are a very active orienteering family, during the summer of 1981. This fondue was one of the highlights of her stay!

100 ml of white wine per person
1 clove garlic
¼ to ½ lb. of cheese per person (5 parts Gruyère to 1 part
    Emmentaler or Appenzell)
1 tsp. lemon juice
1 tbsp. cornstarch
pepper
nutmeg
1 shot kirsch

Cut cheese into small cubes and toss in cornstarch. Rub inside of pot with garlic clove. Add wine and heat on the stove until it bubbles. Then add the cheese, a little at a time, stirring until it melts. Add the rest of the ingredients; stir until the fondue is smooth and heated through. Pour into cheese fondue dish or chafing dish and place on a portable burner that can be brought to the table to keep the fondue hot and bubbling.

Serve with cubes of crusty French bread. Spear bread with long-handled fondue forks and dip away!

Tradition has it that if a lady loses her bread in the fondue, she pays a kiss to the nearest man; if a man loses his bread, he provides the next bottle of wine. It is considered unethical to make anyone lose his or her bread!

Susan Budge, Waterloo, Ont

Brown Rice Soufflé

Because this soufflé contains rice, it doesn't rise as much, or fall as easily either!

3 tbsp. butter *or* margarine
3 tbsp. all-purpose flour
$^1/_2$ tsp. salt
dash of cayenne pepper
$^3/_4$ cup milk
$^1/_2$ lb. medium *or* old Cheddar cheese, grated
4 eggs yolks, well-beaten
$1^1/_3$ cups cooked brown rice
4 egg whites
1 small bunch of fresh broccoli

Steam broccoli and chop enough to make 1 cup. Butter a 2-quart casserole or soufflé dish. Melt butter or margarine in a medium saucepan over medium heat. Stir in flour, salt, and cayenne. Reduce heat and slowly add milk, stirring constantly. Cook and stir until boiling, very thick, and smooth.

Remove saucepan from heat and mix in cheese. Return to *low* heat and stir mixture until cheese is melted. Gradually stir some of the hot mixture into well-beaten egg yolks, then stir all back into saucepan. Remove from heat and fold in rice.

Beat egg whites until stiff but not dry. Fold into cheese mixture along with broccoli, then turn into casserole or soufflé dish. Bake at 350°F until browned on top and set in the middle, about 50 minutes.

Serves 4 to 6.

Vegetable Pie

A once-a-week favourite at our house! This is so simple and delicious that we overlook the fact that the recipe contains a commercially prepared mix.

2 bunches fresh broccoli *or* 1 small fresh cauliflower
¹/₂ cup chopped *or* finely-sliced onions
¹/₂ cup chopped green pepper
¹/₂ cup sliced fresh mushrooms
1 cup grated strong Cheddar cheese
1¹/₂ cups milk
³/₄ cup tea biscuit mix
3 eggs
¹/₂ tsp. salt
¹/₄ tsp. pepper
pinch of tarragon (optional)
¹/₄ cup grated strong Cheddar cheese, for topping

Lightly grease a 10-inch pie plate or quiche pan. Chop broccoli or break cauliflower into small flowerets. Steam about 5 minutes and drain. Mix broccoli or cauliflower, onions, green pepper, mushrooms, and cheese in pie plate or quiche pan.

Beat remaining ingredients for about 1 minute with a hand beater. Pour over the cheese and vegetables. Top with ¹/₄ cup grated Cheddar cheese.

Bake in 400°F oven until golden brown and knife inserted in centre comes out clean, about 50 minutes. (Do not underbake.) Let stand 5 minutes before serving.

Makes 6 servings.

Variation: Frozen vegetables may be used; thaw completely and *drain well* but do not cook. Experiment with other vegetables such as sliced carrots or zucchini. This pie is a good way to use leftover vegetables.

Ann Budge, Belfountain, Ont

Meatless/Legumes

Nut and Seed Patties

Mix these up the night before and they will be ready to pop into the pan after your late afternoon workout. Experts say that peanuts are one of the most nutrient-dense foods for your dollar. Other nuts could be substituted for peanuts.

1 cup unsalted peanuts
$^1/_2$ cup sesame seeds
$^1/_2$ cup sunflower seeds
$^1/_2$ cup grated Parmesan cheese
$^1/_4$ cup wheat germ
3 tbsp. lemon juice
1 to 1$^1/_2$ tbsp. soy sauce
1 onion, finely chopped
2 cups mushrooms, finely chopped
$^1/_4$ cup snipped fresh parsley
2 to 3 tsp. vegetable oil

Place nuts and seeds in a food processor or blender and grind until very fine. Spread powdered nuts on a cookie sheet and toast in a moderate oven until lightly browned. Pour nuts into a large mixing bowl and add cheese, wheat germ, lemon juice, and soy sauce. Mix well.

Mix onions, mushrooms, and parsley with vegetable oil. Add to nut mixture and combine well. Refrigerate 24 hours. Form into patties and coat with wheat germ. Brown in a lightly-greased frying pan over low-medium heat. Served with colourful vegetables.

Makes 10 to 12 medium patties.

Home-Style Baked Beans

A banquet when served with Boston brown bread and coleslaw!

1½ lb. dry navy beans
9 cups water
½ tsp. ground ginger
2 stalks celery, thinly sliced
1 onion, chopped
1 green pepper, chopped
1 cup tomato sauce *or* stewed tomatoes
½ cup brown sugar
½ cup maple syrup
2 tsp. dry mustard *or* 1 tbsp. prepared mustard
2 tbsp. blackstrap molasses
1 tsp. salt
8 slices of lean bacon, diced
3 apples, peeled and diced
1 clove garlic, cut into 4 pieces

Rinse beans and discard imperfect ones. Soak remaining beans in 9 cups of water overnight. Add ginger and simmer 1½ to 2 hours, until skins pop when gently pressed between thumb and finger.

Drain beans and pour into a bean crock or heavy casserole with a lid. Add remaining ingredients and stir well. For a tight fit, cover with a piece of foil before putting lid on.

Bake beans for 8 hours in a 250°F oven. Check occasionally and stir to see if a little more water is needed. Remove cover and foil for final hour of cooking.

Makes 8 to 10 servings.

Three-Bean Chili

2 cups dry soybeans	2 beef bouillon cubes
1 cup dry pinto *or* pink beans	2 tbsp. vegetable oil
1 cup dry chick peas	3 medium onions, chopped
7 cups water	2 green peppers, chopped
4 cups stewed tomatoes, chopped	2 tbsp. chili powder

Wash and drain beans and chick peas. Put beans and peas into a 5-quart heavy pot. Add water and bring to a boil. Reduce heat, cover, and simmer 2½ hours.

Add tomatoes and bouillon cubes. Heat oil in a large skillet and sauté onions and green peppers until tender. Stir into bean mixture along with chili powder; cover and simmer 1 hour longer. Leftovers will freeze well.

Makes 9 servings.

Lynda Sidney, Sudbury, Ont

Falafels

Falafels are the Middle Eastern version of our hamburgers. Adjust the seasonings to suit your taste. If you are in a hurry, use canned chick peas; but often there is satisfaction in making something from scratch. Chick peas are also known as "ceci beans."

2$\frac{1}{2}$ cups uncooked chick peas
4 medium onions
2 to 4 cloves garlic
$\frac{1}{2}$ cup chopped parsley
2 tsp. cumin
2 tsp. coriander
1 tsp. baking powder
salt and pepper
dash of cayenne pepper
pita breads
shredded lettuce and yogurt, for garnish

Rinse chick peas and discard imperfect ones. Cover remaining peas with 2$\frac{1}{2}$ times their volume of water and let stand overnight. The next day simmer until just tender, about four hours. Add more water if needed.

Put cooked peas, onions, and garlic through a food chopper. Mix remaining ingredients (except pita breads and garnishes) and combine with pea mixture. Refrigerate for an hour.

Form patties and fry as you would a hamburger. Serve in pita bread halves. Add shredded lettuce and yogurt as a garnish.

Serves 4.

Tofu Patties

1 lb. tofu	1 tsp. Worcestershire sauce
4 tbsp. vegetable oil	¼ cup chopped walnuts *or*
1 small onion	sunflower seeds
1 stalk celery	½ tsp. salt
1 clove garlic	pinch of black pepper
½ cup dry bread-crumbs	¼ tsp. thyme
¼ cup chopped parsley	wheat germ
1 egg	

Place tofu in a colander and top with a small plate on which is placed a heavy object such as a tin of juice. Let stand to drain for an hour or so. Chop onion and celery finely. Mince garlic.

Heat 2 tbsp. of oil in a small skillet over medium heat and add onion, garlic, and celery. Sauté until soft, then allow to cool.

Mash tofu. Add vegetable mixture and bread-crumbs, parsley, egg, Worcestershire sauce, nuts, salt, pepper, and thyme. Blend well with fork. Form 12 small patties. Coat each patty with wheat germ.

Heat remaining oil in a large heavy frying pan over medium heat. Fry patties until heated through, turning to brown both sides.

Serves 6.

Tofu in Pita Breads

Tofu (soybean curd) is a relatively new food, low in cholesterol and carbohydrates, high in protein, and relatively inexpensive.

1 block of tofu	2 tsp. sunflower *or* sesame oil
2 green onions with tops	alfalfa sprouts
3 fresh mushrooms	parsley
½ tsp. soy sauce	4 to 6 whole-wheat pita breads

Dice onions and mushrooms and sauté in sunflower or sesame oil until golden. Beat tofu and soy sauce together with a fork and add to vegetables in the pan. Stir and heat through. Add finely-chopped parsley and alfalfa sprouts just before serving. Cut a small slice off the top of each pita bread and pull open to form a pocket, spoon tofu mixture into the pocket, and they are ready to eat!

Julie DePass, Oakville, Ont

Vegetables

Green Beans with Croutons

4 cups fresh green beans
2 tbsp. vinegar, any flavour
2 tsp. liquid honey
$^1/_2$ to $^3/_4$ cup Croutons (recipe follows)
2 to 4 tbsp. freshly-grated Parmesan cheese

Cut beans into 1-inch pieces and steam until tender-crisp. Grease a shallow baking dish and add beans. Stir in vinegar and drizzle honey over beans. Add croutons and toss. Sprinkle cheese on top. Bake at 450°F for 15 minutes. Place under broiler for a minute or two to brown top.

Makes 8 servings.

Croutons

dried bread cubes
1 clove garlic (optional)
vegetable oil

Make your own croutons by sautéing dried bread cubes in a generous amount of vegetable oil until lightly browned. A garlic flavour may be added by marinating a clove of garlic in the oil for at least an hour before sautéing.

Croutons may also be made by tossing bread cubes in oil and browning them in a 350°F oven, stirring occasionally.

Stir-Fried Fresh Green Beans

4 cups fresh green beans
4 green onions
2 tbsp. peanut oil
$^1/_2$ tsp. ginger
$^1/_2$ tsp. sugar
3 drops Tabasco sauce
2 tbsp. sesame seeds
2 tbsp. vinegar
salt and pepper

Toast sesame seeds. Cut beans into 1-inch pieces. Slice green onions. Heat oil in a wok or a large, heavy frying pan over high heat. Add beans, stirring constantly for 3 minutes or so. Mix remaining ingredients and add to wok. Heat for 3 minutes, tossing now and then.

Makes 8 servings.

Cabbage 'n' Apples

1 green *or* red cabbage
$^1/_4$ cup butter
1 large onion
$^1/_2$ tsp. salt
$^1/_4$ tsp. pepper
3 tbsp. vinegar
3 apples, peeled
$^1/_3$ cup toasted sunflower seeds *or* other nuts
yogurt, for garnish (optional)

Shred cabbage coarsely and add to melted butter in a large saucepan. Add chopped onion, seasonings, and vinegar. Cover and simmer over low heat for 20 minutes, stirring occasionally. Chop apples and add, continuing to cook until apples are tender, about 15 to 20 minutes. Stir frequently. Add toasted sunflower seeds or other chopped nuts and toss. Servings may be topped with a dab of yogurt.

Makes 4 to 6 servings.

Baked Beets

Much more interesting than the name might suggest!

12 medium-sized fresh beets
2 onions
¼ cup sugar
¼ tsp. salt
¼ tsp. paprika
3 tbsp. butter
1 tbsp. lemon juice
⅓ cup water

Peel and slice beets. Grate or slice onions. Grease a 7-inch baking dish. Place beets in layers. Sprinkle with sugar, salt, and paprika. Dot with butter. Mix lemon juice and water and pour over beets. Top with onions. Cover dish tightly and bake at 400°F for 30 minutes or until tender. Gently stir a couple of times during baking.

Makes 5 servings.

Harvard Beets

Excellent with ham or turkey, especially at Christmastime. The dry mustard and ginger are not necessary, but add them if you like a little more zip!

1½ cups diced or sliced canned beets
1 tbsp. cornstarch
⅓ cup white *or* brown sugar
¼ cup white vinegar
¾ cup juice from canned beets (Add water to make ¾ cup
    if necessary.)
pinch of dry mustard *or* ground ginger (optional)

Mix cornstarch, sugar, and optional spices together in a heavy-bottomed saucepan. Stir in vinegar and juice and/or water. Cook over low heat, stirring until thick and clear. Add diced or sliced canned beets. Heat through. Keep hot in the top of a double boiler if necessary.

Makes 4 servings.

Crunchy Broccoli Flowerets

Broccoli cooked this way will be bright green and still crunchy. A nice accompaniment to cold meat!

¹/₂ **cup plain yogurt**
¹/₂ **tsp. Worcestershire sauce**
broccoli flowerets, enough for 4 servings
³/₄ **cup combination of bread-crumbs** *or* **cereal crumbs, grated
    Parmesan cheese, and sesame seeds**
pinch of freshly-ground black pepper

In one bowl, mix yogurt and Worcestershire sauce; in a second bowl, combine crumbs, cheese, sesame seeds, and pepper. Dip broccoli into yogurt, then into crumb mixture. Place on greased baking sheet. Bake at 375°F for 10 to 12 minutes or until crumbs are crisp and broccoli is cooked to the degree of crunchiness you like. Serve immediately.

Serves 4.

Broccoli and Whole-Wheat Noodles

This may be prepared in a wok or a heavy frying pan.

1 bunch of fresh broccoli   ¹/₄ **tsp. thyme**
2 tbsp. vegetable oil   **dash of pepper**
¹/₂ **onion**   ¹/₂ **cup sunflower seeds**
3 cups mushrooms   **whole-wheat noodles**
¹/₄ **tsp. salt**   **grated Parmesan cheese**
¹/₂ **tsp. rosemary**

Chop onion, slice mushrooms, and toast sunflower seeds.
    Break broccoli into flowerets and chop a portion of the stems. Heat oil over medium heat. Sauté onions for a few minutes. Add broccoli stems and stir a minute longer. Now add mushrooms, seasonings, and sunflower seeds, and stir 1 more minute. Add ¹/₄ cup of water and place broccoli flowerets on top. Reduce heat, cover, and steam for about 15 minutes. Stir gently. Serve over hot cooked whole-wheat noodles. Sprinkle with grated Parmesan cheese.

Makes 4 or 5 servings.

Broccoli and Mushrooms

An interesting way to serve broccoli.

2 bunches of fresh broccoli
1 cup chicken stock
¼ lb. bacon
2 cups fresh mushrooms
1 small can water chestnuts
¼ cup slivered almonds
½ tsp. salt
⅛ tsp. pepper

Cook broccoli in chicken stock until tender-crisp. Drain and set aside ⅓ cup of the cooking stock. Chop broccoli into bite-sized pieces. Slice mushrooms and water chestnuts. Chop bacon and partially cook it in a skillet. Drain off fat. Then add mushrooms, water chestnuts, almonds, and seasonings. Cook and stir until mushrooms are tender. Add broccoli and stock. Stir gently and cook until heated through.

Makes about 8 servings.

Broccoli Pudding

2 large bunches of broccoli
1 cup mayonnaise
1 tbsp. fresh lemon juice
1 cup medium White Sauce (See page 99.)

Steam broccoli until tender-crisp; drain and chop to make 6 cups. Combine broccoli, mayonnaise, lemon juice, and white sauce in a casserole dish. Bake for 30 minutes at 350°F.

Makes 6 servings.

Barb Pearson, Hamilton, Ont

Glazed Parsnips

Parsnips can be rather anaemic looking, but this glaze really gives them pizzazz!

6 to 8 medium parsnips
¼ cup butter
½ tsp. salt
½ cup orange, pineapple, *or* ginger marmalade
¼ tsp. ginger (Omit if using ginger marmalade.)
1 seedless orange, for garnish

Cut peeled parsnips into 2-inch sticks. Place in boiling, salted water and simmer until tender. Drain, reserving ¼ cup of cooking water, and set aside.

Melt butter in saucepan. Add marmalade, ¼ cup reserved cooking water, and ginger, then mix well. Simmer 5 minutes. Add parsnips and toss gently to coat well with the glaze. Place parsnips in serving dish and spoon remaining glaze over them. Garnish with orange slices cut in half.

Serves 6.

Carrot Casserole

6 to 8 large carrots
¼ cup brown sugar
2 tbsp. fresh lemon juice
½ tsp. grated lemon rind (optional)
½ cup liquid honey
½ tsp. cinnamon
⅛ tsp. ground cloves
¼ cup raisins
¼ cup chopped walnuts *or* hazelnuts

Cut carrots into ¼-inch slices. Bring ¼ cup water to the boil. Add carrots to water, cover tightly, and bring back to the boil. Reduce heat and simmer about 10 minutes, until carrots are almost tender. Drain, reserving cooking water. Place carrots in a buttered baking dish. Combine cooking water with remaining ingredients. Pour over carrots and dot with butter. Bake 30 minutes at 300°F, basting 3 or 4 times.

Makes 6 servings.

Carrot-Turnip Medley

A good idea for people who dislike either cooked carrots or cooked turnip: combined they are great!

carrots
freshly-grated nutmeg (optional)
turnip
butter

Peel carrots and turnip; boil or steam in separate pots until fork-tender. Combine in one pot and mash coarsely together with a potato masher until the two vegetables are fairly well mixed. Add a little butter and perhaps a pinch of nutmeg. Heat through and serve.

Make-Ahead Turnip-Apple Bake

A most welcome recipe at Christmastime or Thanksgiving or any time you are entertaining a crowd. In many Canadian homes, turnip is traditionally served with Christmas dinner. This recipe's greatest asset is that it can be put together two days ahead and merely reheated.

2 to 3 medium turnips
1 cup applesauce *or* 2 or 3 finely chopped apples
4 tbsp. butter (at room temperature)
4 tsp. sugar
1 tsp. salt
$1/4$ tsp. black pepper
2 eggs, lightly beaten
$1^3/4$ cups soft bread-crumbs
2 tbsp. melted butter

Peel turnip, removing all traces of green, and slice as apples for a pie. Cook in boiling water until tender. Mash turnip or purée in food processor. Stir in applesauce or chopped apples, 4 tbsp. butter, sugar, salt, pepper, and eggs. Combine well.

Spoon into a greased 2-quart baking dish and top with the soft bread-crumbs mixed with the melted butter. When casserole is cooked, cover and refrigerate. Remove 1 hour before dinner and heat uncovered in a 350°F oven for 30 minutes or so.

Serves 12.

Ann Budge, Belfountain, Ont

Spaghetti Squash au Gratin

This interesting squash is becoming more popular as people are learning what to do with the long spaghetti-like strands.

1 medium-large spaghetti squash	1½ cups shredded Swiss cheese
1 medium onion	¼ tsp. salt
2 tbsp. butter	¼ tsp. freshly-ground pepper
	pinch of freshly-grated nutmeg

With a skewer, prick squash through to the middle in a dozen places. Set in a low baking dish and bake at 350°F for 1½ hours. Turn squash over after 45 minutes. Slice off ⅓ of the top lengthwise and carefully remove seeds and any liquid. Use a fork to scrape spaghetti-like fibres carefully from both pieces of squash. Drain pieces of shell upside down in a colander.

Sauté chopped onion in butter until soft. Put squash in a bowl and add onion, cheese, salt, pepper, and nutmeg. Mix gently but well. Return squash mixture to larger squash shell (discard the smaller piece) and bake at 350°F for 20 to 25 minutes or until heated through and bubbling.

Makes 6 servings.

Ann Budge, Belfountain, Ont

Spaghetti Squash with Tomato Sauce

1 spaghetti squash	1 tsp. basil
1 onion, chopped	1 tbsp. fresh parsley
1 clove garlic, minced	½ tsp. lemon juice
butter *or* vegetable oil	salt and pepper
5 medium tomatoes, peeled, seeded, and chopped	

Sauté chopped onion and minced garlic in butter or oil. Add tomatoes and their juices, herbs, lemon juice, salt, and pepper. Simmer briefly and set aside.

Simmer whole squash in a large pot of water for 30 minutes. Pierce end with a fork to test to see if it is tender. Cut squash in half lengthwise. Carefully remove the seeds. Scoop out the spaghetti-like fibres and pile on a plate. Toss with a little oil and pour the hot sauce over the squash.

Serves 6.

Squash and Peach Bake

A good autumn vegetable dish to serve with ham, pork chops, or basic meat loaf.

2½ cups sliced, peeled butternut squash *or* vegetable marrow
3 fresh peaches, peeled and sliced
1 to 2 tbsp. butter
1 to 2 tbsp. brown sugar
dash of salt
grated fresh nutmeg *or* allspice

Alternate layers of squash and peaches in a greased shallow baking dish. Top with dabs of butter and sprinkle with brown sugar, salt, and spices. Cover and bake at 350°F for 45 minutes to 1 hour.

Serves 5 or 6.

Baked Green Tomatoes

Wondering what to do with all those green tomatoes still on the plants at the end of the season? Baked this way, they are great!

3 to 4 green tomatoes
1 large onion (optional)
salt and pepper
⅓ cup grated Parmesan cheese
¾ cup fresh bread-crumbs
3 tbsp. butter
¼ tsp. *each* of basil, oregano, and thyme
1 tbsp. butter

Slice *unpeeled* tomatoes into ½-inch thick slices. Slice onion thinly. Grease a low baking dish and arrange tomatoes and optional onion so they are overlapping. Sprinkle with salt and pepper.

Melt 3 tbsp. butter in a small frying pan. Brown bread-crumbs lightly. Stir in herbs. Sprinkle over top of tomatoes and onions. Top with grated Parmesan and dot with 1 tbsp. butter. Bake at 350°F for 45 minutes or until tomatoes and onions are tender.

If you have many green tomatoes, prepare additional dishes of Baked Green Tomatoes. Bake 40 minutes, cool, and freeze. To serve, partially thaw and bake until well heated through.

Serves 3 or 4.

Cucumber or Zucchini Boats

An excellent way to use left-over rice!

4 medium cucumbers *or* zucchini
1 tomato
1¹/₂ cups cooked white *or* brown rice
¹/₃ cup plain yogurt
2 tbsp. Dijon mustard
¹/₄ tsp. thyme *or* savory
¹/₄ tsp. marjoram *or* basil
2 tbsp. chopped chives *or* parsley
salt and pepper
¹/₂ cup dry bread-crumbs
¹/₂ cup freshly-grated Parmesan cheese
2 tbsp. butter

Peel cucumbers but not zucchini. Cut lengthwise, and scrape out the seeds with a spoon. Peel, seed, and chop tomato. Mix rice, yogurt, tomato, mustard, and herbs. Season with salt and pepper.

Place cucumbers or zucchini on a rack in a low baking dish. Pour ¹/₂ cup of water into dish. Fill boats carefully with rice mixture. Sprinkle with bread-crumbs and cheese. Spoon melted butter over top. Bake uncovered at 375°F for 30 to 45 minutes.

Makes 6 to 8 servings.

Zucchini and Tomatoes

Couldn't be simpler or more delicious!

zucchini
tomatoes
onions
cheese
bacon (optional)
bread-crumbs (optional)
oregano (optional)

Arrange layers of sliced zucchini, tomatoes, and onions in a greased shallow baking dish. Top with slices of cheese and partially cooked bacon drained on a paper towel, *or* with grated cheese mixed with bread-crumbs and seasoned with oregano. Bake at 350°F for 1 hour.

Zucchini Bake

This solves the problem of what to do with a bumper crop of zucchini or a near giveaway at your local market.

8 medium zucchini
1 onion
2 tbsp. vegetable oil
3 tbsp. flour
2 tsp. baking powder
¼ tsp. salt
dash of cayenne pepper
1½ cups grated Mozzarella cheese
½ cup cottage cheese
1 tbsp. basil
olives, sliced (optional)

Slice zucchini and onion. Sauté zucchini and onion in vegetable oil in a large frying pan. Mix remaining ingredients, and add the zucchini and onions. Mix well but gently. Pour into a greased 9 x 9-inch baking dish. Bake at 350°F for 35 minutes. Let stand for 15 minutes before cutting into squares to serve.

Serves 9.

Country Corn Pudding

Best when made with kernels of corn cut right from the cob, but you may use frozen or canned corn. Always a favourite with everyone!

¼ **cup butter**
3 tbsp. flour
1½ cups milk
2 eggs
1 tbsp. chopped parsley
¼ **cup finely-chopped green** *or* **sweet red pepper**
salt and pepper
3 cups corn kernels
2 to 3 thin slices of ham
2 to 3 thin slices of Cheddar *or* **Mozzarella cheese**

Melt butter over medium heat in a medium saucepan. Add flour and stir until smooth, then stir and cook 1 more minute. Slowly add milk, stirring constantly. Cook, continuing to stir, until sauce has thickened. Remove from heat and set aside to cool slightly.

Meanwhile, beat eggs in a glass bowl. Gradually whisk sauce into eggs, mixing well after each addition. Stir in parsley, chopped pepper, salt, and pepper. Add corn and stir to mix thoroughly. Spoon into a greased 2-quart baking dish and spread evenly.

Cut ham and cheese slices into 1-inch squares. Arrange squares in a checker-board pattern on top of corn mixture. Bake at 350°F for 20 to 30 minutes, until the centre is set.

Makes 4 to 6 servings.

Creamed Stinging Nettles

Perhaps if orienteers eat enough nettles, there won't be any left to sting us!

stinging nettles
White Sauce (recipe follows)

Don a pair of rubber gloves. Then away you go and gather young nettle tops when they are about 6 inches high.

Wash nettles under running water. Boil, with a minimal amount of water, for a couple of minutes. The boiling will cause the nettles to lose their stinging properties.

Drain off the water and chop the nettles into small pieces. Add to white sauce and serve with pork chops. Delicious!

White Sauce

2 tbsp. butter
2 tbsp. all-purpose flour
1 cup milk
¹/₄ tsp. salt
other seasonings (optional)

Melt butter over low heat. Stir in flour. Cook, stirring, for a few minutes. Slowly stir in milk. Keep stirring until sauce is creamy and thickened. Season with salt and other seasonings, as desired.

Nora Reid, Winnipeg, Man

Traditional Ratatouille

This is the traditional sauté method for preparing ratatouille.

1 medium eggplant
1 tsp. salt
¹/₄ cup vegetable oil
1 onion
2 cloves garlic
1 green pepper
1 cup chopped zucchini
3 tomatoes
2 tsp. basil
salt and pepper
2 tbsp. chopped parsley

Chop onion and green pepper. Mince garlic. Peel, seed, and chop tomatoes. Peel eggplant and cut into ¹/₂-inch slices and then into cubes. Sprinkle with salt and leave to stand 15 minutes. Rinse eggplant and dry with paper towels. Heat oil in frying pan and sauté eggplant until lightly browned. Remove eggplant from pan. Sauté onion, garlic, green pepper, and zucchini for 5 minutes. Return eggplant to pan and add all remaining ingredients. Simmer over low heat for 20 minutes, until almost all of the liquid from the vegetables has evaporated.

Serves 4 or 5.

Nicole Roy, Montreal, Qué

Steamed Ratatouille

Many ratatouille recipes call for sautéing the vegetables. This one is a little different.

2 tbsp. corn oil
3 cloves garlic
3 large onions
4 green peppers, seeded and quartered
1 medium eggplant
5 small zucchini
5 medium tomatoes
salt and pepper

Slice garlic, onions, and tomatoes thickly. Slice eggplant and zucchini into ¼-inch slices.

Place oil and a clove of garlic in the bottom of a deep heavy pot and heat for a few minutes. Layer the following, sprinkling salt and pepper over each layer: onion, green pepper, eggplant, garlic, zucchini, and tomatoes. Fill the pot with layers and add a few drops of oil to the surface, cover, and cook over low heat for 30 to 35 minutes. Gently move contents with a wooden spoon from time to time. Cook final 5 minutes uncovered.

Serves 6.

Layered Vegetable Casserole

A delicious herbed vegetable dish; attractive, too, especially when baked in a glass ovenwear soufflé dish. This is a good buffet dinner dish. Triple the amount of herbs if you are using finely-chopped fresh herbs.

3 tbsp. butter
4 potatoes (preferably new)
1 tsp. dried sage *or* savory
1 tsp. dried tarragon *or* oregano
pinch *each* of salt and pepper
1 green pepper
2 sweet red peppers

⅔ cup frozen peas, thawed
1 onion
½ cup uncooked long-grain rice
3 medium zucchini
4 tomatoes
1 cup grated Swiss cheese

Scrub and slice potatoes into ¼-inch slices, dice peppers, slice onion thinly, and slice tomatoes thickly.

Grease a 10-cup glass baking dish with a little butter or vegetable oil. Place half the potato slices in overlapping rows on the bottom. Dot with a little butter and sprinkle with a pinch of herbs and salt and pepper. Add layers of half the peas, onion, peppers, rice, and zucchini in that order. Dot with butter and sprinkle with herbs and seasonings. Repeat layers, sprinkle with seasonings, and arrange tomatoes on top.

Cover (with foil if dish does not have a cover) and bake in a 350°F oven for at least 1½ hours, until potatoes are tender. Remove casserole from oven, uncover, and sprinkle with cheese. Replace cover and return to oven for about 10 minutes until cheese has melted. Allow casserole to stand, covered, for 10 minutes before serving. Garnish with sprigs of fresh herbs or parsley.

Serves 6 to 8.

Farmer's Market Medley

Simple, colourful, and delicious!

½ **cup chicken stock**
2 cups cut green *or* **yellow beans**
6 carrots
3 medium zucchini
3 onions
1 green pepper
1 tsp. dried basil *or* **1 tbsp. fresh basil, chopped**
salt and freshly-ground pepper

Place chicken stock in a saucepan. Cut carrots into 2-inch sticks. Add beans and carrots to stock. Bring to a boil, reduce heat, and simmer for 2 to 3 minutes. Slice zucchini and onions; cut green pepper into strips. Add zucchini, onions, and green pepper. Continue to simmer for 5 minutes, stirring occasionally. Vegetables should be tender-crisp. Sprinkle basil, salt, and pepper over vegetables; toss and stir to mix well. Serve, spooning any remaining liquid over vegetables.

Serves 6.

Sweet Potatoes with Apricots, Canadian Style

A side dish that will turn leftover cold turkey or ham into something special. It may be prepared the day before and refrigerated until two hours before serving time.

14 to 18 dried apricot halves
6 medium sweet potatoes
$^1/_3$ cup pure Canadian maple syrup
$^1/_4$ tsp. herbs (basil, ginger, rosemary, *or* other favourite)
pinch of salt
3 tbsp. butter

Soak apricots in $^3/_4$ cup boiling water while preparing sweet potatoes. Scrub sweet potatoes but do not peel, and boil until barely tender, about 10 to 15 minutes depending on potato size. Drain and allow to cool. When cool, peel and cut into $^1/_2$-inch slices.

Grease a large, low baking dish and arrange sweet potato slices in it. Drain apricots, reserving the soaking liquid, and arrange on top of the sweet potatoes.

Add maple syrup, salt, and herbs of your choice to apricot soaking liquid. Mix and pour over sweet potatoes and apricots. Dot with butter.

Cover baking dish with foil and bake at 350°F for 30 minutes. Uncover and bake another 10 minutes or until potatoes are tender and a nice glaze has formed. During the last 10 minutes, occasionally stir gently.

If prepared the day before, place foil-covered baking dish in refrigerator and remove 2 hours before serving time so it comes to room temperature before baking as instructed above.

Serves 8 to 10.

Barley-with-Vegetables Casserole

1 cup pot barley   **1 apple**
1 small onion   **1 green pepper**
2 medium zucchini   **$^1/_2$ lb. mushrooms**
1 clove garlic   **2 stalks celery**
$^1/_2$ tsp. oregano   **1$^1/_4$ cups stewed tomatoes**
$^1/_2$ tsp. basil   **1 cup grated Cheddar cheese**
2 tbsp. butter

Cook barley according to package directions and allow to cool. Slice zucchini, celery, and mushrooms. Dice apple, green pepper, and onion. Crush garlic clove.

Combine zucchini, onion, garlic, and herbs in a greased casserole. Dot with butter. Cover and bake at 350°F for 15 minutes.

Add barley, apple, green pepper, mushrooms, and celery. Chop tomatoes and add. Mix well.

Bake at 350°F for 45 minutes. Sprinkle with grated cheese and bake 5 more minutes.

Serves 6.

Vegetable Loaf

An interesting way to serve vegetables. Good with cold leftover roast.

4 large potatoes
4 large carrots
$^1/_2$ cup beef *or* chicken stock
$^1/_2$ green pepper, finely chopped
1 small onion, finely chopped
1 cup wheat germ *or* quick-cooking oats
$^1/_4$ cup butter, melted
2 eggs, lightly beaten
salt and pepper
$^1/_2$ tsp. savory, sage, *or* basil
Quick Tomato Sauce (see page 41) *or* Mushroom Sauce (see page 40)

Chop potatoes and carrots finely, combine, and steam until barely tender. Drain thoroughly. Combine stock, wheat germ, vegetables, melted butter, eggs, and seasonings, and spoon into a well-greased loaf pan. Bake at 350°F for 1 hour or until set. Cut into thick slices to serve. Top with **Quick Tomato Sauce** or **Mushroom Sauce.**

Makes 4 servings.

Löcshen Kügel (Noodle Pudding)

A Jewish dish that is often served at holiday time. While it could be a meal in itself, it is perhaps best served as a side dish.

4 eggs
1 tsp. cinnamon
$\frac{1}{2}$ tsp. salt
$\frac{1}{3}$ cup vegetable oil
$\frac{1}{4}$ cup white sugar
$\frac{1}{4}$ cup raisins
1 14-oz. can crushed pineapple, drained
chopped apple (optional)
1 pkg. broad noodles, cooked

Mix ingredients in order given and pour into 9 x 9-inch greased oven-proof glass baking dish. Bake at 350°F for 30 to 40 minutes. For maximum flavour, serve warm rather than hot.

Makes 5 or 6.

Potatoes *Milles Feuilles*

My daughter Susan aptly named this recipe. You'll see why when you make it!

$\frac{1}{2}$ clove garlic
4 fairly large new potatoes
**$1\frac{1}{2}$ to 2 cups grated cheese (Parmesan, Mozzarella, *or* a
    combination)**
salt and pepper
freshly-grated nutmeg
1 large egg
$1\frac{1}{3}$ cups milk
slivers of butter

Butter a $1\frac{1}{2}$-quart casserole dish. Rub with cut garlic clove.

Peel the potatoes and slice them *paper-thin*. (Using a special slicing blade will make it much easier!) Place the potatoes in the dish in neat rows. Sprinkle salt, pepper, nutmeg, and cheese over each layer. Save a little cheese for the top.

Bring the milk to a boil, then pour slowly, while stirring, over the beaten egg. Stir, then pour over the potatoes. Dot the top of the casserole with butter slivers and sprinkle with remaining cheese.

Bake uncovered in a 375°F oven for 45 minutes. Serve immediately.

Makes 4 to 5 generous servings.

P.S. *Milles Feuilles* is French for "a thousand leaves."

Ann Budge, Belfountain, Ont

Mashed Potato and Cottage Cheese Casserole

5 medium-sized potatoes *or* **1¹/₂ cups leftover mashed potatoes**
1 tbsp. warm milk *or* **melted butter**
pinch of garlic salt
3 drops Tabasco sauce
3 tbsp. sesame seeds
1 tbsp. grated onion
1¹/₂ cups low-fat cottage cheese
¹/₃ cup freshly-grated Parmesan cheese
4 eggs
additional Parmesan cheese and sesame seeds
wheat germ

Boil potatoes with skins on to preserve vitamins. Peel when cool enough to handle. Chop potatoes and place in a large bowl. Add milk or butter, garlic salt, Tabasco sauce, sesame seeds, and onion. Mash and combine thoroughly. Now add cottage cheese, Parmesan cheese, and eggs. Mix thoroughly, mashing with a fork.

Spoon mixture into a greased 9-inch baking dish. Spread evenly and sprinkle top with a mixture of Parmesan cheese, sesame seeds, and toasted wheat germ. Bake at 350°F for about 30 minutes or until set.

Serves 6.

Puffy Potato Bake

Nutritionists say that potatoes are the best source of carbohydrates for athletes.

2 cups cooked mashed potatoes
4 tbsp. butter
2 eggs, beaten
³/₄ cup milk
1 large onion, chopped
³/₄ cup grated old Cheddar cheese
4 tbsp. wheat germ
salt and pepper

Sauté chopped onion in 2 tbsp. butter. Season potatoes with salt and pepper. Stir in remaining 2 tbsp. butter and beat potatoes until creamy. Add eggs, milk, and onions. Mix thoroughly. Spoon into a greased casserole or soufflé dish and cover with grated cheese mixed with wheat germ.

Bake at 350°F until light, puffy, and golden brown, about 30 minutes.

Serves 5 to 6.

Scalloped Potatoes with Cheese and Herbs

A delightful blend of herbs and Swiss cheese make this potato scallop something special. Serve it with cold meat such as leftover roast or meat loaf.

3 tbsp. butter
2 onions, finely chopped
2 cloves garlic, minced
3 cups milk
¹/₄ tsp. dried rosemary
¹/₄ tsp. dried basil
¹/₄ tsp. dried oregano
¹/₂ tsp. salt
¹/₄ tsp. black pepper
2 cups grated Swiss cheese
1 cup fresh bread-crumbs
5 medium potatoes

Melt butter in skillet; add onions and garlic. Cook until tender without browning. Reserve.

Heat milk, rosemary, basil, oregano, salt, and pepper. Reserve. Combine cheese with bread-crumbs.

Peel potatoes; slice thinly. Place one-third of potatoes in the bottom of a buttered 2-quart casserole. Spread half of onions over potatoes and sprinkle with a third of cheese mixture. Place another third of potatoes on top, then remaining onions and another third of cheese. Add remaining potatoes, pour milk mixture over, and sprinkle with remaining cheese.

Bake uncovered at 350°F for 1 hour and 35 minutes, or until potatoes are tender when pierced with a knife. Let stand 10 minutes before serving.

Makes 6 or 8 servings.

Courtesy of The Ontario Milk Marketing Board

Potatoes 'n' Apples

Good with ham, pork, or turkey, especially at Thanksgiving time.

¼ **cup butter**
2 cups warm mashed potatoes
2 cups applesauce
2 tbsp. sugar
½ **tsp. nutmeg**
¼ **tsp. salt**

With electric mixer, beat butter into potatoes until potatoes are light and fluffy. Stir in remaining ingredients. Spoon into greased 1½-quart baking dish. Bake at 325°F for 30 minutes or until heated through. Place under broiler for about 3 minutes to brown top.

Serves 6.

Spanish Bulgur

Bulgur is used instead of rice in this recipe to provide an interesting change. Bulgur is available in most natural food stores. It is precooked cracked wheat.

6 green onions
1 clove garlic
$^1\!/_2$ green pepper
$1^1\!/_4$ cups uncooked bulgur
2 tbsp. vegetable oil
1 cup cooked lima beans
$3^1\!/_2$ cups stewed tomatoes
$^1\!/_2$ tsp. paprika
$^1\!/_4$ tsp. salt
$^1\!/_8$ tsp. pepper
dash of cayenne pepper

Chop green onions, garlic, and green pepper. Heat oil in a heavy frying pan and add garlic, onions, pepper, and bulgur. Sauté for 5 minutes. Add remaining ingredients. Cover and bring to a boil. Reduce heat and simmer for 15 minutes or until bulgur is tender and liquid is absorbed. Add a little water if it gets too dry.

Serves 4 to 6.

Baked Bulgur Pilaf

Chopped cooked meat or seafood could be added to this.

1 cup uncooked bulgur
1 onion
1 tbsp. margarine *or* **butter**
2 cups vegetable, beef, *or* **chicken stock**
2 medium carrots
$^1\!/_4$ tsp. salt
$^1\!/_2$ cup chopped almonds *or* **other nuts, toasted**
$^3\!/_4$ cup grated Cheddar cheese

Grate carrots with a medium grater. Sauté chopped onion and bulgur in margarine for 5 minutes. Add the stock, carrots, and salt. Stir well. Pour into a greased covered casserole. Cover and bake at 350°F for 25 minutes. Stir in nuts. Top with cheese and return to oven until cheese melts, about 8 minutes.

Serves 4.

108

Barley and Mushroom Casserole

A tasty substitute for potatoes.

4 to 5 tbsp. butter
1 medium onion
2 stalks celery
$^1/_2$ lb. fresh mushrooms
$^1/_2$ cup pot *or* pearl barley (Pot barley will give a chewier
   texture.)
3 cups well-seasoned chicken *or* beef stock
$^1/_4$ cup slivered almonds
salt and pepper

Chop onion and celery. Slice mushrooms. Lightly toast almonds and set aside.

Sauté onion, celery, and mushrooms in butter until just soft. Add barley, then stir while browning the barley slightly. Place in a greased casserole dish and stir in the toasted almonds.

Heat stock to boiling point and pour over barley and vegetables. Stir to mix well. Add salt and pepper. Cover and bake at 350°F for 30 minutes. Uncover and continue baking until the liquid is completely absorbed. This should take at least another 30 minutes.

Serves 6.

Brown Rice Pilaf

An excellent way to use up leftover brown rice.

3 to 4 tbsp. butter   **$^1/_2$ cup canned water chestnuts**
1 small onion   **2 cups cooked brown rice**
2 stalks celery   **soy sauce (optional)**
$^1/_2$ cup fresh mushrooms

Slice celery, mushrooms, and water chestnuts. Chop onion.

Melt butter in a skillet, add onion and mushrooms, and sauté for 3 to 4 minutes. Add rice, celery, and water chestnuts. Heat through and add salt and pepper to taste. This pilaf is good served with soy sauce.

Serves 6.

Julie DePass, Oakville, Ont

109

Wendy's Wild Rice Casserole

Wendy bought some wild rice in Minnesota *en route* to the 1982 Canadian Orienteering Championships in Manitoba, and treated some Toronto Orienteering Club members to this delicious dish at a potluck supper.

1 cup uncooked wild rice
1 cup uncooked brown rice
1 large onion, chopped
1 cup chopped fresh mushrooms
salt and pepper
3 tbsp. butter

Simmer 1 cup brown rice in 2½ cups salted water in a covered pot for 45 minutes

Stir 1 cup wild rice into 3 cups of boiling water. Boil for 5 minutes. Remove from heat and let soak in same water, covered, for 1 hour. Drain and rinse. Simmer in 3 cups of salted water for 30 minutes or until curly and tender. (When cooked, the dark kernels curl up, exposing a whitish inner part.)

Sauté onion and mushrooms in 3 tbsp. butter in a large frying pan. Add cooked brown rice and wild rice. Sprinkle with salt and pepper to taste. Stir-fry until hot and slightly browned. Turn into a warm casserole dish and serve.

Serves 6.

Wendy Edge, Bowmanville, Ont

Salads

All-Green Summer Salad

This salad is fun because everything in it is green! If you can think of any green vegetables we've missed, go ahead and add them!

lettuce (several varieties)
spinach
green pepper
cucumber
zucchini
chives *or* **green onion tops**
snowpeas
green peas, cooked
green beans, French-cut and cooked tender-crisp
seedless green grapes, halved
alfalfa sprouts, for garnish

Tear, chop, or slice the above and toss together in a large glass bowl. Keep the alfalfa sprouts to garnish the salad after it is tossed with **Garlic-Cucumber Dressing** at serving time. (If you are not a garlic lover, then substitute a creamy salad dressing of your choice.)

Garlic-Cucumber Dressing

2 large cucumbers
1 cup plain yogurt
1 cup commercial sour cream
¹/₂ tsp. finely-minced garlic
¹/₄ tsp. salt
¹/₄ tsp. freshly-ground black pepper

Peel cucumbers, remove seeds, and grate coarsely. Place in a sieve and press out as much juice as possible. Mix yogurt, sour cream, and seasonings with the cucumber. *Chill for several hours to blend seasonings before serving.* Makes enough dressing for a huge salad.

Dick's Tossed Salad

This tops off any meal and sets you up for an evening of work or exercise. If you can keep this to two servings, let Dick know how. He has trouble!

Tear lettuce into bite-sized pieces, then add any or all of the following:

spinach, torn into bite-sized pieces
celery, chopped
carrots, chopped or grated
parsnips, chopped or sliced with a peeler
cabbage, chopped
apples, chopped unpeeled
pears, chopped unpeeled
grapes, halved and pitted, green or red
raisins
shelled sunflower seeds, just a few
walnuts, chopped
garlic powder
sprinkle of dill
light fennel seeds

Sprinkle lightly with sweet pickle juice or salad cider vinegar. Dribble lightly with sunflower oil. Toss. Sprinkle lightly with wheat germ, grated cheese, crumbled blue or feta cheese, or Grape-Nuts® cereal.

Pat de St. Croix, Vineland, Ont

Overnight Salad

A great make-ahead salad.

1 head iceberg lettuce
³/₄ cup sliced fresh mushrooms
1 onion
¹/₂ green pepper
1 300-g pkg. frozen green peas, neither thawed nor cooked
2 tbsp. sugar
2 cups mayonnaise *or* a combination of yogurt and mayonnaise
1 cup grated Cheddar cheese
8 slices of lean bacon

Grape-Nuts® is a registered trademark of General Foods Inc.

Cook bacon until crisp, drain well, and break into bite-sized pieces. Chop onion and green pepper finely. Break up lettuce and put in the bottom of a wide glass bowl. Top with layers of onion, green pepper, mushrooms, and frozen peas. Cover right out to the edges with mayonnaise or yogurt-mayonnaise mixture. Top with cheese and then bacon pieces. Cover bowl tightly with plastic wrap and place in refrigerator overnight. Serve from the bowl, but do *not* mix the salad.

Serves 6 to 8

Summer Vegetable Salad

An excellent make-ahead salad when fresh vegetables abound.

1 small head cauliflower
3 large carrots
1 cup whole cherry tomatoes
2 cups fresh green beans
1 turnip

Divide cauliflower into flowerets. Slice carrots into $1/4$-inch slices. Cut beans into 2-inch pieces. Cut turnips into $1/4$ x 2-inch sticks.

Cook vegetables (except tomatoes) separately until *barely* tender. Drain, then cover immediately with cold water and drain again. Combine with tomatoes.

Dressing

$1/4$ **cup white *or* tarragon vinegar**
$1/4$ **cup finely-minced onion**
1 clove garlic, crushed
$1/2$ **tsp. dried tarragon**
pinch of dry mustard
$1/4$ **tsp. salt**
black pepper
$3/4$ **cup vegetable oil**

Blend dressing ingredients together; pour over vegetables and mix gently. Add salt and pepper to taste. Chill salad for 12 to 24 hours, stirring once or twice.

Serves 6 to 8.

Lynda Sidney, Sudbury, Ont

Christmas Salad

This red and green salad is very attractive on a Christmas buffet table, but don't ignore it other times of the year. It is prepared a day ahead.

1 bunch fresh broccoli
1 head cauliflower
¹/₂ cucumber (seedless variety)
2 cups cherry tomatoes
1 red onion

Wash, cut, and break broccoli and cauliflower into large bite-sized flowerets with stems not more than 1 inch long. Cut unpeeled cucumber into ³/₄-inch chunks. Slice onion. Wash tomatoes and remove any stems.

Blanch or steam broccoli and cauliflower for 2 minutes. Immediately plunge into very cold water to arrest cooking. When cool, drain well. Mix all vegetables together in a large glass bowl.

Dressing

¹/₂ cup vegetable oil
2 tbsp. tarragon *or* red wine vinegar
2 tbsp. lemon juice
1 tsp. Dijon mustard
1 garlic clove, minced
salt and freshly-ground black pepper

Prepare dressing by placing all ingredients in a deep bowl and whisking to combine ingredients well. Pour dressing over vegetables, cover tightly, and refrigerate for 12 to 24 hours. Stir occasionally. Serve chilled or bring to room temperature before serving. You may wish to serve this salad with a slotted spoon.

Serves 8 to 10, depending on the size of the vegetables.

Cool Spinach Salad

A nice light salad. Prepare enough salad for six and toss with this tangy dressing.

spinach leaves, well washed and drained
canned mandarin oranges, drained, *or* fresh orange sections
slivered almonds, toasted
fresh mushrooms, sliced

Combine the preceding in a glass bowl and chill.

Dressing

$^1/_3$ **cup sunflower oil**
3 tbsp. vinegar
2 tbsp. fresh orange juice (not syrup from canned oranges)
1 tsp. or more Dijon mustard

Mix vinegar, orange juice, and mustard. Beat in oil with a fork. Pour over salad at serving time and toss.

Serves 6.

Spinach Salad with Mushroom Dressing

Everyone loves this dressing! Perhaps it's the tarragon flavour!

10 oz. fresh spinach
4 hard-cooked eggs
1 medium onion
12 slices of lean bacon

Wash spinach, dry well, and tear into bite-sized bits. Slice hard-cooked eggs and onions. Cook bacon until very crisp, drain well, and crumble.

In a large glass bowl arrange alternate layers of salad ingredients. Season each layer with salt and pepper. Serve with a bowl of dressing and let folks help themselves.

Dressing

1 10-oz. can mushroom soup
$^1/_4$ **cup water**
$^1/_2$ **cup tarragon vinegar**
1 tsp. dry mustard
$^1/_4$ **tsp. celery seed**
1 tsp. marjoram
dash of Worcestershire sauce

In a saucepan, combine dressing ingredients. Heat 5 minutes, but do not boil, stirring occasionally. Cool and chill.

Serves 6.

Julie DePass, Oakville, Ont

Spinach-Strawberry Salad

The deep green of the spinach and bright red of the strawberries make a cool, refreshing-looking summer salad.

fresh spinach (enough for 6 servings)
1 cup fresh strawberries
$1/2$ cup slivered *or* $1/3$ cup sliced almonds

Wash, dry, and tear up spinach. Place in a glass salad bowl. Wash, dry, hull, and halve strawberries. Add to salad bowl. Lightly toast almonds. Setting a few aside for garnish, add remainder to the salad.

Dressing

$1/2$ cup sunflower oil
$1/4$ cup vinegar (whatever type you wish)
2 tbsp. white sugar
2 green onions, sliced
3 drops of Worcestershire sauce
1 tbsp. poppy seeds
2 tbsp. lightly-toasted sesame seeds

Place all dressing ingredients in a food processor or blender and process until smooth. Pour over salad and toss at serving time. Garnish with reserved almonds.

Serves 6.

Rabbit's Delight

A favourite with young children.

2 cups grated carrots
$1/2$ cup raisins
mayonnaise

Combine carrots and raisins in a bowl. Stir in a little mayonnaise to moisten.

Serves 4 or 5.

Variation: A little plain yogurt may be added along with the mayonnaise. You may also stir in $1/3$ cup chopped walnuts. (Walnuts should be omitted for very young children.)

Barb Pearson, Hamilton, Ont

Dandelion Salad

Next time you rid your lawn of this pesky weed, have a feast!

2 slices of lean bacon
¹/₂ cup unopened dandelion flower buds
2 cups *young* dandelion leaves

Wash and drain dandelion leaves. Cook bacon until crisp, drain well, and crumble. Add flowers and cook in the bacon fat until the flowers burst open. Drain. Combine leaves, bacon, and flowers in salad bowl.

Dressing

2 tbsp. vegetable oil   **salt and pepper**
1 tbsp. vinegar   **1 tsp. tarragon**

Combine oil, vinegar, and seasonings. Pour over salad and toss.

Serves 4.

Bean Salad

1 can kidney beans
1 can chick peas
1 can green beans *or* equivalent amount of steamed cut fresh beans
1 can yellow beans *or* equivalent amount of steamed cut fresh beans
1 small mild onion

Drain beans well.

Dressing

¹/₂ cup sugar   **¹/₂ tsp. prepared mustard**
¹/₂ cup vegetable oil   **¹/₂ tsp. tarragon**
¹/₂ cup vinegar   **¹/₂ tsp. basil**
¹/₄ tsp. salt   **parsley, chopped**

Dissolve sugar in vinegar, then whisk in oil. Mix herbs and add to oil-vinegar mixture. Pour dressing over beans and marinate, covered, overnight in the refrigerator, stirring occasionally. Add *finely* sliced onion rings 1 hour before serving.

Serves 8.

Gillian Bailey, West Hill, Ont

Dilly Beans

6 to 8 cups fresh green beans
salt
$^1/_2$ cup white wine vinegar
$^1/_3$ cup white sugar
$^1/_2$ cup water
1 tbsp. snipped fresh dill *or* 1 tsp. dried dill weed

Snip ends off beans and leave whole. Steam beans until tender-crisp. Rinse immediately with cold water and drain thoroughly. Season with salt. Combine the vinegar, sugar, water, and dill in a small pot; heat and stir until sugar is dissolved. Cool. Pour over cooled beans. Marinate overnight in refrigerator, stirring occasionally.

Makes 8 servings.

Summer Squash Salad

The most common summer squashes are zucchini, vegetable marrow, crookneck, and straightneck squashes. This makes a pleasant, tangy late-summer salad.

4 cups shredded summer squash
2 cups shredded green *or* red cabbage
$^1/_2$ cup minced green onion *or* chives
1 cup finely-diced medium Cheddar cheese

Remove excess moisture from the squash by pressing it lightly between clean tea towels or paper towels. Toss together the squash, cabbage, green onions or chives, and cheese.

Dressing

$^1/_3$ cup sunflower oil
3 tbsp. lemon juice
$^1/_2$ tsp. dill weed
$^1/_2$ cup sunflower seeds *and/or* chopped nuts, lightly toasted
1 clove garlic, pressed (optional)

Mix oil, lemon juice, dill weed, and optional garlic. Pour over salad; add sunflower seeds *and/or* nuts, then toss.

Makes 4 or 5 servings.

Creamy Coleslaw

1 small cabbage
2 carrots
1 small minced onion

Shred cabbage, grate carrot, and mince onion. Combine.

Dressing

²/₃ cup mayonnaise
1 tbsp. sugar
3 tbsp. vinegar
½ tsp. salt
1 tsp. celery seed

Blend dressing ingredients. Toss with vegetables. Chill. Keeps well in the refrigerator.

Serves 5 or 6.

Cabbage Salad

Great for potluck suppers, and keeps well. This recipe makes a large quantity so it may be more practical to halve the ingredients.

2 cabbages
2 onions
2 carrots
celery seed (optional)
salt and pepper

Grate cabbages, onions, and carrots, then toss together.

Dressing

1 cup white vinegar
1 cup vegetable oil
²/₃ cup white sugar

Bring vinegar, oil, and sugar to a boil. Pour over cabbage mixture and refrigerate overnight. At serving time, drain and season with salt, pepper, and celery seed. Will keep in a large glass jar with a tight lid in the refrigerator for 3 weeks.

At least 20 servings.

Flavia Simpson, Hamilton, Ont

Fruit Slaw

Julie brought this to a potluck supper at one of Orienteering Ontario's Annual General Meetings. Many people asked her for the recipe. Here it is!

1 small head cabbage
1 medium apple
$^1/_2$ cup seedless grapes
1 10-oz. can mandarin oranges, drained
$^1/_4$ cup raisins
$^1/_4$ cup chopped walnuts

Shred cabbage. Core apple and cut into 1-inch slices. (If not serving immediately, toss apples in a little lemon juice to keep them from browning. Cortlands don't brown easily.) Cut grapes in half. Mix fruits, nuts, and cabbage. Cover and chill. Toss with the following dressing at serving time.

Dressing

$^1/_3$ cup honey
3 tbsp. lemon juice
1 tsp. celery seeds, poppy seeds, *or* toasted sesame seeds (Each gives quite a different flavour.)
$^1/_2$ cup vegetable oil
$^1/_2$ tsp. dry mustard
$^1/_2$ tsp. paprika
$^1/_4$ tsp. salt

In a blender or food processor place honey, lemon juice, seeds, dry mustard, paprika, and salt. Process until just mixed. With the machine running, gradually pour in the vegetable oil, taking about 1 minute to add. Process for another 15 seconds. The dressing should be slightly thick. Chill.

Serves 8.

Julie DePass, Oakville, Ont

German Potato Salad

So tasty! Worth the last minute preparation.

4 slices of lean bacon
2 cups diced cooked potatoes,
 still warm
2 hard-cooked eggs
1 small onion
mayonnaise

¹/₄ tsp. salt
1 egg, well beaten
¹/₂ tsp. sugar
¹/₈ tsp. dry mustard
2 tbsp. vinegar
2 tbsp. chopped chives

Cook bacon until crisp, drain well, and crumble. To the warm (not hot) bacon fat add the beaten egg, seasonings, and vinegar. Stir until sauce is thick.

Pour over warm potatoes and mix well. Add chopped eggs, bacon, chopped onions, and chives. Stir in mayonnaise to taste. Serve immediately.

Makes 4 servings.

Potato Salad Meal

An excellent salad to take in your cooler on a picnic. Vary the amounts according to the size of your group. Prepared in the cool of the morning, this can also be a delicious supper on a hot summer evening.

2 cups diced cooked potatoes, preferably unpeeled
1 cup diced cooked ham
³/₄ cup diced medium *or* old Cheddar cheese
3 tbsp. chopped parsley
¹/₃ cup cooked corn kernels
¹/₃ cup cooked green peas
2 tbsp. minced onion
¹/₂ cup mayonnaise
¹/₂ cup plain yogurt
¹/₄ tsp. freshly-ground black pepper

Mix together potatoes, ham, cheese, corn, peas, parsley, and onion in a large bowl.

Whisk together mayonnaise, yogurt, and pepper. If dressing is too thick, thin with a little milk.

Pour dressing over ham, cheese, and vegetable mixture, and toss to coat all ingredients evenly. Refrigerate until well chilled.

Serves 4 as a main dish, or 6 as a side dish or buffet salad.

Paul's Favourite Pasta Salad

Always in the Rietzschel's picnic basket at orienteering meets!

4 cups cooked macaroni *or* small shells, drained and cooled
4 radishes, chopped
1 onion, diced
1 or 2 tomatoes, chopped
4 tbsp. mayonnaise
2 stalks of celery, sliced
4 large dill pickles, chopped
¹/₂ cup liquid from dill pickles
4 slices of ham *or* cooked chicken, cut into small pieces

Mix vegetables and ham or chicken in a large bowl, then add liquid from the pickles and mayonnaise, as well as salt and pepper to taste. Mix well. Slowly add cooked pasta and mix again. Refrigerate overnight. Ready to take orienteering! *Bon appétit!*

Serves 4.

Denyse Rietzschel, St. Louis de Terrebonne, Qué

Overnight Macaroni Supper Salad

For a cool patio supper complete in one bowl, try this layered salad. Be sure to prepare it the night before.

2 cups frozen peas, thawed
¹/₂ cup thinly-sliced celery
1 cup uncooked macaroni
1 cup thinly-sliced radishes
¹/₂ cup sliced green peppers
2 cups thinly-sliced carrots
4 green onions, sliced
1 cup grated old Cheddar cheese
3 slices cooked ham, cut into strips
3 hard-cooked eggs, sliced

Dressing

³/₄ cup mayonnaise	3 tbsp. milk
¹/₄ cup sour cream	¹/₄ tsp. salt
¹/₄ cup yogurt	¹/₄ tsp. paprika
1 tsp. prepared mustard	dash of white pepper

Cook macaroni according to package directions, drain well, and cool.

To make dressing, mix all ingredients thoroughly.

To assemble salad, layer all ingredients in a large glass bowl as follows: Start with peas, then celery, and half the macaroni. Top with ¹/₃ cup of salad dressing. Then layer radishes, green peppers, carrots, green onions, remaining macaroni, ¹/₃ cup salad dressing, grated cheese, ham, and egg slices. Top with remaining salad dressing, spreading dressing to edge of bowl to completely cover top layer. Cover and refrigerate overnight.

Makes 4 to 6 servings.

Courtesy of Foodland Ontario

Tuna Macaroni Salad

1 cup cooked elbow macaroni, drained
3 green onions *or* 1 small onion, chopped
1 hard-cooked egg, chopped
4 stalks celery, chopped
1 7¹/₂-oz. can tuna, drained
1 cup mayonnaise *or* ¹/₂ cup mayonnaise and ¹/₂ cup yogurt

Combine all ingredients and chill for 2 to 3 hours. Add more mayonnaise if a more moist salad is desired.

Serves 3 or 4.

Barb Pearson, Hamilton, Ont

Barley Salad

1 cup uncooked barley
3 cups chicken *or* vegetable stock
1 cup cooked chick peas
$^3/_4$ cup chopped unsalted nuts (any variety)
1 large carrot, grated
$^1/_4$ cup chopped parsley
2 tbsp. chopped fresh mint *or* 1 tsp. dried mint
lettuce leaves
carrot curls or chopped parsley, for garnish

Cook barley in boiling stock until tender, about 1 hour. Drain, rinse with cold water, and drain again. Toss chick peas, nuts, grated carrot, parsley, and mint with barley.

Dressing

3 tbsp. vegetable oil
3 tbsp. lemon juice
$^1/_4$ tsp. salt
$^1/_4$ tsp. pepper
$^1/_4$ tsp. dry mustard

With a whisk, beat together vegetable oil, lemon juice, mustard, salt, and pepper. Pour over barley mixture and toss to coat. Chill several hours. Spoon salad into a bowl lined with lettuce leaves. Sprinkle with chopped parsley to garnish. Carrot curls also make a colourful garnish.

Serves 6.

Bulgur and Vegetable Salad

A colourful salad and another use for wholesome bulgur. This is a particularly good wintertime salad.

1 cup uncooked bulgur
$1^1/_2$ cups broccoli flowerets
$^2/_3$ cup homemade chicken stock
3 tbsp. vinegar, any variety
$1^1/_2$ tsp. Dijon mustard
$^1/_4$ tsp. salt
1 clove garlic, minced
$^1/_4$ tsp. ground black pepper
$^1/_3$ cup thinly-sliced radishes
$^1/_3$ cup thinly-sliced celery
$^1/_4$ cup thinly-sliced green onions *or* chives
$1^1/_2$ tbsp. vegetable oil
$^1/_2$ tsp. vinegar, any variety

Steam broccoli until still slightly crisp. Drain well and dry between clean towels. Cut into tiny pieces.

Bring stock, 3 tablespoons of vinegar, mustard, garlic, salt, and pepper to boil in medium saucepan. Add bulgur. Cover and let sit, off the burner, for about 15 minutes or until stock is absorbed by the bulgur.

Place bulgur in a bowl and fluff gently with a fork. Carefully stir in the broccoli, radishes, celery, and green onions. Mix the vegetable oil with $1/2$ tsp. of vinegar and fold carefully into salad. This salad is best served at room temperature.

Serves 6.

Rice and Tuna Salad

The recipe can be extended by simply adding more cooked rice. It is an excellent winter salad.

1 cup uncooked rice
1 7-oz. can tuna fish
3 or 4 large carrots
4 stalks celery
$1/2$ small cabbage
$1/4$ cup chopped parsley
$1/2$ small onion

Drain and break up tuna with a fork. Finely grate cabbage and carrot. Chop celery and onion.

Cook rice according to package directions. Put in a large bowl and allow to cool. Add tuna, carrots, celery, cabbage, parsley, and onion. Toss lightly and chill.

Dressing

$3/4$ cup mayonnaise
1 tbsp. lemon juice
$1/4$ tsp. Worcestershire sauce
$1/4$ tsp. salt
$1/8$ tsp. savory
$1/8$ tsp. marjoram

Combine dressing ingredients and add to salad at serving time. Toss lightly.

Serves 4 to 6.

Ham-Rice Salad

2 cups diced cooked ham
2 cups cooked white *or* brown rice
1 stalk celery
$\frac{1}{2}$ green pepper
$\frac{1}{4}$ cup chopped parsley
3 green onions
1 11-oz. can manderin oranges, drained
$\frac{1}{2}$ cup slivered almonds
$\frac{1}{4}$ cup shredded coconut

Slice celery. Chop green pepper and onions. Lightly toast almonds. Mix all ingredients together.

Dressing

$\frac{1}{3}$ cup vegetable oil
3 tbsp. white *or* tarragon vinegar
2 tbsp. fresh orange juice (not syrup from canned oranges)
1 tsp. to 1 tbsp. Dijon mustard
$\frac{1}{8}$ tsp. salt

One at a time, add other ingredients to vinegar while beating with a fork.

Toss salad with dressing, and sprinkle with additional coconut at serving time.

Makes 6 servings.

Salmon and Yogurt Slimmer

$\frac{1}{2}$ cup plain low-fat yogurt
$\frac{1}{2}$ small cucumber
1 tbsp. green onion, chopped
$\frac{1}{2}$ small clove garlic

salt and pepper
1 can salmon, drained
leafy lettuce

Grate cucumber and mince garlic. Mix together yogurt, grated cucumber, onion, and seasonings. Cover and refrigerate. Serve over flaked salmon on a bed of lettuce. Garnish with sliced cucumber and tomato wedges. *Bon appétit!*

Serves 1. 210 calories per serving.

Denise Rietzschel, St. Louis de Terrebonne, Qué

Avocado and Orange Salad

"A must for Fit To Eat," says Susan.

1¹/₂ large heads of romaine lettuce
1 11-oz. can mandarin oranges *or* fresh orange sections
2 ripe avocados
handful of toasted slivered almonds

Tear lettuce into the size of pieces you like for a salad. Drain canned oranges, or peel fresh oranges and divide into sections, removing the white membranes carefully. Slice avocado close to serving time so it does not discolour. Toss oranges and avocado in a bowl along with almonds.

Dressing

¹/₃ cup vegetable oil
¹/₃ cup orange juice (*not* syrup from canned oranges)
¹/₄ cup white wine vinegar
1 small clove garlic
1¹/₂ tbsp. grated orange peel (optional)
1¹/₂ tsp. basil
1 tsp. sugar
¹/₄ tsp. salt
pepper
yogurt (optional)

Combine dressing ingredients and blend in blender at least one hour before serving to allow flavours to mellow. If you prefer the dressing to be thicker, stir in a little plain yogurt.

At serving time, pour dressing over salad and toss lightly.

Serves 8 to 10.

Susan Budge, Waterloo, Ont

Curried Chicken Salad

3 cups diced cooked chicken
1 cup drained pineapple tidbits *or* dried apricots
$^1/_2$ cup walnut halves *or* slivered almonds
6 green onions
$^1/_4$ cup raisins
$^1/_2$ cup green seedless grapes

If using apricots, cut them into quarters. Slice green onions and cut grapes in half. Lightly toast walnuts or almonds. Combine chicken, fruit, nuts, and onions.

Dressing

$^1/_4$ cup mayonnaise
1 cup plain yogurt
$^1/_3$ cup milk
2 tbsp. lemon juice
1 tbsp. curry powder (or less to taste)
2 tsp. Dijon mustard
$^1/_4$ tsp. salt

Mix mayonnaise and yogurt with a fork, then add milk and lemon juice. Add seasonings last. Mix well. Toss salad with dressing and serve on lettuce leaves.

Serves 10.

Apple Salad

romain lettuce
1 mild-flavoured onion
$^1/_2$ English cucumber, unpeeled
1 Granny Smith apple, unpeeled
$^1/_2$ cup pecan halves *or* coarsely chopped hazelnuts
$^1/_2$ cup raisins
alfalfa sprouts, for garnish

Thinly slice onion, cucumber, and apple. Tear lettuce into pieces and place in a salad bowl. Add remaining ingredients.

Sesame Yogurt Dressing

3 tbsp. tahini (sesame purée)
3 tbsp. apple cider vinegar
¼ cup vegetable oil
¼ cup plain yogurt
juice of ½ lemon
2 tbsp. chopped parsley

Combine the above ingredients and beat with a fork or whisk. Season to taste with salt and pepper.

Pour dressing over salad. Garnish with alfalfa sprouts.

Serves 4.

Waldorf Salad

1 green apple (Granny Smith)
1 red apple
3 or 4 stalks celery
1 cup seedless green grapes
½ cup grated mild cheese
½ cup coarsley-chopped walnuts

Dice unpeeled apples and sprinkle with lemon juice to prevent browning. Slice celery. Cut grapes in half. Toss together celery, grapes, cheese, and apples.

Dressing

¼ cup mayonnaise
¼ cup plain yogurt

Combine mayonnaise and yogurt. Pour over salad and toss to coat.

Refrigerate until serving time. Toast walnuts lightly, add to salad, and toss it again. Serve on a bed of lettuce.

Makes 6 servings.

Three-Fruit Salad

As a light summer lunch, this is tops.

1 large orange
1 banana
1 large apple
lettuce leaves

Peel orange, remove membranes, and cut into bite-sized pieces.
Cut banana into small chunks. Slice apple as you would for a
pie. Mix the fruit and place on lettuce leaves.

Dressing

$^1/_2$ cup cottage cheese
$^1/_4$ cup orange juice
1$^1/_2$ tsp. lemon juice
$^1/_2$ tsp. liquid honey
$^1/_8$ tsp. salt
$^1/_4$ cup toasted sesame seeds

Blend and pour over salad

Serves 2 or 3.

Basic Oil and Vinegar Dressing

1 cup vegetable oil
$^1/_4$ cup wine vinegar *or* tarragon vinegar (recipe follows)
pinch of dry mustard
salt and pepper
1 clove garlic
yogurt (optional)

Mix vinegar, mustard, salt, and pepper. Beat in oil with a fork or
wire whisk. Pour into dressing bottle. Add garlic to bottle.
Remove garlic after 6 to 12 hours, depending on how strong you
wish the garlic flavour to be. Store dressing in refrigerator.
Before using, shake to blend.

For a low-calorie dressing, mix equal portions of dressing
and low-fat yogurt at serving time.

Tarragon Vinegar

white vinegar
tarragon sprigs

Prepare your own tarragon vinegar by stuffing as many fresh tarragon sprigs as possible into a bottle. Fill with luke-warm white vinegar. Cover and place in the sun to steep for 3 weeks or until vinegar is nicely flavoured. Remove tarragon sprigs and replace with a fresh sprig. Cover and store in a cool, dark place. Tarragon is easy to grow in your garden or in a flower pot.

Whipped Dressing

This is a tasty, thick dressing. It's my Dad's favourite!

2 egg yolks
1/4 cup Dijon mustard
1 1/2 cups sunflower oil
1/2 cup white vinegar
salt and pepper

Beat egg yolks until thick and light in colour. Add mustard. Beat until smooth. Add vinegar, salt, and pepper. *Very* slowly add oil while beating. It should take 10 to 12 minutes to add oil. Refrigerate.

Susan Budge, Waterloo, Ont

Yogurt Dressing

This is particularly good on a spinach salad.

1/2 cup plain yogurt
1 clove garlic
1 to 2 tsp. Dijon mustard
1 tbsp. lemon juice
2 tbsp. safflower *or* sunflower oil
salt and pepper
1/2 tsp. liquid honey
1 tbsp. chopped chives *or* green onion tops

Press garlic clove through a garlic press. Mix all ingredients and beat well with a fork or wire whisk. Refrigerate in a tightly-capped bottle.

Tofu Mayonnaise

1 cup tofu
2¹/₂ tbsp. sunflower *or* safflower oil
2¹/₂ tbsp. cider vinegar
1 tsp. Dijon mustard
¹/₄ tsp. salt

Mash tofu with a fork. Blend in other ingredients with a whisk. To achieve the best flavour, let mayonnaise stand 20 minutes before serving. Refrigerate any left-over dressing for a day or two.

Buttermilk Dressing

An excellent dressing for a Calico Salad made with chopped tomatoes, corn cut from the cob, diced red or green peppers, tender-crisp green beans, thinly-sliced red onions, and celery. It is equally good on a lettuce or spinach salad.

1 small clove garlic
1 tbsp. wine vinegar
1 tsp. Dijon mustard
1 cup buttermilk
4 tbsp. vegetable oil
¹/₄ tsp. salt
2 tsp. chopped fresh parsley
2 tsp. chopped fresh dill *or* ¹/₂ tsp. dried dillweed
freshly-ground black pepper

Mince garlic and place in a tightly-lidded bottle. Add mustard and vinegar. Shake well to mix. Add oil and buttermilk and shake again. Add salt, parsley, dill, and a few grinds of pepper. Shake once more and refrigerate.

If you prefer a quicker method, all ingredients may be placed in a food processor and processed until well mixed.

Oriental Dressing

Great on a salad of spinach, sliced mushrooms, bean sprouts, and sliced water chestnuts.

¹/₄ **cup soy sauce**
1¹/₂ tbsp. lemon juice
¹/₂ **tsp. sugar**
pinch of ground ginger
1 tsp. grated onion
²/₃ **cup vegetable oil**
1 tsp. toasted sesame seeds

Combine ingredients. Shake vigorously in a tightly covered dressing bottle.

Carrot Juice Dressing

Carrot juice is finding its way into all kinds of recipes. Here is an excellent use for it — particularly if you are fortunate enough to have a juicer and can prepare your own. This dressing is excellent on a salad of crisp greens.

2 green onions
1 medium tomato
¹/₃ **cup carrot juice, fresh *or* canned**
3 tbsp. sunflower oil
3 tbsp. fresh lemon juice
¹/₃ **tsp. basil**
pinch of salt
pinch of white pepper

Chop green onions and tomato. Place in a blender along with remaining ingredients. Blend until smooth. Refrigerate. Pour liberally over salad greens at serving time and toss.

Makes ¹/₂ cup of dressing

Sesame Dressing

A unique dressing that is particularly suited to salads that include tomatoes. Try it for a change on potato salad!

$^1/_2$ **cup sunflower oil**
$^1/_4$ **cup lemon juice**
2 tbsp. tahini (sesame purée)
1 tsp. soy sauce
1 tsp. dried *or* fresh dill weed

Mix all ingredients well. If you use a blender, do not run it for too long or the dressing will be too thick. If that happens, thin it with additional oil and lemon juice.

Low-Calorie Oil and Vinegar Dressing

Chicken stock replaces some of the oil in this dressing, resulting in lower calorie content.

$^1/_2$ **cup safflower *or* sunflower oil**
$^1/_2$ **cup homemade chicken stock**
3 to 4 tbsp. cider *or* tarragon vinegar
1 tbsp. red wine vinegar
1 tbsp. lemon juice
1 tsp. Dijon mustard
$^1/_2$ **tsp. dill weed (optional)**
1 tsp. chopped parsley
1 tsp. chopped chives *or* green onion tops
salt and pepper

With a fork, mix ingredients in the order given. Shake vigorously in a bottle with a tight lid. Store in refrigerator.

Makes 1$^1/_3$ cups.

Low-Calorie Tomato Juice Dressing

The vegetable oil may be omitted, but it does help the dressing adhere to the salad greens.

$\frac{1}{2}$ cup tomato juice
2 tbsp. lemon juice
1 tbsp. vinegar
1 tbsp. vegetable oil
$\frac{1}{2}$ tsp. prepared mustard
1 tsp. chopped chives *or* green onions
pinch of garlic salt
$\frac{1}{2}$ tsp. Worcestershire sauce
1 or 2 drops Tabasco sauce
1 tsp. liquid honey

Blend all ingredients with a wire whisk, or for a short time in a blender. Store in a tightly-covered bottle in refrigerator. Shake before serving.

Skinny Goddess Dressing

No promises, but it *is* low in calories!

$\frac{1}{2}$ cup low-fat cottage cheese
$\frac{1}{4}$ cup low-fat plain yogurt
1 tbsp. vinegar, any variety
2 tbsp. chopped parsley
$\frac{1}{2}$ garlic clove
$\frac{1}{4}$ tsp. salt
3 drops Tabasco sauce

Put all ingredients in a blender and whirl until smooth. Refrigerate.

Makes $\frac{3}{4}$ cup. 10 calories per tablespoon.

Susan Budge, Waterloo, Ont

Low-Calorie Blue Cheese Dressing

$^1/_4$ **cup blue cheese**
1 tsp. white vinegar
$^1/_2$ **tsp. sugar**
$^1/_4$ **tsp. salt**
$^1/_2$ **cup plain low-fat yogurt**

In a small bowl, crumble and mash cheese with a fork. Mix in vinegar, sugar, and salt. Stir in yogurt. Cover and chill.

Makes $^3/_4$ cup.

Julie DePass, Oakville, Ont

Cookies & Squares

Granola-Bran Cookies

$^1/_2$ **cup vegetable shortening**
$^3/_4$ **cup firmly-packed brown sugar**
1 egg
$^1/_4$ **cup liquid honey**
1 tsp. vanilla
1 cup whole-wheat flour
1 tsp. baking powder
$^3/_4$ **tsp. cinnamon *or* nutmeg**
$^1/_2$ **tsp. salt**
$^1/_3$ **cup raisins**
$^1/_3$ **cup chopped walnuts**
$^1/_3$ **cup prepared dry bran cereal**
$^1/_3$ **cup granola-type cereal**

Cream shortening and sugar. Add egg, vanilla, and honey. Mix dry ingredients together and add to creamed mixture. Drop by spoonfuls onto a greased baking sheet. Flatten slightly with a fork. Bake at 350°F for 10 minutes or until lightly browned.

Makes 3 dozen cookies

Sue Brenot, Ottawa, Ont

Sesame-Peanut Butter Balls

¹/₂ **cup freshly-ground peanut butter**
¹/₂ **cup liquid honey**
³/₄ **cup instant skim milk powder**
¹/₂ **cup wheat germ**
1 **tbsp. brewer's yeast**
sesame seeds, toasted

Combine peanut butter, honey, milk powder, wheat germ, and brewer's yeast; blend well. Form into 1-inch balls and roll in sesame seeds to coat outside. Store in tightly-covered container in refrigerator. Really good!

Lynn MacDonald, Dartmouth, NS

Date-Filled Cookies

These cookies, which can be made in a variety of shapes, are always a favourite! When you can manage a few extra calories in your diet, have one with a glass of milk!

1 **cup butter**
1 **cup firmly-packed brown sugar**
1 **cup Demerara sugar**
2 **eggs, beaten**
¹/₂ **tsp. vanilla**
3 **cups all-purpose flour**
1 **cup quick-cooking oats**
2 **tsp. cream of tartar**
1 **tsp. baking soda**
¹/₄ **tsp. salt**
Date Filling (recipe follows)

Cream butter and sugar until fluffy, then beat in eggs. Add vanilla. Mix dry ingredients together. Gradually add dry ingredients to batter. Mix well. Place batter in refrigerator until it is easy to handle, at least an hour.

Date Filling

1¹/₂ **cups chopped dates**   1 **cup orange juice**
grated rind of 1 orange   **dash of salt**
¹/₄ **cup honey**

Cut dates with scissors dipped in hot water. Combine all ingredients in a heavy-bottomed pot. Bring to a boil; then turn heat down and cook until mixture is fairly dry. Allow to cool before spreading on cookies.

Roll out dough to ¼-inch thickness on a floured board. Now there are some choices! Try making some of each.
- Cut into 2-inch or 3-inch rounds. Bake, cool, then put together sandwich-style with date filling.
- Cut into 3-inch rounds. Place about ½ tsp. filling on each circle. Fold over, making a half-moon-shaped cookie. Seal edges with a fork dipped in flour and bake.
- Cut into 2-inch or 3-inch rounds. Place a small spoonful of filling in centre of 1 circle, then top with another. Seal edges with a fork dipped in flour and bake.
- Spread rolled-out dough with filling and roll up like a jelly roll. Refrigerate roll, wrapped in waxed paper, for a couple of hours. Slice ¼-inch thick and bake.

Place cookies on greased baking sheets and bake in a 350°F oven for 10 to 15 minutes, depending on the size of the cookies. Bake until cookie is just set, being careful not to overcook. Remove from oven and leave on baking sheet for a few minutes. Then remove to finish cooling on a rack.

Butterscotch Chipits® Honey Granola Cookies

Soft cookies with a chewy texture.

½ **cup margarine**
½ **cup honey**
1 egg
1 tsp. vanilla
1 cup all-purpose flour
½ **tsp. baking soda**
½ **tsp. salt**
1½ **cups granola-type cereal**
1 cup (175-g pkg.) Butterscotch Chipits®

Cream margarine with honey. Beat in egg and vanilla. Stir together flour, baking soda, and salt. Gradually blend into creamed mixture. Stir in granola cereal and Butterscotch Chipits®. Drop from a medium spoon onto greased baking sheets. Bake at 350°F for 10 to 12 minutes.

Makes about 3 dozen cookies

Courtesy of Nabisco Brands Ltd

Chipits® is a registered trademark of Nabisco Brands Ltd.

Orange-Chocolate Chip Cookies

A delicious new twist to an old favourite!

¹/₃ **cup vegetable shortening**
¹/₃ **cup margarine** *or* **butter**
¹/₃ **cup firmly-packed brown sugar**
3 tbsp. white sugar
1 egg
1 tsp. vanilla
1 cup all-purpose flour
¹/₂ **tsp. baking soda**
¹/₄ **tsp. salt**
finely-grated rind of 1 medium orange
³/₄ **to 1 cup semi-sweet pure chocolate chips**
¹/₂ **cup chopped nuts** *or* **raisins (optional)**

Cream together shortening, margarine, and sugars. Beat in egg and vanilla. Combine flour, baking soda, salt, orange rind, chocolate chips, and nuts or raisins. Stir this dry mixture into the creamed mixture. Drop by spoonfuls (teaspoons or tablespoons, depending on the size of cookie you wish) onto *ungreased* baking sheets. Bake at 375°F for 10 to 12 minutes.

Makes 2 to 3 dozen cookies, depending on the size. This recipe doubles well.

Shelagh MacDonald, Mississauga, Ont

Old-Fashioned Soft Molasses Cookies

1 cup brown *or* **white sugar**
1 cup molasses
1 cup vegetable shortening
4 cups all-purpose flour *or* **3¹/₂ cups whole-wheat flour**
2 tsp. baking soda
1 egg
1 cup boiling water
1 tsp. cinnamon
¹/₂ **tsp. ground cloves**
¹/₂ **tsp. salt**
1 cup raisins *or* **currants**

Soak raisins or currants in 1 cup of boiling water for about 1 hour. Drain, reserving water for adding to cookie batter. Chill water in refrigerator.

Melt shortening and cream with sugar and molasses. Stir baking soda into 1 cup flour and add to batter. Stir in egg and chilled water drained from raisins or currants.

Sift together remaining flour, cinnamon, cloves, and salt. Stir into creamed mixture along with raisins or currants.

Refrigerate for 1 hour; then drop by tablespoonfuls onto a *well-greased* cookie sheet. Bake at 375°F for 12 to 15 minutes. Cookies will still be very soft in the centre when done; be careful not to overbake them.

Makes 4 to 5 dozen.

In-Training Cookies

These cookies, which are high in calories, are permissible only after an all-day cycle or cross-country ski, or a long training run!

$^1/_2$ **cup butter** *or* **margarine**
$^1/_2$ **cup smooth peanut butter**
1 cup white sugar
1 cup firmly-packed brown sugar
2 eggs
$^1/_2$ **cup milk**
1 tsp. vanilla
$^7/_8$ **cup whole-wheat flour**
1 cup all-purpose flour
1 tsp. baking soda
$^1/_4$ **tsp. salt**
$^1/_4$ **cup semi-sweet chocolate chips**
$2^1/_2$ **cups quick-cooking oats**
$^1/_2$ **cup raisins**

Blend butter, peanut butter, and sugars until smooth. Beat in eggs, milk, and vanilla. Sift flour, baking soda, and salt; then add to batter. Mix well and add chocolate chips, oatmeal, and raisins.

Drop by tablespoonfuls on *ungreased* cookie sheets. Bake at 350°F for 15 minutes.

Makes about 40 large cookies.

Colin's Cookies

We understand these cookies are a big hit at the Fitness and Amateur Sports Centre floor parties at 333 River Road, Ottawa. Colin has become famous for them!

Colin says that this is a great TV-watching recipe for when one is resting one's well-exercised muscles. It takes about 10 minutes to make the dough. After putting the cookies in the oven, you can watch TV or listen to long-playing records; the length of one side of a record or the time between TV commercials is just about the ideal time for a batch of cookies to bake. Two periods of a hockey game and the entire batch of cookies is ready!

1 egg, beaten
1 cup butter *or* margarine
1 cup white sugar
½ cup firmly-packed brown sugar
1 cup all-purpose flour
1¾ cups quick-cooking oats
½ cup raisins (optional)
¾ cups flaked coconut *or* slivered
    almonds (optional)
1 tsp. baking powder
1 tsp. baking soda

Beat together egg, butter, and sugars. Cream well. Mix flour with baking powder and baking soda, then with remaining ingredients, and stir into batter. Take small portions between the palms of the hands and roll into small balls. Place the balls about 3 inches apart on a greased cookie sheet. The heat soon melts the balls into nice round shapes. Bake at 350°F for 12 to 15 minutes or until golden.

Makes 50 to 60.

Colin Kirk, Ottawa, Ont
Executive Director
Canadian Orienteering Federation

Anzac Biscuits

This is an old Australian recipe named for the Australia-New Zealand Army Corps.

$^1/_2$ **cup butter**
1 tbsp. honey *or* **golden syrup**
2 tbsp. boiling water
1 tsp. baking soda
1 cup rolled oats (*not*** quick-cooking)**
1 cup flaked coconut
1 cup whole-wheat *or* **all-purpose flour**
$^1/_2$ **cup firmly-packed brown sugar**

Melt butter and honey over low heat. Add boiling water mixed with baking soda. Mix dry ingredients. Pour liquid mixture over dry ingredients. Blend well.

Drop teaspoonfuls of dough onto greased baking sheets. Bake in a 300°F oven for 20 minutes. Leave to cool, then remove from baking sheet.

This recipe doubles easily.

Robyn Rennie, Vancouver, BC

Whole-Wheat Peanut Butter Cookies

$^1/_2$ **cup butter** *or* **margarine**
$^1/_2$ **cup liquid honey**
$^1/_2$ **cup firmly-packed brown sugar**
1 egg
1$^1/_4$ cups whole-wheat flour
1 tsp. baking powder
1 cup peanut butter
chocolate *or* **carob chips (optional)**

Cream together peanut butter, butter or margarine, brown sugar, and honey. Beat in egg. Combine flour and baking powder and add to creamed mixture. Add chocolate or carob chips if desired. Roll dough into small balls and place on a greased cookie sheet. Flatten with a fork dipped in vegetable oil or water.

Bake at 350°F for 15 minutes.

Makes about 3 dozen medium cookies.

Jenny Birchell, Hamilton, Ont

Team Bus Cookies

A good nutritious cookie to take on the team bus!

1½ cups vegetable shortening
2 cups firmly-packed brown sugar
1½ cups all-purpose flour
2 tsp. baking powder
¼ tsp. baking soda
½ tsp. salt
¾ cup natural bran
1½ cups quick-cooking rolled oats
½ cup flaked coconut

Cream together shortening and sugar. Thoroughly mix dry ingredients.

Add the dry ingredients to the creamed mixture. Drop by spoonfuls onto a greased baking sheet. Bake for 10 to 15 minutes at 375°F.

Makes about 5 dozen medium cookies.

Ann Urquhart, Fredericton, NB

Stokely Creek Cookies

Phyllis Burrell-Elyk, the resident culinary artist at Stokely Creek Ski Touring Centre in Goulais River, Ontario, bakes these daily as they are a staple in their hungry skiers' Lunch-Munch! They also appear piled high on huge trays at the finish of the annual 30-km Wabos Wilderness Cross-Country Ski Loppet. Phyllis was happy to give us the recipe when we asked for it.

1 cup seedless raisins
⅔ cup butter
1 cup firmly-packed brown sugar
1 cup white sugar
2 tbsp. vanilla
2 eggs
1 tsp. baking soda
½ tsp. salt
1½ cups whole-wheat flour
1½ cups all-purpose flour
1 cup peanuts

Pour boiling water over raisins and set aside for approximately half an hour. Then drain, discarding water. Combine flours, baking soda, and salt. Put all ingredients in a large bowl and work well with hands. Make balls the size of an egg and place on *ungreased* cookie sheets. Flatten with a fork. Bake in 350°F oven for 15 minutes. Cool cookies on a rack.

Phyllis Burrell-Elyk, Goulais River, Ont

Colossal Oatmeal Carob Chip Cookies

The carob chips could be replaced with pure chocolate chips.

4¹/₄ cups whole-wheat flour
3¹/₂ tsp. baking soda
1 tsp. salt
6¹/₄ cups rolled oats
2¹/₂ cups shortening (preferably soy oil margarine)
3³/₄ cups Demerara *or* firmly-packed brown sugar
5 eggs
1¹/₂ tsp. pure vanilla extract
2¹/₄ cups carob chips

Combine flour, baking soda, salt, and oats in a large bowl. Stir to blend well.

In another large bowl cream shortening and brown sugar. Beat in eggs and vanilla. Add flour mixture, mixing until combined. Stir in carob chips.

Drop dough by ¹/₃-cupfuls 6 inches apart on a greased cookie sheet. Flatten each cookie with a fork, but leave thick because the cookies will spread. Bake at 350°F for 12 to 15 minutes or until done. Cool before removing from cookie sheet.

Makes about 40 huge cookies.

Julie DePass, Oakville, Ont

Apricot Bars

Yummy!

1 cup firmly-packed dried apricots
¼ cup liquid honey
½ cup water
½ cup sliced almonds
1 tsp. almond extract
1 cup rolled oats
1½ cups whole-wheat flour
½ tsp. baking soda
¼ tsp. salt
¾ cup firmly-packed brown *or* Demerara sugar
¾ cup vegetable shortening
1 cup plain yogurt
2 tbsp. rolled oats, for topping

Cut apricots into small pieces with scissors. Place apricots, water, and honey in a small pot. Heat until boiling. Cover and simmer, stirring occasionally, for about 15 minutes or until apricots are very tender. Allow to cool. Add almond extract and almonds.

Whirl oats in a blender until finely ground. Combine oats, flour, baking soda, sugar, shortening, yogurt, and salt. Beat ingredients with an electric mixer or by hand until they are well blended.

Grease a 9 x 13-inch pan. With dampened fingers or a dampened knife, carefully spread half of oats mixture into the pan. Spread with cooled apricot mixture. Drop remaining oat mixture by small spoonfuls evenly over top and spread with a dampened knife to cover filling completely. (This is a little tricky and requires patience!) Top with 2 tbsp. rolled oats.

Bake at 350°F for about 30 minutes or until the top springs back when lightly touched. Cool completely before cutting into bars.

Nutritious Apricot Squares

Made with nutritious ingredients galore!

1 cup dried apricots	¹/₂ cup wheat germ
¹/₃ cup liquid honey	¹/₈ tsp. salt
¹/₃ cup molasses	1 cup raisins
¹/₂ cup vegetable oil	¹/₂ cup sunflower seeds
1¹/₂ cups rolled oats	orange *or* other fruit juice,
1 cup whole-wheat flour	if necessary
3 tbsp. soy flour	

Cut apricots into small pieces with scissors. Beat honey, molasses, and oil to combine well. In a large bowl combine oats, flours, wheat germ, and salt. Pour in the honey mixture and stir to mix thoroughly. Add apricots, raisins, and sunflower seeds, then mix completely. If mixture seems too stiff, add a little fruit juice.

Press into a well-greased 9 x 9-inch baking pan. Bake 20 minutes in a 375°F oven. Cool in pan, cut into squares, and EAT!

Susan Budge, Waterloo, Ont

Raisin Squares

The butter tart lover's alternative!

1 cup raisins
¹/₃ cup margarine *or* vegetable shortening
²/₃ cup firmly-packed brown sugar
2 tbsp. molasses
1 egg
¹/₂ cup all-purpose flour
¹/₄ tsp. salt
¹/₄ tsp. baking soda
³/₄ cup rolled oats

Sift flour, salt, and soda. Melt margarine or shortening; then add sugar, flour mixture, molasses, and egg, beating to combine. Stir in raisins and oats.

Pour into greased 8 x 8-inch or 9 x 9-inch pan. Bake at 350°F for 25 minutes. The squares may not appear cooked, but remove after this amount of time. (They should not be dry.) Allow squares to cool before cutting.

Banana Bars

My mother nearly always has a pan of these in the refrigerator.

1 cup dates
$^1/_2$ cup butter
1 cup white *or* brown sugar (*or* less)
2 eggs
1 tsp. almond extract
2 cups sliced very ripe bananas
1 cup whole-wheat flour
$^3/_4$ cup all-purpose flour
1 tsp. baking powder
$^1/_4$ tsp. salt
$^1/_4$ tsp. baking soda
$^1/_2$ cup slivered almonds
icing sugar

Cut dates into small pieces using scissors dipped in hot water. Cream butter and sugar. Beat in eggs one at a time, beating until mixture is fluffy. Add almond extract. *Stir* in bananas. Sift dry ingredients and stir into batter. Add dates and almonds. Spread in a greased 9 x 13-inch baking pan. Bake at 350°F for 30 minutes. While warm, sprinkle very lightly with icing sugar. Cut into bars. These keep well in the refrigerator.

Ann Budge, Belfountain, Ont

Partridgeberry Squares

These were a big hit at the 1979 Canadian Orienteering Championships in Newfoundland! Partridgeberries are tart red berries that grow like blueberries on low bushes.

1 cup butter	2 tbsp. brown sugar
1 cup grated Cheddar cheese	pinch of salt
2 cups all-purpose flour	partridgeberry jam

Cream butter and cheese. Add flour, sugar, and salt. Beat to blend well. Press three-quarters of the mixture into a 9 x 9-inch greased pan. Spread with partridgeberry jam. Sprinkle with the remaining mixture. Bake at 350°F for 20 to 25 minutes. Cool and cut into squares.

Barb Taylor, St. John's, Nfld

Oatcakes

A Nova Scotia specialty!

3 cups rolled oats
3 cups all-purpose flour
1½ cups vegetable shortening
1 cup white sugar
2 tsp. salt
1 tsp. baking soda
¾ cup cold water

Combine dry ingredients. Work in shortening by cutting with a knife, then rubbing with tips of fingers until fine. Gradually add water to form a dough that is not too sticky to roll. Roll to ¼-inch thickness on a pastry board, using rolled oats on the board instead of flour. Cut into squares, place on cookie sheet, and bake in a 350°F oven for about 15 minutes.

Makes 3 to 4 dozen.

Mary Russell, Tantallon, NS

Granola Squares

Kids love these — both making them *and* eating them!

½ cup honey
½ cup smooth *or* crunchy peanut butter
1 cup unsweetened flaked coconut
½ cup chopped unsalted peanuts
3 cups granola-type cereal

In a large heavy pot, heat honey and peanut butter until melted. Stir until well blended. Add all remaining ingredients and mix well. Press onto a greased cookie sheet. Refrigerate and cut into squares.

Lynda Sidney, Sudbury, Ont

No-Bake Granola Bars

Because these are high in calories, they are permitted for consumption only after a long ski-orienteering course on a cold winter day or other endurance event.

$^1/_2$ **cup white sugar**
$^1/_3$ **cup corn syrup**
3 cups crunchy granola-type cereal
$^1/_2$ **cup raisins**
$^1/_2$ **cup unsalted peanuts**
1 cup semi-sweet chocolate chips (optional)

In a heavy saucepan blend sugar and corn syrup over medium-low heat, stirring constantly until mixture comes to a boil.

Boil gently for 2 or 3 minutes, stirring until sugar syrup begins to thicken. It is vital that the syrup boil for no longer than 3 minutes, or until a candy thermometer registers 220°F.

In this next step *you must work quickly* in order to get the mixture into the pan before it hardens. Into saucepan with syrup pour granola, raisins, and nuts. Quickly stir mixture until it is coated with sugar syrup, then press into a greased 9 x 9-inch square pan. Melt chocolate chips over very low heat and spread over granola bars, if you wish.

Julie DePass, Oakville, Ont

Nutritious Chewy Squares

3 eggs
1 cup liquid honey
1 cup chopped walnuts
1 cup unsweetened shredded coconut
1 cup chopped dates
$^3/_4$ **cup whole-wheat flour**
$^1/_4$ **cup wheat germ**

Beat eggs well and add honey. Stir in flour and wheat germ. Mix well. Add nuts, coconut, and dates, combining well with batter. Press into a greased 9-inch square pan. Bake for 20 minutes at 350°F. Cut into squares while still warm.

Barb Pearson, Hamilton, Ont

Good-Health Fudge

If you usually shun the empty calories of traditional fudge, you'll likely appreciate this one.

1 cup freshly-ground peanut butter
1 cup honey
1 cup carob powder
$^{1}/_{2}$ cup sunflower seeds
$^{1}/_{2}$ cup chopped raisins
$^{1}/_{2}$ cup toasted sesame seeds
$^{1}/_{2}$ cup unsweetened shredded *or* flaked coconut
$^{1}/_{2}$ cup chopped nuts (preferably walnuts *or* soynuts)

Heat peanut butter and honey in a heavy pot until just melted. Blend thoroughly. Add carob powder. Mix well.

Add remaining ingredients. Press into buttered 9 x 11-inch pan. Chill 2 hours; then cut into squares.

Patti Konantz, Winnipeg, Man

Wheat-Germ Squares

Delicious and nutritious!

3 eggs
$^{7}/_{8}$ cup firmly-packed brown sugar
$^{1}/_{4}$ cup vegetable oil
$^{1}/_{2}$ cup natural bran
2 tbsp. molasses
2 to 3 tsp. vanilla
1 cup skim milk powder
1$^{1}/_{2}$ cups wheat germ
$^{1}/_{4}$ tsp. salt
$^{1}/_{2}$ tsp. baking powder
$^{1}/_{2}$ cup sesame seeds, for topping

Beat eggs, vegetable oil, and brown sugar until well blended. Add molasses and vanilla. Mix dry ingredients together thoroughly and add to liquid ones. Spoon into greased 9 x 9-inch pan. Spread evenly and sprinkle with sesame seeds. Bake in a 325°F oven for 22 to 25 minutes.

Sheila Smith, Waterloo, Ont

Energy Bars

No doubt these have provided Sheila with plenty of energy!
Sheila, a past Canadian orienteering champion, was a member of
Canada's National Orienteering Team to the World
Championships from 1974 to 1982.

2 cups whole-wheat flour
¹/₂ cup firmly-packed brown *or* Demerara sugar
¹/₄ cup instant skim milk powder
¹/₄ cup wheat germ
1 tsp. baking powder
1 cup raisins
1 cup dried apricots
¹/₂ cup sunflower seeds, lightly toasted
¹/₃ cup chopped walnuts, almonds, *or* pecans
2 eggs
¹/₃ cup vegetable oil
¹/₄ cup liquid honey
¹/₄ cup molasses
2 tbsp. sesame seeds, for topping

Cut apricots finely with scissors. Combine dry ingredients. Add
fruit, nuts, and sunflower seeds. In another bowl, beat eggs with
oil, honey, and molasses. Add to dry ingredients and blend well.
Spread in greased 9 x 9-inch pan. Sprinkle with sesame seeds.
Bake at 350°F for 30 to 35 minutes. Cool and cut into bars with a
sharp knife.

Sheila Smith, Waterloo, Ont

Cakes

Date Cake

Lots of calories and, oh, so good! A rich, moist cake that doesn't need an icing.

3/4 **cup whole-wheat flour**
1 tsp. baking soda
1 tsp. cinnamon
1 tsp. ground cloves
1 cup boiling water
2 cups rolled oats
3/4 **cup butter**
2 cups firmly-packed brown sugar
2 eggs, lightly beaten
1 1/2 **cup dates**
1 cup chopped walnuts

Cut dates finely with scissors dipped into hot water. Sift flour, baking soda, and spices into a large bowl and set aside. Pour boiling water over oats, mix well, and cool slightly. Then stir in butter. When butter is melted, add sugar, eggs, dates, and walnuts. Mix completely. Pour oatmeal mixture into dry ingredients and mix well.

Bake in a greased 9 x 9-inch or 9 x 13-inch pan at 350°F for about 45 minutes. Be careful not to under-bake. Cake must be set in the centre.

Date and Orange Cake

1 cup firmly-packed dates
1 orange
$\frac{1}{2}$ tsp. vanilla
$1\frac{1}{2}$ cups all-purpose flour
2 tsp. baking powder
$\frac{1}{2}$ tsp. baking soda
$\frac{1}{2}$ cup butter
$\frac{3}{4}$ cup firmly-packed brown sugar
2 eggs
$\frac{1}{2}$ cup plain yogurt

Squeeze juice from orange and add water if necessary to make $\frac{1}{3}$ cup. Add vanilla to orange juice. Remove white membranes from orange peels. Chop peel and dates in a food chopper. Add orange juice to date mixture. Sift dry ingredients and set aside. Cream butter with sugar. Beat in eggs. Combine butter and date mixtures. Fold in flour mixture alternately with yogurt.

Grease an 8 x 8-inch pan. Pour in batter and bake in a 350°F oven for about 1 hour or until a toothpick inserted near the centre of the cake comes out clean.

Fridge Cake

This English recipe is a good source of energy! It appeared in a recent issue of the British Orienteering Federation's magazine, so somebody else must like it too!

$\frac{1}{2}$ lb. crumbled digestive cookies
$\frac{1}{4}$ lb. butter *or* margarine
1 tbsp. corn syrup
2 tbsp. instant chocolate drink powder
$\frac{1}{4}$ lb. semi-sweet pure chocolate

Melt butter; then mix in crumbled cookies, syrup, and chocolate drink powder. Press into a 9-inch square cake pan and flatten with a knife. Melt chocolate over very low heat or in a double boiler and spread over the top. Using a knife, outline portions in the chocolate before it hardens.

Barb Pearson, Hamilton, Ont

Prune and Nut Cake

A cake with substance and lots of usable calories. Great for an athlete in serious training!

1½ cups pitted prunes
1½ cups vegetable oil
1 cup Demerara sugar
1 cup white sugar
5 eggs, beaten
1½ tsp. vanilla
1½ cups all-purpose flour
1½ cups whole-wheat flour
2 tsp. cinnamon
1½ tsp. baking soda
1 tsp. salt
1½ cups buttermilk
1½ cups chopped lightly-toasted nuts

Using scissors, cut prunes into 4 or 5 pieces. Toss with ⅛ cup of the flour.

In a large bowl, mix oil, sugar, eggs, and vanilla. In a smaller bowl, blend remaining flour, cinnamon, baking soda, and salt.

Add flour mixture to egg mixture and stir well, by hand, to blend. Stir in buttermilk, then prunes. Finally, add nuts and stir until well mixed.

Pour into a greased and floured 9 x 13-inch cake pan. Bake at 350°F for about 1 hour, or until a toothpick inserted into the cake comes out fairly clean. Remove cake from oven, let it sit for one minute, then pour glaze over top. Allow cake to sit several hours to absorb the glaze.

Glaze

½ cup butter
½ cup buttermilk
½ cup Demerara sugar
1 tsp. baking soda
1 tsp. vanilla

In a medium saucepan, melt butter, then add buttermilk. Stir in sugar and baking soda. Boil 1 minute. Remove from heat. Allow to cool while cake is baking. When glaze is cool, stir in vanilla.

Apple Cake

This is best the day after it is baked. It's a moist cake that keeps well in the refrigerator. Great for after orienteering!

2 eggs, well beaten
1 to 2 cups sugar
3 cups all-purpose flour *or* **2⅝ cups whole-wheat flour**
3 cups sliced peeled apples
1 cup vegetable oil
½ tsp. salt
1 tsp. baking soda
1 tsp. cinnamon
1 tsp. vanilla
½ cup firmly-packed brown sugar

Beat eggs, sugar, and vanilla. Add dry ingredients, then apples and vegetable oil.

Grease and flour a 9 x 13-inch pan. Pour in batter. Sprinkle top with ½ cup brown sugar. Bake at 300°F for about an hour.

To serve as a dessert, cut in large squares and top with yogurt into which has been folded a little cinammon and grated orange peel.

Ann Budge, Belfountain, Ont

Newfoundland Blueberry Cake

As many orienteers know, blueberries grow in abundance in Newfoundland; the bushes are a little tricky to run through! This cake is superb.

½ cup margarine *or* **butter**
2 eggs, separated
2 tsp. baking powder
2 cups white sugar
3 cups all-purpose flour
1 cup milk
2 cups fresh blueberries

Cream margarine and sugar. Add egg yolks. Sift flour and baking powder, then add to butter mixture alternately with 1 cup of milk. Fold in beaten egg whites. Gently fold in blueberries. Bake in a large greased tube pan at 375°F about 50 to 60 minutes.

Serve warm, cool, plain, or frosted! This cake freezes very well.

Barb Taylor, St. John's, Nfld

Light Carrot Cake

This light and fluffy carrot cake is made with cooked carrots. It was a hit at a recent Toronto Orienteering Club potluck supper. In fact, several Juniors are known to have had four pieces each!

2 cups sifted cake flour
¹/₂ tsp. salt
2 tsp. baking powder
¹/₂ tsp. baking soda
¹/₂ tsp. cinnamon
¹/₂ tsp. nutmeg
¹/₂ tsp. ginger
¹/₂ tsp. ground cloves
1¹/₂ cups firmly-packed brown sugar
¹/₂ cup vegetable shortening, softened
³/₄ cup well-mashed cooked carrots
¹/₂ cup milk
2 eggs
¹/₄ cup milk

Sift flour, baking powder and soda, and spices into a large bowl. Beat brown sugar, shortening, carrots, and ¹/₂ cup milk at medium speed on electric mixer for 2 minutes. Stir in flour mixture. Add eggs and ¹/₄ cup milk and beat 2 more minutes.

Spread batter into a greased 9 x 13-inch pan and bake at 350°F until top springs back when touched lightly in the centre, about 35 minutes. Cool in pan and ice with the following icing.

Raisin-Nut Frosting

3 cups sifted icing sugar
¹/₃ cup soft butter
1¹/₂ tsp. pure vanilla extract
3 tbsp. milk (approximately)
¹/₃ cup chopped raisins
¹/₂ cup chopped walnuts

Blend sugar, butter, and vanilla. Add enough milk to make a mixture that spreads easily. Beat until fluffy and stir in raisins and nuts.

Riny Geddes, Toronto, Ont

Supreme Carrot-Pineapple Cake

No one ever tires of a good carrot cake!

1¹/₂ cups vegetable oil
4 eggs
2 cups white sugar
2 cups all-purpose flour
2 tsp. baking powder
1¹/₂ tsp. baking soda
¹/₂ tsp. salt
2 tsp. cinnamon
2 cups grated carrots
1 cup drained canned crushed pineapple
¹/₂ cup chopped walnuts

Beat sugar and oil. Add eggs one at a time, mixing well after each addition. Mix dry ingredients and add to batter. Mix well. Stir in carrots, pineapple, and nuts.

Pour into a greased 9 x 13-inch baking pan. Bake at 350°F for 35 to 40 minutes. Ice if you desire with the following icing.

Cream Cheese Icing

¹/₂ cup margarine *or* butter
1 8-oz. pkg. cream cheese
3¹/₂ cups icing sugar
1 tsp vanilla

Beat together and spread on cooled cake.

Barb Pearson, Hamilton, Ont

Rhubarb Cake

1 to 1¹/₂ cups white sugar
¹/₂ cup vegetable oil
3 eggs
1 tsp. baking soda
1 tsp. cinnamon
¹/₄ tsp. cloves
¹/₄ tsp. allspice

dash of salt
1 cup all-purpose flour
1 cup whole-wheat flour
¹/₃ cup skim milk
2 cups diced rhubarb
¹/₃ cup brown sugar
¹/₃ cup sunflower seeds

Beat vegetable oil and white sugar. Add eggs one at a time. Mix flours, baking soda, and spices, and add alternately with milk. Add rhubarb and mix gently. Spread batter in a greased 9 x 13-inch pan.

Mix brown sugar and sunflower seeds, then sprinkle on unbaked batter. Bake 35 minutes at 350°F.

Jenny Birchell, Hamilton, Ont

Honey Cake

A nice moist cake with an intriguing flavour. Top with applesauce or stewed rhubarb for dessert.

¼ cup white sugar
¼ cup firmly-packed brown *or* Demerara sugar
½ cup vegetable oil
3 eggs
1 cup cold coffee
1 tsp. baking soda
1 cup liquid honey
1⅛ cups whole-wheat flour
1¼ cups all-purpose flour
2 tsp. baking powder
¼ tsp. nutmeg
½ tsp. cinnamon

Cream sugar and oil. Beat in eggs one at a time. Stir soda into coffee, then add to batter. Add honey. Sift together dry ingredients and add to honey mixture. Pour into a greased 10-inch tube pan. Bake at 350°F for 45 to 60 minutes. Drizzle with lemon glaze while cake is still slightly warm, or top wedges with homemade applesauce or stewed rhubarb.

Lemon Glaze

¼ cup lemon juice
¼ cup liquid honey
grated lemon peel (optional)
2 tsp. cornstarch
2 tbsp. water

Mix ingredients in a small saucepan and bring to a boil. Lower heat and cook, stirring, until clear. Allow glaze to cool. If it is too thick, thin it with a *little* hot water.

Friendship Cake

Friendship cakes have become very popular. They are fun to make, especially as a family activity, and not nearly as complicated as appears at first glance. I came across this recipe in Mary McGrath's column, "Recipe Exchange," which appears weekly in the *Toronto Star*. Mary says it is one of her most requested recipes; people panic when they lose it!

Starter Mixture

1 tsp. white sugar
2 cups warm water (110°F)
1 envelope active dry yeast
5 cups all-purpose flour
1½ cups white sugar
3 cups milk

Day 1: Dissolve sugar in ½ cup warm water in a medium-sized non-metal bowl. Sprinkle yeast into water and let stand 10 minutes. Stir, then add 1½ cups water and 2 cups flour. Beat until smooth. Cover with plastic wrap and let sit overnight on the kitchen counter.

Day 2: Stir 1 cup all-purpose flour, 1 cup milk, and ½ cup sugar into Starter Mixture. Cover loosely with a piece of waxed paper and refrigerate.

Days 3 and 4: Stir until smooth once each day.

Day 5: Stir 1 cup all-purpose flour, 1 cup milk, and ½ cup sugar into Starter Mixture. Cover loosely and refrigerate.

Days 6 to 9: Stir well once each day.

Day 10: Stir in 1 cup all-purpose flour, 1 cup milk, and ½ cup sugar.

To keep your starter going, keep 1 cup yourself and start again at Day 2. Remove 3 cups of Starter Mixture and give 1 cup to each of 3 friends along with copies of the following two recipes.

Cake

²/₃ cup vegetable oil
3 eggs
2 cups all-purpose flour
¹/₂ cup white sugar
¹/₂ cup firmly-packed
   brown sugar
1 cup milk
1¹/₂ tsp. cinnamon
¹/₂ tsp. baking powder
¹/₂ tsp. salt

1 tsp. vanilla
1¹/₄ tsp. baking soda
1 cup Starter Mixture
1 cup chopped apple
1 cup chopped nuts
1 cup raisins
1 cup grated carrot
¹/₂ cup flaked *or*
   shredded coconut

To 1 cup Starter Mixture add oil and eggs, then milk and vanilla, beating well after each addition. Mix dry ingredients together and add. Beat until smooth. Add apple, nuts, raisins, carrot, and coconut, then mix well.

Pour batter into a greased tube pan. Bake at 350°F for 45 to 60 minutes. Cool 10 minutes on a rack, then turn out to finish cooling. Cake may be topped with **Lemon Glaze** (see page 159).

Starter Banana Bread

1 cup Starter Mixture
¹/₂ cup butter
¹/₂ cup white sugar
1 cup mashed very ripe banana
2 eggs
2 cups all-purpose flour
¹/₂ tsp. salt
1¹/₄ tsp. baking soda
¹/₃ cup raisins

Do *not* turn on oven to pre-heat!

Cream butter and sugar until light and fluffy. Beat in eggs, one at a time. Add banana and Starter Mixture. Sift dry ingredients and stir into batter. Add raisins. Let batter sit for 10 minutes. Then stir and turn into greased 9 x 5 x 3-inch loaf pan. Put into a *cold* oven. Turn oven to 350°F and bake cake 50 to 60 minutes. Remove from oven and let stand 10 minutes, then turn out onto wire rack to cool.

Sourdough Chocolate Cake

A chocolate cake with a tangy difference!

$^1\!/_2$ cup **Sourdough Starter (see page 214)**
1 cup **water (110°F)**
$1^1\!/_2$ cups **whole-wheat flour**
1 cup **firmly-packed brown sugar**
$^1\!/_4$ cup **instant skim milk powder**
$^1\!/_2$ cup **margarine** *or* **butter**
1 tbsp. **brewer's yeast (from natural food shop)**
$^1\!/_3$ cup **cocoa powder**
1 tbsp. **soy flour**
1 tsp. **cinnamon**
$^1\!/_2$ tsp. **salt**
$1^1\!/_2$ tsp. **baking soda**
2 tbsp. **vegetable oil**
1 tsp. **vanilla**
2 **eggs**

Heat a large bowl by filling it with hot water for a few minutes.
Empty bowl and add **Sourdough Starter**, water, flour, and milk
powder. Set aside for 2 to 3 hours in a warm place until mixture
is bubbly.

Cream sugar and margarine until light and fluffy. Mix
brewer's yeast, cocoa, soy flour, cinnamon, salt, and soda. Add
to creamed mixture along with oil and vanilla. Stir until well
blended. Beat in eggs. Add chocolate mixture to sourdough
mixture, stirring until well blended.

Pour into well-greased 9 x 9-inch pan. Bake at 350°F for 25 to
30 minutes or until centre springs back when lightly touched.
Cool thoroughly on rack before removing cake from pan.

Mother Hamilton's Chocolate Cake

Note the unexpected ingredients here: beets!

1½ cups sugar *or* 1 cup liquid honey
3 eggs
1 cup vegetable oil
1½ cups finely-grated cooked beets
3 squares pure semi-sweet chocolate
¾ cup whole-wheat flour
1 cup all-purpose flour
1½ tsp. baking soda
¼ tsp. salt
¼ tsp. vanilla

Melt chocolate over very low heat or in a small double boiler and set aside to cool. Beat together sugar or honey and eggs. Add oil, beets, and chocolate; then mix thoroughly.

In another bowl, mix flour, baking soda, and salt. Combine with the chocolate mixture. Add vanilla and stir again.

Pour into a greased 9 x 9-inch pan. Bake 50 to 60 minutes in a 350°F oven.

Jennifer Hamilton, Winnipeg, Man

Creamy Fruit Frosting

This recipe was posted on the wall of my dentist's waiting room! A good icing with low sugar content.

4 oz. cream cheese
1 tbsp. liquid honey
2 tbsp. berries mashed with 1 tbsp. milk, *or* 2 tbsp. orange *or* grape juice

Beat all ingredients together with a mixer until smooth. Chill to stiffen. Makes enough for an 8-inch or 9-inch cake.

Old-Fashioned Gingerbread

Delicious served with a topping of stewed rhubarb or homemade applesauce. A true autumn favourite!

$^1/_2$ **cup white sugar**
$^1/_2$ **cup molasses**
$^1/_4$ **cup butter**
2$^1/_4$ cups all-purpose flour
$^7/_8$ **cup hot water**
$^1/_2$ **to 1 tsp. ginger**
1 tsp. baking soda
$^1/_4$ **cup finely-chopped candied** *or* **preserved ginger (optional)**
$^1/_2$ **cup raisons**

Melt butter and blend with sugar and molasses. Add flour and stir until thoroughly mixed.

Mix hot water, ginger, and baking soda, then add all at once to flour mixture. Blend together. Add raisins, then chopped ginger if you are a ginger lover.

Pour batter into a well-greased 8 x 8-inch or 9 x 9-inch pan. Bake at 350°F for 30 to 35 minutes or until done.

Puddings
& Other Desserts

Scandinavian Fruit Soup

From the homeland of orienteering comes this popular "soup." It is usually a dessert, but may be served before the main course, particularly in the summertime, as it is traditionally served chilled.

½ lb. (about 16) dried pitted prunes
½ lb. (about 18) dried apricots
3 fresh apples, diced
¼ cup Demerara sugar *or* brown sugar
6 cups any fruit juice *and/or* apple cider
1 cinnamon stick
2 tbsp. cornstarch
white wine, red wine, *or* brandy (optional)
yogurt, for garnish

Combine fruits, sugar, 6 cups fruit liquid, and cinnamon stick. Simmer until fruit is very tender. Remove cinnamon stick and purée fruit with liquid in a blender or food processor in small batches.

Return fruit purée to saucepan. Add 2 tbsp. cornstarch dissolved in a little cold water. Cook, stirring, until clear-looking. Chill and serve very cold. At serving time, a tablespoon of wine or brandy per serving may be added. Top with a dab of plain yogurt, if you wish.

Makes 6 servings.

Lemon Pudding

A simple yummy pudding that originated in Grandmother's day. When baked, a cake layer will be on the top and a lemon sauce on the bottom!

½ **cup sugar**
2 **tbsp. all-purpose flour**
2 **eggs, separated**
¼ **tsp. salt**
1 **cup milk**
1 **lemon**

Squeeze lemon and carefully grate peel, avoiding the white part. Mix flour, sugar, and salt. Beat in egg yolks, then milk. Stir in lemon juice and peel.

Beat egg whites until stiff and fold into batter. Turn into a baking dish and place in a larger pan of hot water. Bake at 325°F for about 1 hour.

Serves 4.

Spiced Blueberries

This is a favourite summer dessert from our good friend Lee Lindsay of Montreal. Perhaps you are lucky enough to be able to pick your own wild berries, but Lee says that this simple recipe makes even those large, tasteless cultivated berries quite acceptable!

2 **cups blueberries**
¼ **cup white sugar**
½ **cup water**
½ **tsp. fresh lemon juice**
1 **2-inch cinnamon stick**
3 **whole cloves**
dash of salt (optional)

Place sugar, water, lemon juice, spices, and salt in a small saucepan. Boil for one minute. Meanwhile wash and drain blueberries. Strain syrup to remove spices, then pour over berries. Chill, and serve garnished with mint leaves or over ice-cream.

Serves 3 or 4.

Lemon Snow

A light, delicious dessert whose popularity has endured for generation after generation.

1 envelope unflavoured gelatin
¼ cup cold water
1 cup boiling water
1 cup white sugar
pinch of salt
1 whole lemon
2 egg whites, at room temperature (Reserve yolks for Custard Sauce.)
Custard Sauce (See page 170.)

Soak gelatin in ¼ cup cold water for 5 minutes, then stir to dissolve. Stir gelatin and cold water into 1 cup boiling water until gelatin is completely dissolved. Immediately add sugar, salt, juice, and finely-grated peel of 1 lemon. Let cool slightly, then pour into a glass bowl. Refrigerate until almost set, but not quite completely firm. Be sure to allow to set until this stage is reached; this is the key to success with this dessert!

When gelatin mixture is ready, beat egg whites with a pinch of salt until stiff but not dry. Beat gelatin mixture gradually into egg whites with an electric mixer.

Pour into chilled serving bowl and refrigerate until serving time. Serve with a pitcher of **Custard Sauce.**

Serves 6.

Roberta Sellars, Mt. Albert, Ont

Five-Minute Orange Mousse

This refreshing dessert couldn't be simpler and is loved by children!

³/₄ cup thawed, undiluted frozen orange juice
    concentrate (1 6-oz. tin)
1¹/₂ tbsp. unflavoured gelatin
²/₃ cup very hot water
¹/₄ cup white sugar
2 cups crushed ice
coconut (optional)
raisins (optional)
pure chocolate chips (optional)

Place water and gelatin in a blender and blend for 20 seconds. Add sugar and blend for 30 seconds. Add orange juice and crushed ice and blend another 30 seconds. Before pouring into dessert dishes, you may quickly stir in unsweetened coconut, or a few raisins or chocolate chips. Children love to find surprises in their dessert!

Pour into 4 or 5 dessert dishes or parfait glasses. Within a minute or so the mousse will be set. Garnish with anything you like, such as a slice of orange, a sprinkle of grated chocolate or coconut, or a dab of yogurt.

Serves 4 or 5.

Ricotta Cheesecake

Serve this topped with fruit-flavoured yogurt or plain yogurt and fruit, such as raspberries, strawberries, peaches, or crushed pineapple.

3 cups low-fat ricotta cheese
1 lemon
3 medium-sized eggs
³/₄ cup buttermilk
³/₄ cup brown *or* Demerara sugar, *or* liquid honey
1¹/₂ tsp. pure vanilla extract
pinch of salt

Place a pan of water in the oven and preheat to 375°F. Squeeze lemon, removing any seeds. Grate peel of lemon carefully (or use a lemon zester), avoiding the white part.

Place all ingredients into a blender. Blend until well combined. Be sure to scrape the sides of the blender well several times. If your blender is small, it may be best to blend this in two batches, then mix both halves together.

Pour into a lightly-greased 9-inch spring-form pan. Bake for 40 to 45 minutes or until set. Do not underbake.

Makes 6 generous wedge-shaped servings or 8 average-sized ones.

Rashimalai

Sue got this delicious East Indian recipe from a neighbour who used to serve it for afternoon tea. It is pronounced "rash mal ee."

1 lb. ricotta cheese, drained
1 cup white sugar
rose water essence (optional)
1 385-ml can evaporated milk
¹/₂ tsp. cardamom
pistachio and almond pieces

Mix sugar and cheese. Put mixture into a square pan and bake in the oven at 350°F for 30 to 35 minutes, until cheese is dried out but *not* browned. Cut cheese into squares and place in a serving dish.

Make a mixture of evaporated milk and cardamom powder. A little rose water essence may be added if you wish. Pour milk mixture over the cheese squares. Sprinkle with pistachio and almond pieces. Allow milk to soak in. Refrigerate. This is served as a pudding in a dessert dish.

Makes 6 servings.

Sue Waddington, Hamilton, Ont

Pioneer Bread Pudding

Use your imagination and try other fruits in place of apples.
Even bananas are good in this version of an old-time recipe from
pioneer days, when dry bread was never wasted.

2 cups bread cubes, preferably egg bread
4 apples, preferably cooking apples
3 eggs
¹/₃ cup white sugar
2 cups milk
pinch of salt
¹/₄ tsp. freshly-grated nutmeg
1 tsp. cinnamon
2 tbsp. butter, melted
¹/₂ tsp. vanilla *or* almond extract
¹/₂ cup raisins *or* unsweetened coconut
Custard Sauce (recipe follows)

Cut bread into ¹/₂-inch cubes. If cubes are not dry, dry them in a
225°F oven for a few minutes. Egg bread is best for this pudding
as it is denser. Peel and slice apples very thinly (¹/₈-inch). You
should have about 2 cups of slices.

Beat together the following ingredients: milk, eggs, sugar,
salt, spices, vanilla or almond extract, and 1 tbsp. melted butter.
Stir in raisins or coconut and bread cubes.

Pour the above mixture into a greased 1¹/₂-quart baking dish.
Toss apple slices with the remaining tbsp. of butter, then arrange
neatly on top of bread mixture. Sprinkle with a little cinnamon.
Do not cover baking dish.

In a 350°F oven, place a large baking pan. Into this pan set
the filled baking dish. Add ³/₄-inch of hot water to larger pan.
Bake about 1 hour or until a knife inserted in the middle of the
pudding comes out clean. Serve with warm **Custard Sauce.**

Serves 5 or 6.

Custard Sauce

³/₄ cup milk
2 egg yolks
2 tbsp. sugar
pinch of salt
¹/₂ tsp. vanilla, *or* grated orange *or* lemon peel

Scald milk in the top pot of a double boiler over direct heat. Remove from heat. Beat egg yolks well with a small wire whisk and blend in sugar and salt. Gradually stir in scalded milk.

Return mixture to double boiler top and cook over simmering water, stirring constantly, until mixture coats a silver spoon and is slightly thick. Cool slightly, then stir in vanilla or peel.

Makes 1 cup.

Down-to-Earth Carrot Pudding

Carrots for dessert? Why not? They're good for you!

1½ **cups finely-grated carrots**
½ **cup brown** *or* **Demerara sugar**
1 **cup whole-wheat flour**
1 **tsp. baking powder**
1 **tsp. baking soda**
½ **tsp. ginger**
¾ **tsp. freshly-grated nutmeg**
1 **tsp. cinnamon**
2 **tbsp. butter**
1 **egg**
1 **cup buttermilk**
1 **cup raisins** *or* **currants**
½ **cup chopped almonds** *or* **other nuts**

Grate carrots. Melt butter in heavy-bottomed saucepan, add carrots, cover the pot, and cook carrots over medium heat until tender, about 10 minutes. Allow carrots to cool slightly.

Combine dry ingredients in a large bowl. Beat egg lightly with a fork and blend into buttermilk. Stir into dry ingredients. Fold in carrots, raisins, and nuts. Spoon into a greased 1½-quart baking dish. Bake uncovered at 350°F for 35 to 45 minutes. Pudding must be set and firm in the centre. Remove from oven and allow to cool while eating your main course. Serve with one of the following toppings.

Serves 8.

Yogurt Topping. Mix plain yogurt with a dash of cinnamon and a little finely-grated lemon or orange peel.

Custard Sauce. See **Custard Sauce** (page 170). In place of vanilla, add 1½ tsp. finely-grated lemon peel.

Indian Pudding

A favourite sustaining dessert of the pioneers of our country. The name suggests that they acquired a version of the recipe from the Indians.

2 cups milk (skim is fine) ¼ tsp. ground ginger
½ cup yellow cornmeal   ½ tsp. cinnamon
1 cup water   ¼ cup molasses
½ cup molasses   2 tsp. butter

Scald milk (heat it almost to boiling point) in a medium saucepan. Add cornmeal to water and stir well. Stir cornmeal mixture into hot milk along with ½ cup molasses and ginger and cinnamon. Cook over low-medium heat, stirring constantly, until smooth and thickened.

Pour into a greased 1-quart low baking dish or oven-proof cast-iron frying pan. Do not cover. Place in a 300°F oven and bake for about 1 hour. Pudding will be thick and have a golden-brown crust on top. Slow cooking is the secret to success with this dessert.

Remove from oven and top with 2 tsp. butter and ¼ cup molasses. Allow to cool ½ hour, then serve.

Serves 4 or 5.

Traditional Rice Pudding

Two recipes are included here. The first one is for using leftover cooked rice when you have greatly misjudged the quantity for dinner the night before! The second is a traditional baked rice recipe. Brown rice gives an interesting nutty flavour as well as being more nutritious.

Rice Pudding using Cooked Rice

3 cups cooked rice
3 cups milk
½ cup sugar
sprinkle of cinnamon, nutmeg, *or* grated lemon rind
dash of salt
2 tbsp. butter
1 tsp. vanilla extract
½ cup raisins, currants, *or* chopped dates

Combine all ingredients except vanilla in a heavy saucepan. Cook over medium heat, stirring frequently so the bottom doesn't stick, until thickened, about 25 minutes. Add vanilla and stir. Spoon into serving dishes. Serve hot or cold, topped with a sprinkling of Demerara sugar, maple syrup, **Custard Sauce** (see page 170), or fruit-flavoured yogurt.

Serves 6.

Traditional Baked Rice Pudding

6 tbsp. uncooked long-grain rice
3 tbsp. white _or_ brown sugar
4 cups cold milk
¼ tsp. salt
nutmeg _or_ cinnamon
½ cup raisins, chopped dates, chopped dried apricots, _or_ chopped dried apples

In a well-greased baking dish, place the rice, milk, fruit, salt, and sugar. Sprinkle to taste with grated nutmeg or cinnamon. Bake in a 300°F oven for 1½ hours. Long, slow baking is the secret to a creamy pudding. Stir several times during the first hour of baking to remove the film that forms on top. Serve hot with Demerara sugar, milk, or warm maple syrup. A light lemon-flavoured **Custard Sauce** (see page 170) is also good.

Serves 4.

Fruit and Nut Ricotta

A quick and easy, creamy, tasty, and wholesome dessert!

1 13-oz. pkg. ricotta cheese
⅛ to ¼ cup white, brown, _or_ Demerara sugar
1 egg yolk, beaten with a fork
2 tbsp. orange juice
1 tsp. grated orange peel
1 cup dried fruit and nut mix

Stir sugar, egg yolk, juice, and peel into cheese and combine well. Stir in fruit and nut mix. Chill.

Makes 6 servings.

Spiced Dried Fruit Dessert

Drying of fresh fruits at home is quite popular these days. If you dry your own, you will appreciate this recipe!

2¹/₂ to 3 cups mixed dried fruit
6 cups water
¹/₂ cup raisins *or* currants
2 3-inch cinnamon sticks
4 whole cloves
1 seedless orange
¹/₃ cup white *or* brown sugar
2 tsp. quick-cooking tapioca
2 tbsp. fresh lemon juice
3 to 4 tbsp. brandy (optional)

Pour water into a large saucepan. Add dried fruit, raisins or currants, cloves, and broken-up cinnamon sticks. Cut orange into thin slices, cutting each slice in half; discard end slices. Add orange slices to pot. Cover and bring to the boiling point. Lower heat and simmer for about 20 minutes, until fruit is tender.

Mix sugar with tapioca. Stir gradually into fruit. Bring back to a simmer, cover, and allow to simmer for 10 to 15 minutes, until fruit is soft and liquid has become slightly thickened. Stir in lemon juice and optional brandy. Remove orange slices, cloves, and cinnamon stick. Serve warm, perhaps with a small scoop of vanilla ice cream, or refrigerate and serve chilled.

Makes 6 to 8 servings.

Yogurt Fruit Topping

A nice topping for fresh fruit, particularly strawberries or a compote of mixed melon balls. As an alternative, the fruit could be dipped into the topping for greater child-appeal.

1 cup plain yogurt
2 tbsp. liquid honey
1 tsp. grated orange peel (just the zest) *or* 3 tbsp. finely-ground
    almonds
2 tbsp. orange juice
1 tsp. lemon juice
1 tbsp. toasted sesame seeds
cinnamon *or* nutmeg (optional)

Add honey to yogurt. Stir well, then add orange peel or almonds, orange juice, and lemon juice to the yogurt. Finally, stir in the sesame seeds. A little sprinkling of cinnamon or nutmeg is a nice addition. Make the topping at least an hour or two ahead of serving time and place in refrigerator to mellow.

Yogurt Fruit Dessert

$\frac{1}{2}$ **cup dried apricots**
$\frac{1}{2}$ **cup dried peaches**
$\frac{1}{2}$ **cup dried pears**
1 piece cinnamon stick
6 cups water
1 cup unsweetened pineapple juice, apple juice, *or* **orange juice**
1 cup plain yogurt
2 tbsp. lemon juice
2 tbsp. brown sugar
2 tbsp. liquid honey

Simmer fruit and cinnamon stick in water until fruit is tender, about 20 minutes. Remove cinnamon stick. Cut fruit into small pieces. Add the fruit juice. Whirl the mixture in a blender or food processor. Add 1 cup yogurt, lemon juice, brown sugar, and honey. Process just enough to mix. Serve chilled, topped with an extra dab of yogurt.

Serves 4 or 5.

Marianne Skarborn, Fredericton, NB

Berry (or Fruit) Grunt

A hearty, irresistible dessert for a cool, rainy summer day, especially at the cottage. Perhaps you will be fortunate enough to be able to pick the berries yourself or pull the rhubarb from your own garden. Try other fruits such as peaches or raspberries.

4 cups blueberries, *or* 2 cups strawberries and 2 cups rhubarb
$1/2$ cup sugar
$1/2$ cup water for blueberries *or* $1/4$ cup for strawberries and
**   rhubarb**
$1/2$ to 1 tsp. lemon juice
2 cups all-purpose flour
4 tsp. baking powder
$1/2$ tsp. salt
1 tsp. white sugar
1 tbsp. vegetable shortening
1 tbsp. butter
$1/4$ to $1/2$ cup milk

Cut rhubarb into 1-inch pieces. Hull and halve strawberries. Place fruit, $1/2$ cup sugar, water, and lemon juice into a 10-inch skillet. Over medium heat, bring to a boil. Reduce heat, cover, and simmer 5 to 10 minutes, stirring occasionally, until fruit is tender and there is plenty of juice.

Meanwhile sift together flour, baking powder, salt, and sugar. With 2 knives or a pastry blender, cut in the shortening and butter. Add enough milk to make a soft biscuit dough.

With fruit simmering, drop dough by tablespoonfuls on top. Cover tightly and cook about 15 minutes *without peeking*. Serve hot, with a scoop of ice cream if you wish.

Makes 6 servings.

Rhubarb with Crumbly Crust

This version of an old favourite is a more nutritious one because of the oats, whole-wheat flour, and wheat germ in the topping. Other fruits may be used in place of rhubarb. If a less tart fruit is used, reduce the amount of sugar added to the fruit.

6 to 8 cups rhubarb cut into ³/₄-inch pieces
1 egg
2 tbsp. orange juice
¹/₄ cup raisins (optional)
1 cup white sugar *or* **¹/₂ cup white and ¹/₂ cup brown sugar**
2 tbsp. all-purpose flour
¹/₄ tsp. ginger, nutmeg, *or* **cinnamon**

Place rhubarb and optional raisins into a large bowl. In a small bowl, combine lightly beaten egg, orange juice, sugar, flour, and spices. Pour over rhubarb and toss thoroughly. Turn into a greased 1¹/₂-quart casserole or an 8-inch square glass baking dish.

Topping

1 cup rolled oats
¹/₂ cup whole-wheat flour
¹/₄ cup wheat germ
¹/₂ cup brown sugar
¹/₂ tsp. nutmeg
1 tsp. cinnamon
¹/₄ tsp. salt
¹/₂ cup butter, chilled

Combine all topping ingredients except butter. Cut the butter in with a pastry blender or two knives. Sprinkle topping over rhubarb mixture. Bake at 375°F for about 45 minutes, or until fruit is tender and topping is lightly browned.

Makes 8 servings.

Variation: Chunks (about 1 inch in length) of banana make an interesting addition to the rhubarb in this recipe. Sliced strawberries could be added to the rhubarb.

Apple-Peanut Butter Crisp

Peanut butter is always a favourite with little kids, and big ones too! If you can't disassociate bananas and peanut butter, add a sliced banana to the apples.

6 large apples	**¹/₂ cup whole-wheat flour**
¹/₂ cup raisins (optional)	**¹/₄ cup crunchy peanut butter**
1 sliced banana (optional)	**2 tbsp. butter**
¹/₃ cup water	**³/₄ cup brown or Demerara sugar**

Peel and slice apples, placing them in a greased low baking dish. Mix in raisins, and banana slices if they are to be included. Pour ¹/₃ cup water over fruit. Mix sugar and flour, then use 2 knives to cut in the peanut butter and butter. Mixture will resemble coarse crumbs. Sprinkle crumbs over fruit. Bake at 350°F for about 40 minutes.

Makes 6 servings.

Mr. Burt's Hot Chocolate Sauce: The World's Best!

Every now and then chocolate lovers (and that's nearly everybody!) get a craving for a superb chocolate sauce, even though we all know it contains many "empty" calories. Here's a recipe for what has to be the best chocolate sauce in the world! Mr. Burt was the chef at King's Hall, Compton, Québec, from 1936 to 1968. "Compton" was a country boarding school for young ladies in the Eastern Townships of Quebec. Chocolate Sauce was a Sunday dinner ritual, poured from large jugs onto vanilla ice cream and voraciously devoured by the girls! Pity the girls at the far ends of the tables — often there was little left! When cooked to perfection, Mr. Burt's Hot Chocolate Sauce forms a slightly sticky coating on the cold ice cream. No words can describe this delight! Now and then the girls had a mid-week taste-treat — Mr. Burt's Hot Chocolate Sauce on **Cream Puffs** (recipe follows).

Thanks, Mr. Burt, for allowing us to include your recipe.

3 squares unsweetened chocolate	**3 cups white sugar**
6 tbsp. melted butter	**pinch of salt**
1 cup boiling water	**1¹/₂ tsp. vanilla extract**
6 tbsp. corn syrup	

Melt butter over low heat and soften chocolate in it. Add boiling water very slowly, stirring all the time. Boil one or two minutes. Add corn syrup and sugar, stir to dissolve, and boil 10 minutes (no longer, no less). Cool a little and stir in salt and vanilla. While still warm, pour over vanilla ice cream or **Cream Puffs.** To reheat left-over sauce, heat in the top of a double boiler. Smaller quantities may be prepared by cutting the quantities by one-third or two-thirds.

Cream Puffs

1 cup water
¹/₂ cup butter
1 cup all-purpose flour
4 eggs
Custard Filling (recipe follows) *or* **whipped cream**

Bring water and butter to a boil in a medium saucepan over high heat. Allow to come to a full rolling boil. Turn heat to low. Add flour all at once, stirring vigorously. Stir until ingredients form a ball leaving the sides of the pot, about 1 minute. Remove from heat.

Add eggs, one at a time. Beat well after each addition and continue beating until mixture is velvety and smooth. Drop by spoonfuls about 3 inches apart onto ungreased baking sheets making 8 to 12 puffs, depending on the size you wish.

Bake in 400°F oven for about 40 to 50 minutes or until golden, crisp, dry to touch, and light when picked up. Remove from oven and cool thoroughly on racks.

At serving time, cut tops off puffs and pull out any soft dough from the centre. Fill with whipped cream or the following thick **Custard Filling.** Replace the tops and pour warm chocolate sauce over top!

Custard Filling

¹/₂ cup sugar	**2 cups milk**
dash of salt	**4 egg yolks**
¹/₃ cup all-purpose flour	**2 tsp. vanilla**

Mix sugar, salt, and flour in a heavy saucepan. Gradually blend in milk, stirring until smooth. Cook over medium heat, stirring constantly, until boiling. Boil 1 minute while stirring constantly.

Beat egg yolks lightly. Gradually stir at least half the hot mixture into the egg yolks. Stir back into saucepan and return to medium heat. Stir constantly until custard just reaches the boiling point. Cool, then stir in vanilla.

Cranberry-Pear Pie

A yummy pie that's a little different!

pastry for a 9-inch pie shell and lattice top
4 or 5 medium fresh pears
¹/₂ cup dates
3 tbsp. whole-wheat flour
dash of nutmeg
¹/₄ tsp. cinnamon
1 12-oz. jar whole cranberry sauce
1 tbsp. lemon juice
1 tbsp. butter

Prepare pastry and line a pie plate with it, keeping enough for a lattice top. Chop dates. Peel and slice pears into a bowl with the dates, flour, cranberry sauce, lemon juice, cinnamon, and nutmeg; toss well. Spoon into the pastry-lined pie plate. Dot with butter.

Cover filling with a lattice top. Seal and flute edge. To prevent over-browning, cover edge of pastry with a strip of foil. Remove foil a few minutes before pie is done. Bake at 450°F for 10 minutes, then for about 35 minutes at 350°F or until pears are tender.

Makes 6 servings.

Lee Wisener, Eden Mills, Ont

Fresh Fruit Ice

A cold fruit ice is a delicious summer dessert. This recipe can be made with any fresh fruit: peaches, cantaloupe, apples, berries, watermelon, pears, bananas, kiwis, pineapple, or any others you can think of!

4 cups cut-up fresh fruit   **¹/₂ cup water**
1 cup white sugar   **2 tbsp. lemon juice**

Whirl fruit in a blender or food processor and set aside. Boil sugar and water for 10 minutes; cool *thoroughly*. Add sugar syrup to fruit. Stir in lemon juice. Put in metal bowl and freeze for 1 hour. Break up and whirl in a blender or food processor until smooth. Freeze again for 4 hours.

Makes 9 servings, 115 calories each.

Heather Budge, London, Ont

Fruit Gelatin

A replacement recipe for commercial fruit-flavoured gelatins, which are essentially sugar, water, and artificial fruit flavouring, and hence of little nutritional value.

1 tbsp. unflavoured gelatin
¼ cup cold water
¾ cup boiling water
1 cup fruit juice
diced fruit *or* berries (Gelatin will not set if *fresh* pineapple is used.)
a little sugar, if desired

Soak gelatin in cold water to soften. Add boiling water and stir until dissolved.

Add 1 cup of any fruit juice (apricot or peach nectar; grape, orange, cranberry, or canned pineapple juice). Add a little sugar if necessary.

Pour into moulds or dishes and chill. When gelatin has become the consistency of unbeaten egg whites, fold in diced fruit or berries. Chill.

Makes 4 servings.

Banana ''Ice Cream''

A delicious pure, sugarless, fatless "ice cream"! Served in a cone or a dish, it is hard to beat! Omit the nuts if serving to very young children.

6 medium very ripe bananas
2 tbsp. liquid honey
1 tsp. lemon juice
¼ cup finely chopped almonds *or* other nuts, toasted lightly for more flavour

Peel bananas, then slice and freeze. When frozen, put into a food processor (or blender, but a processor will make a fluffier ice cream) and add honey and lemon juice. Process until creamy. Fold in nuts, and serve immediately as "soft ice cream." Freeze until firm if you prefer a more solid "ice cream."

Makes 6 servings.

Frozen Fruit Yogurt

1 tsp. unflavoured gelatin
1 tbsp. lemon juice
2 tbsp. water
1 cup strawberries, raspberries, sliced peaches, or blueberries;
    or 1 small sliced banana
1 tbsp. sugar
1 cup plain yogurt
2 egg whites (optional)
2 tbsp. sugar (optional)

Soften gelatin in lemon juice and water. Heat over hot water, stirring until gelatin dissolves. Remove from heat. Add fruit, yogurt, and sugar, and mix lightly.

Pour into a blender or food processor and blend until mixture is fairly smooth. Little pieces of fruit are fine. Pour mixture into a metal bowl and place in freezer.

At this point there is a choice. If a lighter texture is desired, beat egg whites to soft peaks. Gradually add the 2 tbsp. sugar and beat until stiff peaks form. When mixture in the freezer is partly frozen around the edges, beat with an electric mixer until fluffy. Fold in egg whites, and return to freezer in a covered bowl.

The alternative is to freeze the fruit mixture solid. When ready to serve, remove bowl from freezer and allow mixture to soften just enough so that it can be beaten with an electric mixer. Beat until creamy but still quite thick and frozen. Serve immediately.

Makes 4 servings.

Muffins

Norma's Yogurt Muffins

This excellent recipe comes from our good friend Norma Thurston of Calgary, Alberta. We think these muffins are particularly outstanding with fresh blueberries.

2 cups yogurt *or* buttermilk
2 tsp. baking soda
1 cup firmly-packed brown sugar
2 eggs
1 cup vegetable oil
2 cups natural bran
2 tsp. vanilla
2 cups all-purpose flour *or* 1 cup all-purpose and ⁷/₈ cup
    whole-wheat flour
4 tsp. baking powder
¹/₂ tsp. salt
1 cup unsweetened blueberries, chopped dates, raisins, nuts,
    chopped dried apricots, *or* any other dried fruit or nuts

Mix yogurt and baking soda in a medium bowl and set aside to foam.

In a large bowl, beat together sugar, eggs, and oil. Add bran and vanilla. Sift together flour, baking powder, and salt. Add to sugar mixture alternately with yogurt, stirring just enough to blend ingredients.

Fold in berries, fruits, or nuts. Fill greased muffin tins ³/₄ full. Bake at 350°F for about 35 minutes.

Makes about 20 medium muffins.

Ann Budge, Belfountain, Ont

Oatmeal Muffins

1 cup rolled oats (*not* quick-cooking)
1 cup buttermilk
$^7/_8$ cup whole-wheat flour
$^1/_2$ tsp. salt
$^1/_2$ tsp. baking soda
1 tsp. baking powder
$^1/_2$ cup vegetable oil
$^1/_2$ cup firmly-packed brown sugar
1 egg
$^1/_2$ cup chopped dates, prunes, *or* dried apricots

Combine oats and buttermilk in a large bowl and let stand for 5 minutes. In another bowl, thoroughly mix flour with baking soda and baking powder. Beat together oil, sugar, and egg; then add to buttermilk mixture. Stir in dry ingredients, mixing only long enough to moisten. Fold in dates, prunes, or apricots. Spoon into 10 or 12 greased muffin tins and bake in a 400°F oven 15 to 20 minutes.

Susan Budge, Waterloo, Ont

Graham Muffins

$^1/_2$ cup sifted all-purpose flour
1 tsp. baking powder
1 tsp. baking soda
$^1/_4$ tsp. salt
1 egg
$^3/_4$ cup firmly-packed brown sugar
$^1/_2$ cup buttermilk *or* $^1/_2$ cup milk mixed with $^3/_4$ tbsp. lemon juice
$^1/_2$ cup yogurt
$1^1/_2$ cups graham flour
$^1/_2$ cup bran *or* wheat germ
$^1/_2$ cup chopped dates
2 tbsp. vegetable oil

Sift flour, baking powder, baking soda, and salt together. In another bowl, beat egg, then add sugar, buttermilk, and yogurt. Stir in sifted ingredients, graham flour, bran, and dates. Add vegetable oil and stir lightly. Spoon into 12 greased muffin tins and bake at 400°F for 12 to 15 minutes.

Wheat Germ-Raisin Muffins

$^1/_2$ cup white *or* brown sugar
$^1/_2$ cup margarine *or* butter
1 cup milk
1 egg
$1^1/_4$ cups whole-wheat flour
2 tsp. baking powder
$^1/_2$ tsp. nutmeg
$^1/_2$ tsp. cinnamon
$^1/_8$ tsp. salt
$^3/_4$ cup wheat germ
1 cup raisins
3 tbsp. molasses

Cream sugar and margarine until fluffy. Add milk and blend, then stir in egg. Combine flour, salt, baking powder, nutmeg, cinnamon, and wheat germ, then add to creamed mixture. Do not overmix. Stir in molasses and raisins. Fill greased muffin tins $^2/_3$ full. Bake at 425°F for 20 to 25 minutes.

Makes 12 muffins.

Whole-Wheat Date Muffins

A nice crusty nutritious muffin!

1 egg
1 cup plain yogurt
$^1/_3$ cup sunflower oil
1 cup whole-wheat flour
$^1/_3$ cup graham *or* soy flour, *or* combination
$^1/_3$ cup yellow cornmeal
1 tsp. baking soda
$^1/_4$ tsp. salt
3 tbsp. brown sugar
$^1/_2$ cup dates, finely chopped

Beat egg, yogurt, and oil. Combine dry ingredients with chopped dates and add to liquid ingredients. Stir until dry ingredients are *just* moistened. The batter should still be lumpy. Fill greased muffin tins $^3/_4$ full and bake at 350°F for 25 minutes or until muffins are well browned.

Makes about 10 medium muffins.

Oat-Cranberry Muffins

The subtle blending of tart fruit and spice makes these muffins interesting.

³/₄ **cup whole-wheat flour**
³/₄ **cup all-purpose flour**
1 cup rolled oats (*not* quick-cooking)
¹/₂ **cup firmly-packed brown sugar**
1 tbsp. baking powder
¹/₂ **tsp. salt**
1 tsp. cinnamon *or* ³/₄ tsp. nutmeg
1 cup fresh cranberries (cut in half)
¹/₄ **cup butter**
1 cup milk
1 egg

Combine dry ingredients well. Sprinkle cranberries with 1 tbsp. of dry ingredients, stir, and set aside.

Melt butter over low heat. Remove from heat and stir in milk, then egg. Mix well.

Stir butter mixture into dry ingredients. Mix lightly but well, then fold in cranberries. Spoon into greased muffin cups.

Bake 20 to 25 minutes at 325°F until lightly browned. Let stand 5 minutes before removing from pans.

Makes about 10 muffins.

Wheat Germ-Prune Muffins

When I mentioned to my cross-country ski friend Angela Hohban of Mississauga, Ontario, that we were publishing a cookbook, she said she had a great muffin recipe for us. Here it is; thanks Angie! The recipe is correct: there is **no** flour!

¹/₄ **cup vegetable oil**
¹/₄ **cup blackstrap molasses**
3 tbsp. honey
2 eggs
³/₄ **cup milk**
1 tsp. baking soda
2¹/₂ **cups wheat germ**
¹/₂ **tsp. *each* cinnamon, nutmeg, and ginger**
1 tsp. baking powder
¹/₂ **cup or more chopped prunes**

Mix milk and baking soda, then add oil, molasses, honey, and eggs. Set aside. Mix together wheat germ, spices, baking powder, and prunes.

Add dry ingredients to liquid ones and mix just until well moistened. Bake in greased muffin tins at 350°F for 20 minutes or until done.

Makes 12 small or 8 large muffins.

Ann Budge, Belfountain, Ont

Orange Muffins

1 large orange (not a thick-skinned variety or a mandarin)
¹/₂ cup orange juice
¹/₂ cup dates *or* raisins
1 egg
¹/₂ cup butter *or* margarine, melted and cooled
1 cup all-purpose flour
¹/₂ cup whole-wheat flour
¹/₃ to ¹/₂ cup white *or* brown sugar
1 tsp. baking soda
1 tsp. baking powder

Sift together dry ingredients. Wash orange and cut into pieces, removing seeds and excess white membranes. Process in blender or food processor until it becomes a thick liquid. Add juice, chopped dates or raisins, egg, and butter; process until thoroughly mixed. Make a well in dry ingredients and pour in liquid from blender. Stir until dry ingredients are just moistened. Bake 15 minutes at 400°F.

Makes about 14 muffins.

Jeanette Sokol, Toronto, Ont

Cheesy-Cornmeal Muffins

Delicious when served piping hot, these muffins have a crusty top and are great with soup or main course.

1½ cups all-purpose flour
½ cup yellow cornmeal
1 tbsp. baking powder
pinch of cayenne pepper
½ tsp. salt
1 cup milk
1 egg
¼ cup butter, melted
1¼ cups grated sharp Cheddar cheese

Thoroughly mix flour, cornmeal, baking powder, salt, and cayenne pepper.

Beat egg with milk and melted butter, then add to dry ingredients. Stir gently until thoroughly mixed.

Fold in 1 cup of grated Cheddar cheese. Spoon batter into greased muffin tins. Sprinkle 1 tsp. of the remaining cheese on each muffin and bake at 425°F 15 to 20 minutes or until golden. Serve hot from the oven or reheat before serving.

Makes 9 or 10 muffins. These muffins freeze well.

Ann Budge, Belfountain, Ont

Corn-Cheese Muffins

Big, puffy muffins! Delicious with soup for lunch.

⅞ cup whole-wheat flour
1 cup all-purpose flour
3 tsp. baking powder
¼ cup white sugar
¼ tsp. salt
2 eggs
1 10-oz. can cream-style corn
½ cup milk
¾ cup grated medium *or* old Cheddar cheese
¼ cup vegetable shortening *or* butter, melted
¼ cup finely-chopped sweet red pepper *or* chopped pecans

In a large bowl, combine flours, sugar, baking powder, and salt. Beat eggs well and blend in corn, milk, cheese, melted shortening, and red pepper or pecans. Add corn mixture to dry mixture, stirring until just moistened. Spoon into greased muffin tins, filling to the top. Bake at 400°F for 30 minutes or until golden brown.

Makes 10 to 12 large muffins. Best served while still warm or reheated before serving.

Cornmeal-Raisin Muffins

These muffins are rather mild in taste, as cornmeal muffins usually are. If you like a stronger flavour, add grated orange peel, nutmeg, or whatever flavouring you fancy. Crispy, crumbled bacon could be added instead of the raisins.

1^1/$_2$ **cups raisins, preferably Thompson**
2 cups cornmeal
3 cups buttermilk
2^2/$_3$ cups all-purpose flour
2 tsp. baking soda
2 tsp. baking powder
1 tsp. salt
2 eggs
1 cup vegetable oil
1 cup liquid honey

Soak raisins in 2 cups of boiling water for a few minutes, then drain well in a colander. Stir cornmeal into 2 cups of the buttermilk and set aside.

Thoroughly mix flour, baking soda, salt, and baking powder.

Beat eggs; then beat in oil, honey, and remaining 1 cup of buttermilk. Add to cornmeal mixture, then add this batter to flour mixture. Add drained raisins. Stir until dry ingredients are just moistened.

Spoon into greased muffin cups. Bake at 400°F for about 20 minutes.

Makes 2 dozen muffins.

Podborski Muffin Mix

Steve Podborski, Canada's alpine skiing super-star, says these are his favourite muffins. His mother, Jackie, is happy for us to print the recipe. Could being raised on these muffins be the secret to Steve's success? This batter will keep up to four weeks refrigerated in a tightly closed jar, but do not freeze the batter.

²/₃ **cup wheat germ**
3 cups natural bran
3 cups 100% Bran®
3 cups boiling water
1 cup margarine (*not* butter)
2 cups firmly-packed brown sugar
1 cup white sugar
¹/₂ **cup molasses**
4 eggs
4 cups buttermilk
2 cups raisins *and/or* chopped dates
5 cups all-purpose flour
3 tbsp. baking soda (yes, 3 *tbsp.*)
1 tsp. salt

Mix wheat germ, bran, and bran cereal in a bowl. Add boiling water. Stir and set aside.

Cream margarine and sugars in a very large bowl. Add molasses. Beat in eggs one at a time. Add buttermilk and blend thoroughly. Stir in raisins and/or dates.

Mix together flour, baking soda, and salt. Gradually stir into batter. Stir in the bran-water mixture. Mix *thoroughly.* Spoon batter into several large glass containers. Cover and refrigerate at least 24 hours before baking the first batch.

Fill greased muffin tins ³/₄ full. Bake in preheated 375°F oven for 25 to 30 minutes, until golden brown.

Makes 5 dozen medium muffins.

100% Bran® is a registered trademark of Nabisco Brands Ltd.

Overnight Bran Muffins

These superb muffins are prepared ahead of time but baked at the last minute. The longer they wait, the lighter they will be!

3 eggs
$^1/_2$ cup firmly-packed brown sugar *or* Demerara sugar
$^3/_4$ cup molasses
$^1/_4$ cup pure maple syrup
4 tsp. baking soda
$3^1/_2$ cups milk
$1^1/_4$ cups vegetable oil
4 tsp. baking powder
$^1/_2$ tsp. salt
4 cups natural bran
4 cups whole-wheat flour
2 cups raisins

Beat eggs well. Add sugar, molasses, maple syrup, milk, vegetable oil, and baking soda. Mix well.

Combine flour, salt, baking powder, and bran, then add to sugar mixture, stirring until just moistened. Fold in raisins. Spoon mixture into well-greased muffin tins and cover with plastic wrap. Refrigerate 12 to 24 hours. Bake in a preheated 400°F oven for 15 to 20 minutes.

Makes 3 dozen muffins.

Bran Muffins

$2^3/_4$ cups all-purpose flour
4 tsp. baking powder
$^1/_4$ tsp. salt
$^1/_3$ cup vegetable oil
1 egg
$^1/_4$ cup soft butter
3 tbsp. molasses
3 tbsp. honey
$1^1/_4$ cups milk
$^1/_3$ cup natural bran
$^1/_2$ cup raisins
1 to 2 tsp. finely-grated
    orange peel (optional)

Mix flour, baking powder, and salt in a large bowl. Beat remaining ingredients in a separate bowl. Stir liquid ingredients and orange rind if used into dry ingredients just enough to mix thoroughly. Fill 12 greased muffin tins $^3/_4$ full. Bake 20 minutes at 375°F.

Makes 12 muffins.

Frances Bryan, Fredericton, NB

Big Buck Muffins

A hearty muffin, as the name implies.

I

2 cups bran
2 cups buttermilk *or* 2 cups milk and 2 tbsp. vinegar

II

²/₃ cup vegetable oil
2 eggs
³/₄ cup brown sugar *or* ¹/₃ cup honey
2 tsp. baking soda
1 tsp. salt
1¹/₂ cups grated vegetables: parsnips, carrots, squash, *or*
    zucchini
handful of raisins
handful *each* of walnuts, sesame seeds, and sunflower seeds

III

2 cups whole-wheat flour (could include ¹/₂ cup wheat germ)
2 tsp. baking powder

Mix **I** and let stand. Mix **II** in order given. Mix **III**.
    Finally, mix **I** and **II** together, then add **III**. Mix quickly and
spoon into greased muffin tins. Bake at 350°F for 35 minutes.

Makes 18 to 24 muffins.

Ian Lowe-Wylde, Waterloo, Ont

Bran, Carrot, and Fruit Muffins

Loaded with nutritious ingredients. The choices of fruit and
liquid give these muffins a variety of flavours.

3 eggs, lightly beaten
²/₃ cup vegetable oil
¹/₃ cup brown *or* Demerara sugar
¹/₄ cup molasses
1 cup grated scrubbed, unpeeled carrots
¹/₃ cup currants
1 cup puréed *or* mashed fruit (applesauce *or* bananas are good)
1¹/₄ cups liquid (juice, sweet apple cider, milk, *or* buttermilk)

2 cups natural bran
$^1/_2$ cup wheat germ
1$^1/_2$ cups whole-wheat flour
2 tsp. baking powder
1 tsp. baking soda

Combine lightly beaten eggs, vegetable oil, sugar, molasses, carrots, currants, fruit purée, and liquid. Stir in bran and wheat germ, then set aside while sifting together flour, baking powder, and baking soda. Stir flour mixture into the liquid mixture. Fill greased muffin cups three-quarters full and bake in a 375°F oven until nicely browned, about 25 minutes.

Makes 18 to 20 muffins.

Carrot Muffins

Muffins for carrot-cake lovers!

2 cups all-purpose flour
$^1/_2$ tsp. salt
1 tsp. cinnamon *or* $^3/_4$ tsp. nutmeg
1 tsp. baking powder
2 tsp. baking soda
$^7/_8$ to 1$^3/_4$ cups white *or* brown sugar
1 cup vegetable oil
3 eggs
1 tsp. vanilla
2 cups grated scrubbed, unpeeled carrots
1 cup sunflower seeds *or* chopped walnuts
1 14-oz. can crushed pineapple
1 cup flaked unsweetened coconut
1 cup dates *or* raisins

Drain pineapple, reserving juice.
    Mix dry ingredients and form a well in centre. Beat together oil, vanilla, and eggs; mix into dry ingredients. If batter seems too dry, add a couple of tablespoons of pineapple juice. Fold in carrots, nuts, pineapple, coconut, and chopped dates or raisins. Turn into greased muffin tins. Bake at 350°F until set.

Makes 24 muffins.

Brenda Russell, Ottawa, Ont

Banana-Pineapple Muffins

The addition of pineapple gives the ever-popular banana muffin a new look and taste.

$^{1}/_{2}$ **cup butter** *or* **vegetable shortening**
$^{3}/_{4}$ **cup white** *or* **brown sugar**
1 egg
1 tsp. pure vanilla extract *or* $^{1}/_{2}$ **tsp. almond flavouring**
1 cup all-purpose flour
$^{1}/_{3}$ **cup whole-wheat flour**
1 tsp. baking soda
$^{1}/_{2}$ **tsp. baking powder**
$^{1}/_{2}$ **to** $^{3}/_{4}$ **tsp. grated nutmeg (fresh, if possible)**
$^{1}/_{2}$ **cup drained canned crushed pineapple**
1 cup mashed very ripe bananas
flaked unsweetened coconut (optional)

Cream butter or shortening and sugar until fluffy. Beat in egg and vanilla. Sift together remaining dry ingredients. Mix pineapple and banana together. Mix dry ingredients into creamed mixture one-third at a time, alternating with the pineapple-banana mixture. Stir lightly to blend but do not overmix. Spoon into greased muffin tins and sprinkle with coconut, if desired. Bake at 375°F for 25 minutes. Remove muffins from tins and cool on racks. Best while still warm.

Makes 1 dozen muffins.

Banana-Peanut Butter Muffins

2 medium very ripe bananas
$^{1}/_{2}$ **cup peanut butter (smooth** *or* **crunchy)**
2 eggs
$^{1}/_{2}$ **cup liquid honey**
$^{1}/_{2}$ **cup vegetable oil** *or* $^{1}/_{3}$ **cup if peanut butter is very oily**
1 tsp. pure vanilla extract
$^{3}/_{4}$ **cup all-purpose flour**
$^{3}/_{4}$ **cup whole-wheat flour**
1 tbsp. baking powder
$^{1}/_{2}$ **tsp. baking soda**
$^{1}/_{2}$ **tsp. salt**
$^{1}/_{2}$ **cup chopped unsalted peanuts**

Mash bananas. In a large bowl place eggs, honey, oil, banana, peanut butter, and vanilla. Beat until well combined.

In another bowl mix flours, baking powder, baking soda, peanuts, and salt. Add flour mixture to egg mixture and stir until just combined. Spoon into greased muffin tins. Bake until lightly browned, about 20 minutes, in a 400°F oven. Remove muffins and cool on a rack.

Makes 10 muffins.

Mom's Banana Muffins

My mother's recipe makes the best banana muffins we have ever tasted!

$^{1}/_{2}$ cup whole-wheat flour
$^{1}/_{2}$ cup all-purpose flour
$^{1}/_{4}$ tsp. baking soda
$2^{1}/_{2}$ tsp. baking powder
$^{1}/_{2}$ tsp. salt
$^{1}/_{2}$ cup white sugar
$^{1}/_{4}$ cup brown *or* Demerara sugar
$^{3}/_{4}$ cup quick-cooking rolled oats
$^{1}/_{3}$ cup chopped nuts
$^{1}/_{2}$ cup raisins
1 large very ripe banana
1 egg
$^{1}/_{2}$ cup milk
3 tbsp. butter, melted

Mix dry ingredients, including nuts and raisins, in a large bowl. Mash banana. Beat together egg, milk, melted butter, and banana. Carefully stir liquid ingredients into dry ones, mixing only until dry ingedients are just moist. Fill 10 to 12 greased muffin tins. Bake at 375°F for about 20 minutes.

Makes 10 to 12 muffins.

Ann Budge, Belfountain, Ont

Apple Muffins

1 cup whole-wheat flour
1 egg
1 to 2 apples
1½ tsp. baking powder
¼ tsp. salt
1 tbsp. brown sugar
½ cup milk
2 tbsp. vegetable shortening, melted
1 tsp. cinnamon

Sift flour, salt, sugar, baking powder, and cinnamon into a bowl. Peel and chop apples and add to dry ingredients. Beat egg with milk and melted shortening and add to dry ingredients. Mix together with a fork. Spoon into 6 greased muffin cups. Sprinkle tops with a little extra cinnamon and bake at 425°F for 15 to 20 minutes. Serve hot.

Makes 6 muffins.

Christina Day, Ottawa, Ont

Mango Muffins

A recipe from Hawaii!

2 cups all-purpose flour
2 tsp. baking soda
2 tsp. cinnamon
½ tsp. salt
1 cup white *or* brown sugar
3 large eggs
¾ cup vegetable oil
1½ tsp. vanilla extract
¼ cup raisins
2 cups chopped mangos *or* other fruit *or* applesauce
finely-chopped nuts, for topping

Sift flour, cinnamon, baking soda, and salt. Mix in sugar. Beat together eggs, oil, and vanilla; add to dry ingredients. Stir in raisins and mangos. Fill greased muffin cups and sprinkle with nuts. Bake at 350°F for about 32 minutes.

Makes approximately 15 muffins.

Nicole Roy, Montreal, Qué

Blueberry Muffins

A Newfoundland favourite!

1 egg
¼ cup vegetable oil
½ cup milk
1½ cups all-purpose flour
½ cup sugar
2 tsp. baking powder
½ tsp. salt
1 cup unsweetened fresh blueberries

Beat egg lightly. Stir oil and milk into beaten egg. Combine dry ingredients and add to egg mixture, stirring just enough to moisten. Carefully fold in blueberries. Spoon into 10 greased muffin tins. Bake at 400°F for 25 to 30 minutes.

Makes 10 muffins

Barb Taylor, St. John's Nfld

Whole-Wheat Pumpkin Muffins

3 cups whole-wheat flour
1 cup white sugar
1 cup instant skim milk powder
4 tsp. baking powder
½ tsp. salt
1 tsp. cinnamon
1 tsp. nutmeg
¼ tsp. ground cloves
2 eggs
1 cup water
1 cup canned pumpkin *or* puréed cooked fresh pumpkin
½ cup vegetable oil
1 cup raisins

Blend dry ingredients. Beat together eggs, water, pumpkin, and vegetable oil; stir in raisins. Add liquid ingredients to dry ingredients. Stir gently until moistened. Spoon into greased muffin tins. Bake in a 400°F oven for 15 to 17 minutes.

Makes about 2 dozen muffins.

Jenny Birchell, Hamilton, Ont

Hiker's Muffins

A tidy way to take your "gorp" along. "Gorp" is a mixture of nuts and dried fruit that hikers usually munch for energy along the trail.

1½ cups very hot water
¼ cup Barbados *or* blackstrap molasses
½ cup rolled oats
½ cup bran
6 tbsp. Demerara sugar
1 cup whole-wheat flour
¼ cup soy *or* graham flour
3 tbsp. wheat germ
½ cup instant skim milk powder
1 tsp. baking powder
½ tsp. baking soda
½ tsp. salt
⅓ cup vegetable oil
2 eggs
2 tsp. pure vanilla extract
½ cup chopped walnuts, pecans, *or* peanuts
½ cup sesame *or* sunflower seeds
1 cup raisins *and/or* currants
½ cup unsweetened coconut
½ cup or more dates, cut up
½ cup or more apricots, cut up

Add molasses to very hot water in a large bowl; stir in bran and oats. Let sit 15 minutes. In a second bowl combine sugar, flours, milk powder, wheat germ, baking soda, baking powder, and salt. To the molasses mixture add oil, eggs, and vanilla. Beat until well blended. Stir in dry ingredients and combine well but do not overmix. Fold in coconut, nuts, raisins, and chopped dates and apricots. Spoon into greased or paper-lined muffin tins. Bake at 350°F for about 20 minutes.

Makes about 18 good-sized muffins.

Yeast Breads

Chris' Brown Bread

Working time for this bread is about 20 minutes. While the dough rises, find something else to do: lift a few weights, do some stretching exercises, ride your stationary bicycle, or whatever, says Chris!

2 cups warm water (110°F)
2 tsp. honey
2 envelopes active dry yeast
³⁄₄ cup milk
¹⁄₃ to ¹⁄₂ cup molasses
¹⁄₂ cup vegetable oil
¹⁄₂ tsp. salt
6 to 7 cups whole-wheat flour (Several cups of rye flour *or* rolled oats may be substituted.)
¹⁄₂ cup wheat germ
¹⁄₂ cup bran

Dissolve honey in warm water and sprinkle yeast on top. Let sit 10 minutes, then stir well with a fork.

Meanwhile scald milk and stir in molasses, vegetable oil, and salt. Cook to lukewarm (110°F) and stir in yeast mixture.

Mix together flour, wheat germ, and bran. Stir into batter. Knead the dough well on a floured surface. Place dough in a greased bowl and turn once to grease all sides. Cover and let dough rise until doubled. Punch down and shape into 2 loaves. Let rise again in greased pans until nearly doubled.

Bake at 375°F for about 35 minutes. Cool on racks.

Chris Reid, Edmonton, Alta

Daphne's Company Bread

Before you shudder with visions of bending over a hot stove for hours, let me say that this bread is easy to make, and if it doesn't rise as much as bakery bread, what the heck! It's tasty and packed with nutrition.

1 tbsp. honey *or* maple syrup
¹/₂ cup warm water
1¹/₂ tbsp. active dry yeast
2 tbsp. butter
2 tbsp. honey *or* maple syrup
2 cups liquid (milk, water, *or* water drained from boiled
    potatoes)
2 tsp. salt
2 eggs, beaten (optional)
1 cup soy flour (optional)
1 tbsp. wheat germ (optional)
6 to 7 cups whole-wheat flour (approximately)
1 cup grated cheese *or* grated carrots; sunflower seeds *or*
    soybean nuts

Dissolve 1 tbsp. honey or maple syrup in warm water. Sprinkle dry yeast on top. Put in a warm place for 10 minutes, after which it should have doubled in volume.

Meanwhile, melt butter in a saucepan. Add 2 tbsp. honey or maple syrup, then add 2 cups liquid and heat to lukewarm. Pour into a large bowl. Add salt, then beaten eggs if you want them.

Add yeast mixture and 1 cup whole-wheat flour and beat for 100 strokes.

At this point, add the optional cup of soy flour and 1 tbsp. of wheat germ, if you wish. Add whole-wheat flour until stiff enough to turn onto a board. Leave for a few minutes; it will be easier to work with after a brief rest. (Meanwhile I wash my bowl and butter it well.) Knead for 10 minutes, adding flour as needed. (Pardon the pun!) You should use about 6 to 7 cups of flour in all; it will depend on the consistency of the flour. (Sometimes I use rye flour instead; then the bread doesn't rise as much.) The dough should be springy and just a little sticky.

Put dough into a greased bowl and turn it so the top is greased, then cover it with a damp cloth and put it into a warm place to rise. I use the top of my wood stove in the winter. In the summer it can be a problem to find a warm enough place, but a sheltered spot in the sunshine will do. (One day I found my cat curled up in my bread dough!) It will take an hour or so of rising to double the volume, depending on the temperature (it should be close to 86°F). Now is the time to go skiing or running, or do your housework if you must.

When the dough has risen, punch it down to remove air pockets. Now I add whatever is on hand: a cup of grated cheese, grated carrots, sunflower seeds, or soybean nuts. Knead into dough. Divide dough into 2 equal parts and put into greased loaf pans. Cover again with a damp cloth and put in a warm spot to rise until doubled (about 1 hour).

Bake at 375°F for 15 minutes. Reduce to 350°F. Bread will be done if, when you tap the bottom of the loaf, it sounds hollow. If not, return bread to pan and pan to oven again for a few more minutes. Cool on racks.

The extras I add after the first rising to give the bread more nutrition will prevent it from rising as much as it otherwise would, but I believe bread should add more to our diet than just air!

Daphne Tomblin, New Lowell, Ont

Kneadless Oatmeal Bread

A good bread for the novice yeast-bread maker. By varying the spice or seeds, you can give this bread whatever flavour you like.

1 tsp. sugar
¼ cup warm water (110°F)
1 envelope active dry yeast
¾ cup boiling water
½ cup quick-cooking rolled oats
3 tbsp. butter *or* margarine
¼ cup honey *or* molasses
1 tsp. salt
1 egg, beaten
½ tsp. nutmeg, cinnamon, dill seeds, linseeds, caraway seeds,
   ***or* sesame seeds**
1 cup whole-wheat flour
¼ cup skim milk powder
1 cup all-purpose flour

Dissolve sugar in warm water. Sprinkle yeast over water and let stand 10 minutes, then stir well.

While waiting for yeast to dissolve, stir boiling water, rolled oats, butter or margarine, honey or molasses, and salt in a large bowl until butter is melted. Cool to lukewarm.

Add egg, dissolved yeast, nutmeg or cinnamon or seeds, whole-wheat flour, skim milk powder, and ½ cup all-purpose flour to rolled oat mixture. Beat hard with a wooden spoon for 2 minutes.

Add as much as needed of remaining flour and beat well. Turn into a greased or paper-lined loaf pan. Cover with a damp tea towel and let rise in warm place until dough has risen to 1 inch below top of pan, about 1½ hours.

If the dough is slow to rise in the pans, let it sit in the oven while the oven heats to 375°F. If it rises satisfactorily in a warm place, bake in a preheated 375°F oven until loaf sounds hollow when tapped, about 35 to 45 minutes. Turn out of pan and cool on a rack.

Oatmeal-Raisin Bread

Bring some to your next orienteering meet and share it with your favourite meet director, suggests Pat.

1 envelope active dry yeast
$^1/_2$ tsp. sugar
$^1/_2$ cup warm water (110°F)
2 cups rapidly boiling water
1 cup rolled oats
2 tbsp. butter *or* margarine
$^3/_8$ cup molasses
$^1/_2$ tsp. salt
$^1/_2$ tsp. cinnamon *or* ground ginger
3 cups whole-wheat flour
$^1/_2$ cup wheat germ
$^2/_3$ cup raisins
2 to 3 cups all-purpose flour

Dissolve sugar in warm water and sprinkle yeast on top. Tap once or twice to mix. Let stand 10 minutes and stir well.

Pour the rapidly boiling water over the oats in a large bowl. Stir in the butter or margarine and let cool. Add the molasses, cinnamon or ginger, and salt. Add yeast mixture to oatmeal mixture. Mix well. Start adding whole-wheat flour and wheat germ, beating hard at each addition. Sprinkle a little flour over the raisins and mix, then add raisins to batter. Add just enough all-purpose flour to make a soft dough.

Turn onto a generously floured board and knead until smooth and satiny. Place in a greased bowl and turn once to grease both sides. Cover and let stand in a warm place until doubled in bulk, about 1 hour. Shape into 2 loaves. Place in greased bread pans. Cover and let rise until doubled. Bake in a 350°F oven for about 50 to 60 minutes or until browned. Turn out and cool on rack.

Pat de St. Croix, Vineland, Ont

Oatmeal-Molasses Bread

This bread is delicious toasted.

¼ **cup warm water (110°F)**
½ **tsp. white sugar**
1 envelope active dry yeast
2 cups quick-cooking rolled oats
1 tbsp. butter
1 tsp. salt
¼ **cup brown sugar**
3¾ **cups boiling water**
½ **cup molasses**
about 6 to 7 cups whole-wheat flour
melted butter, for brushing loaves when cooked

Dissolve yeast and ½ tsp. sugar in ¼ cup warm water. Sprinkle yeast on water, tap gently, and let sit 10 minutes. Stir to dissolve well.

Put butter, salt, brown sugar, and oats in a large bowl. Pour on 3¾ cups boiling water. When cooled to lukewarm, add yeast mixture. Mix well. Add molasses and mix again.

Add flour until mixture is no longer sticky and is smooth and satiny. Don't worry if it takes more or less flour than suggested. Knead for 5 or 6 minutes.

Place in a well-greased bowl and turn to grease all sides. Cover with a clean tea towel. Leave on counter overnight. In the morning knead a few minutes. Divide into 3 parts and shape into 3 loaves. Put in greased loaf pans. Cover with a tea towel and let rise 1½ hours. Bake at 350°F for about 45 to 50 minutes. Remove from pans and cool on racks. To soften the crust, brush top of loaves with melted butter when removed from the oven. This bread freezes very well.

Marcia Urquhart, Fredericton, NB

Whole-Grain Molasses Bread

4$\frac{1}{2}$ to 5 cups all-purpose flour
2 envelopes dry Rapidmix® yeast
$\frac{1}{3}$ cup molasses
5 cups whole-wheat *and/or* light rye flour
2 tsp. salt
3 cups warm water (110°F)
$\frac{1}{2}$ cup vegetable oil
1 beaten egg white (optional)
poppy or sesame seeds (optional)

In a large bowl, combine 4 cups all-purpose flour with yeast. Mix molasses, oil, 3 cups warm water, and 2 teaspoons salt and add to flour mixture. Beat by hand for 5 minutes, or on low speed of electric mixer for 30 seconds, then 3 minutes at high speed. Stir in whole-wheat and/or rye flour and as much of the remaining all-purpose flour as you can mix in with a spoon.

Turn out on floured surface and knead for 8 to 10 minutes or until dough is smooth and not too sticky. Place in a greased bowl and turn once to grease all sides. Cover and let rise until doubled in bulk (50 to 60 minutes).

Punch dough down to remove air. Divide into 3 equl parts. Shape and place in 3 greased 8 x 4-inch loaf pans or 3 greased 1$\frac{1}{2}$-qt. casseroles or soufflé dishes. Cover and let rise till nearly doubled, 40 to 50 minutes. If desired, brush tops with beaten egg white, sprinkle with poppy or sesame seeds. Bake at 375°F for 40 to 50 minutes.

Makes 3 loaves.

Lynda Sidney, Sudbury, Ont

Rapidmix® is a registered trademark of Nabisco Brands Ltd.

Beer Rye Bread

A soft-crusted, light-textured bread with a malt and caraway flavour.

1 tsp. granulated sugar
¼ cup warm water (110°F)
1 envelope active dry yeast
¾ cup beer
2 tbsp. firmly-packed brown sugar
2 tbsp. margarine
1 tsp. salt
1 tsp. caraway seeds
1½ cups all-purpose flour
1 cup rye flour

Dissolve granulated sugar in warm water. Add yeast and let stand 10 minutes, then stir well. Meanwhile heat beer, brown sugar, margarine, and salt until margarine melts. Cool to lukewarm. Add to dissolved yeast with caraway seeds and all-purpose flour. Blend, then beat for 2 minutes at medium speed of electric mixer. Using a wooden spoon, stir in rye flour until well blended. Spread evenly into a greased 9-inch round pan. Cover and let rise until doubled in bulk, about 45 minutes. Bake at 375°F for 25 to 30 minutes.

Makes 1 loaf.

Courtesy of Nabisco Brands Ltd

Three-Grain Dark Rye Bread

A pumpernickel-type bread.

1¹/₂ **cups boiling water**
¹/₄ **cup brown sugar**
¹/₄ **cup vegetable shortening**
1 tsp. cocoa
1 tbsp. instant coffee
1 tbsp. salt
¹/₂ **cup yellow cornmeal**
1¹/₂ **tsp. caraway seeds (optional)**
2 tsp. white sugar
1 cup lukewarm water (110°-115°F)
2 envelopes active dry yeast
2 cups dark rye flour
2 cups whole-wheat flour
1¹/₂ **cups all-purpose flour**
1 egg white
1 tbsp. water

Pour boiling water into a large mixing bowl. Add brown sugar, shortening, cocoa, coffee, and salt, stirring until shortening has melted. Now add cornmeal and caraway seeds and set aside to cool.

Dissolve 2 tsp. white sugar in 1 cup lukewarm water. Sprinkle yeast over top. Let stand for 10 minutes to bubble up. Then stir with a fork and add to cornmeal mixture.

Stir in rye flour and whole-wheat flour. With floured hands, work in all-purpose flour. Turn onto a lightly floured board and knead dough. Add all-purpose flour as you knead until dough is silky and not sticky and will not take any more flour. Shape into a smooth ball.

Place in a large greased bowl and turn to grease all sides. Cover with greased waxed paper and a damp tea towel. Set in a draught-free area until doubled in bulk (1¹/₄ hours). Punch down and knead on floured board for two minutes. Divide in half and form two round loaves. Place on greased baking sheet; allow to rise until doubled in bulk.

Brush with an egg white lightly beaten with 1 tbsp. of water for a crusty top. Bake in a 375°F oven for 45 to 55 minutes. Bread will be cooked if it sounds hollow when tapped lightly on the bottom.

Wendy Edge, Bowmanville, Ont

Granola Bread

The granola gives this bread a nice nutty taste.

2 tsp. honey *or* pure maple syrup
2 cups warm water (110°F)
2 tbsp. active dry yeast
³/₄ cup plain yogurt *or* buttermilk
¹/₄ cup liquid honey *or* maple syrup
¹/₄ cup vegetable oil
2 tsp. salt
4¹/₂ to 6 cups all-purpose flour
2 cups granola-type cereal (with raisins *or* other dried fruit)

Mix the 2 tsp. honey or maple syrup with warm water. Sprinkle yeast into water and let stand 10 minutes, then stir with a fork. Mix yogurt or buttermilk, ¹/₄ cup honey or maple syrup, oil, salt, and 3 cups of flour. Add yeast mixture and beat with an electric mixer for 2 minutes, or by hand for 5 minutes.

Add granola and mix well. Gradually add the remainder of the flour. Knead by hand for 5 minutes. Place in a large greased bowl and turn once to grease all sides.

Cover and let rise in a warm place for 1 hour or until doubled. Punch down and divide in half. Form into 2 loaves and place in greased loaf pans. Cover with a tea towel and let rise in a warm place for 45 minutes. Bake at 375°F for 45 minutes.

Cheddar Yeast Bread

Cheddar bread is practical since it makes a complete snack. It is delicious toasted and has a wonderful aroma while baking.

2 cups hot water (125°F)
¹/₄ cup vegetable oil
¹/₄ cup honey
8 cups whole-wheat flour
1 tbsp. (1 envelope) Rapidmix® yeast
2 eggs
4 cups grated sharp Cheddar cheese
1 cup yogurt

Put the hot water in a large bowl and add the oil and honey. Blend in 4 cups of whole-wheat flour, 1 cup at a time. Then stir

Rapidmix® is a registered trademark of Nabisco Brands Ltd.

in the yeast, cheese, lightly-beaten eggs, yogurt, and the additional flour until you can't stir it with a wooden spoon.

Transfer the dough to a floured surface and knead 5 to 10 minutes, adding flour if necessary, until dough is satiny. Oil a bowl, put the dough in, and turn it over. Cover with a damp tea towel and let rise in a warm, draught-free place until doubled in bulk. Punch down and let rise again. Shape into 3 medium loaves.

Bake on a greased baking sheet in a 350°F oven for an hour. The bread is done when tapping on the bottom of the loaf sounds hollow.

Suat Tuzlak, Calgary, Alta

Cracked Wheat Bread

1 cup warm water (110°F)
2 tsp. white sugar
2 envelopes active dry yeast
2 cups water *or* milk
¼ cup liquid honey
2 tsp. salt
2 to 3 tbsp. vegetable oil
1 cup cracked wheat
2 cups whole-wheat flour
4 cups all-purpose flour
melted butter

In a small bowl dissolve sugar in warm water. Sprinkle yeast over top. Let stand 10 minutes, until foamy, and stir with a fork.

In a large bowl place water or milk, honey, salt, oil, cracked wheat, 2 cups all-purpose flour, and yeast mixture. Beat until smooth.

Beat in whole-wheat flour and 2 more cups of all-purpose flour. Knead with hands for 10 minutes, working in more flour if necessary, until dough is smooth and satiny. Place in a greased bowl, turning once. Let rise for 1½ hours, until doubled. Punch dough down. Divide into 2 or 3 parts depending on the size of your pans. Form loaves and place in 2 or 3 greased loaf pans and let rise again until doubled, 1½ hours. Brush tops of loaves with melted butter. Bake in 375°F oven for 40 to 50 minutes. Cool on racks.

Wendy Edge, Bowmanville, Ont

Sesame Bread

2 envelopes active dry yeast
¾ cup warm water (110°F)
1 tsp. sugar
3 cups milk
⅓ cup vegetable oil
¼ cup molasses
⅓ cup firmly-packed brown sugar
⅔ cup sesame seeds
¼ cup cornmeal
3 cups whole-wheat flour
2 eggs, lightly beaten
1 tbsp. salt
6½ to 7 cups all-purpose flour
1 tbsp. sesame seeds

In a very large bowl, dissolve sugar in warm water. Sprinkle yeast on top, tap several times, and let sit for 10 minutes. Stir well with a fork.

Heat milk to lukewarm. To yeast mixture add lukewarm milk, oil, molasses, brown sugar, ⅔ cup sesame seeds, cornmeal, whole-wheat flour, eggs (reserve 1 tbsp. to brush loaves with), and salt. Beat until smooth. Cover with a clean tea towel and let rise in bowl for half an hour in a draught-free location.

Now beat in 6 cups all-purpose flour. Place 1 cup of flour on board and knead until dough is smooth and will not absorb any more flour.

Cut dough into 3 equal parts and form loaves. Place in greased 9 x 5-inch loaf pans. Brush *unrisen* loaves with 1 tbsp. beaten egg and sprinkle with additional sesame seeds. Let rise 1½ to 2 hours or until doubled in bulk. Bake at 350°F for 35 to 40 minutes.

Lynda Sidney, Sudbury, Ont

Pumpernickel Bread

Dark and delicious! The potatoes make this a very heavy bread.

3 medium-sized potatoes,
   peeled
3 cups water
³/₄ cup yellow cornmeal
1 cup blackstrap molasses
2 tbsp. butter
3 tbsp. cocoa
4 to 5 tbsp. caraway seeds

1 tsp. salt
2¹/₂ tsp. active dry yeast
1 tsp. white sugar
4 cups light rye flour
3 to 4 cups whole-wheat flour
2 tbsp. egg white, lightly beaten
1 tbsp. caraway seeds

Place peeled potatoes in a saucepan and cover with 3 cups water. Cover, bring to the boil, reduce heat, and simmer until potatoes are soft. Drain, reserving cooking water. Mash potatoes until all lumps have disappeared and set aside.

Place ¹/₂ cup of the potato water (at 110°F) in a measuring cup and dissolve 1 tsp. sugar in it. Sprinkle yeast on top, tap sides of cup, and let sit 10 minutes. Stir to mix.

Place 2 cups of the potato water in a saucepan and stir in cornmeal. Cook over low heat, stirring, until mixture thickens (about 5 minutes). Cool slightly.

Into cornmeal mixture stir molasses, butter, cocoa, 4 to 5 tbsp. caraway seeds, and salt. Combine thoroughly, then stir in potatoes. Beat for 2 minutes with electric mixer.

Place cornmeal-potato mixture into a large bowl. Stir in yeast. Begin adding rye flour, one cup at a time, mixing well after each addition. Then add whole-wheat flour until dough is of a consistency to knead. Turn dough onto a floured board and knead for 15 minutes or longer, adding flour when necessary. Dough should be elastic and smooth.

Place in a greased bowl, turning dough to grease all sides. Cover with a damp tea towel and let rise in a warm spot until doubled, about 1¹/₂ hours. Turn out onto a board, punch down, and knead for 1 to 2 minutes. Divide dough in half and form two round loaves. Place on a greased baking sheet, cover with a tea towel, and allow to rise again for 30 minutes. Brush with lightly-beaten egg white and sprinkle with additional 1 tbsp. caraway seeds. Bake at 350°F for 45 to 55 minutes. When cooked, bread will sound hollow if tapped on the bottom.

Anadama Bread

Legend has it that a poor fisherman off the coast of Maine had a very lazy wife. Every night he came in very hungry from long hours of fishing, hoping to find better food than the cornmeal mush and molasses she usually served him. One night, finding the same thing, he stormed over to the stove, added yeast and flour to the mush, and baked it, muttering, "Anna-dama!" ("Anna, damn her!")

This bread is golden in colour, quite moist, and makes the most delicious toast!

1 cup yellow cornmeal	$^1/_2$ cup warm water (110-115°F)
1 cup milk	2 envelopes active dry yeast
1 cup boiling water	about 6 cups all-purpose flour
3 tbsp. butter	1 tbsp. milk
$^1/_2$ cup molasses	1 tbsp. butter, melted
2 tsp. salt	

Bring 1 cup of water to the boil in a medium saucepan. Mix cornmeal with 1 cup milk, then slowly add to boiling water. Cook, stirring with a wire whisk, 2 or 3 minutes until mixture thickens and is smooth. Remove from heat, beat in butter, all but 1 tbsp. molasses, and salt; then set aside. Combine remaining 1 tbsp. molasses with the warm water and sprinkle yeast on top. Let sit 10 minutes, then stir. Stir yeast mixture into cornmeal mixture and blend well.

Add flour, 1 cup at a time, beating after each addition. When dough is smooth and elastic, knead on a lightly-floured board for about 8 minutes. Grease a bowl and place dough in it; turn dough once. Cover loosely and let stand in a warm place 1 to 1½ hours or until doubled. Punch dough down, knead 1 minute, and divide dough between two greased 8 x 4-inch pans. Cover again and let rise until doubled. Bake at 350°F for 45 to 50 minutes, until bread sounds hollow when tapped on the bottom. Remove loaves from pans and cool on a rack. If you wish, brush loaves with a mixture of 1 tbsp. of melted butter and 1 tsp. milk while they are still hot.

This bread freezes very well. When bread has been frozen, thaw at room temperature and heat, wrapped in foil, 10 minutes in a 350°F oven.

Pulla Bread

This is an attractive Finnish braided bread.

³/₄ **cup milk**
¹/₂ **cup white sugar**
1 tsp. salt
¹/₃ **cup butter**
¹/₂ **tsp. ground cardamon**
2 eggs
1 tsp. white sugar
¹/₂ **cup warm water (110°F)**
1 envelope active dry yeast
5 to 5¹/₂ cups all-purpose flour
2 tbsp. white sugar
1 tbsp. hot coffee

Scald milk. Pour into a large bowl and stir in ¹/₂ cup sugar, salt, butter, and cardamon. Stir until butter melts. Cool to lukewarm. Beat eggs lightly and add.

Meanwhile, dissolve 1 tsp. sugar in warm water. Over this, sprinkle yeast. Let stand 10 minutes, then stir briskly with a fork. Add softened yeast to lukewarm milk mixture and stir.

Beat in 2 cups of flour. Gradually add remaining flour. Knead on a floured surface for 8 to 10 minutes. Shape into a round and place in a greased bowl, turning dough once to grease entire surface. Cover and let rise about 1¹/₂ hours. Punch down and divide in half. Shape each half into three 15-inch ropes and braid together, making 2 braided loaves. Place loaves on a greased baking sheet, cover, and let rise about 1 hour.

Bake in a preheated 375°F oven for 30 to 35 minutes. Upon removing from oven, brush immediately with a glaze of 2 tbsp. sugar dissolved in 1 tbsp. hot coffee. Sprinkle with sugar.

Rena Weiler, Morin Heights, Qué

Brian's Sourdough Starter and Sourdough Bread

Sourdough is a yeasty starter for leavening bread, pancakes, cakes, and muffins. To those who lived in the far north years ago, sourdough became the basis of their "staff of life" as bread could not be made without it. Supply boats came usually only once a year and if the trip was prolonged, the yeast, deactivated because of its sensitivity to extreme cold, would refuse to grow. The yeast in the sourdough starter adapted to conditions and a good strain became prized. Even today, many northerners claim to be using starters that originated before the turn of the century.

Julie DePass, Oakville, Ont

Brian is Brian Maxwell, one of Canada's premier marathon runners, now living in California. Brian says he is honoured to have his recipe in our cookbook. For this we thank him.

Sourdough Starter

½ **cup lukewarm water (110°F)**
1 **tsp. sugar**
1 **envelope active dry yeast (1 tbsp.)**
2 **cups water**
1 **tbsp. sugar**
1 **tbsp. salt**
1¾ **to 2 cups unbleached white** *or* **all-purpose flour**

In a large bowl dissolve 1 tsp. sugar in ½ cup lukewarm water. Add yeast and let stand 10 minutes. Stir well. Add 1 tbsp. sugar and 1 tbsp. salt to 2 cups water. Add liquid to yeast. Add enough flour to make it the consistency of thin pancake batter.

Beat until smooth and let stand in a wide-necked uncovered glass jar covered with damp cheesecloth at room temperature for 3 to 5 days. Beat 2 to 3 times a day. The starter can now be stored in the refrigerator in a tightly-covered glass jar until needed. If it is not used every week, add a tsp. of sugar and/or a little flour and water weekly to make it the consistency of thin pancake batter and to keep it going. Leave uncovered at room temperature for a day or two, then cover and refrigerate again. If the liquid separates from the batter, just stir it up. The sourdough culture will react with starches, produce carbon dioxide, and act as a leavening agent. Always save a little starter, then renew it by adding 1 to 2 tsp. sugar and enough flour and water to make it the consistency of thin pancake batter. Let sit at room temperature, uncovered, for a day or two, then cover and refrigerate. The longer it's kept, the more "sour" it becomes, thereby increasing the flavour of the bread.

Brian's Sourdough Bread

The sugar is consumed in the reaction of the sourdough culture and there is no added fat in this recipe. That makes this bread extremely low in calories and fat and high in carbohydrates and protein, especially if you add sesame seeds.

1 tsp. active dry yeast
1½ cups lukewarm water (110°F)
1 cup starter batter, at room temperature (More starter and less water may be used.)
1 tbsp. salt
5 to 6 cups whole-wheat flour
½ cup sesame seeds (optional)
1 tbsp. sugar

Dissolve yeast in water. Stir in sugar and salt. Add starter batter. Then add approximately 2½ to 3½ cups flour (enough to make the batter the consistency of thick pancake batter.) Beat vigorously. Add sesame seeds. Beat until smooth. The more beating at this stage, the lighter the bread will be.

Let batter sit covered with a damp tea towel for 1 to 2 hours at 70° to 80°F, or 3 to 4 hours at a cooler temperature, or overnight. Batter should appear slightly bubbly. Add 1 to 2 cups more flour and mix. Turn out onto floured board and gradually knead in flour until dough is stiff. Shape into 2 to 4 loaves.

Loaves can be put into plastic bags, tightly closed with air removed, and stored in the refrigerator for 1 to 7 days. The bread will rise slightly and continue to sour. When ready to bake brush tops of loaves with butter before setting on a greased baking sheet to rise and spread, covered with a damp tea towel, for 30 to 60 minutes. When doubled in size, bake at 400°F for 35 to 40 minutes or until brown. Brush top with melted butter upon removing from oven.

Egg Refrigerator Bread

This recipe makes two attractive braided loaves. It's an easy version of this classic yellow bread.

2 envelopes active dry yeast	1 tbsp. salt
1/2 cup warm water (110°F)	3 tbsp. butter, melted
1 tsp. sugar	3 eggs
1 3/4 cups warm milk	7 to 7 1/2 cups all-purpose flour
2 tbsp. liquid honey	sesame seeds *or* poppy seeds

Dissolve sugar in water, then add yeast and allow to stand for 10 minutes. Stir down with a fork and pour into a large bowl.

Add milk, honey, salt, butter, 2 eggs, and 1 egg yolk. (Reserve remaining egg white to brush braid before baking.) Stir in 2 cups of flour and beat with electric mixer for 2 minutes. Gradually add remaining flour, mixing well by hand after each addition, until a medium-stiff dough is formed. Turn out onto floured surface and knead until smooth and satiny, about 8 to 10 minutes.

Cut dough in half. Make 3 long ropes out of each half. Braid to form 2 loaves. Place on greased baking sheet. Cover with plastic wrap. Place in refrigerator for at least 4 hours but not more than 24 hours. When ready to bake, brush bread with slightly-beaten egg white. Sprinkle with sesame or poppy seeds. Let stand at room temperature for 10 minutes. Bake at 375°F for 25 to 30 minutes or until done. Cool on wire racks.

Cheese-Filled Rolls

1 tsp. sugar	1 tsp. grated lemon rind
1/4 cup warm water (110°F)	3 cups all-purpose flour
1 envelope active dry yeast	1 package (125 g) cream cheese
1/2 cup milk	1 tbsp. lemon juice
1/3 cup margarine	2 tbsp. sugar
1/3 cup sugar	2 tsp. water
1/2 tsp. salt	2 tbsp. sugar
2 eggs	

Dissolve 1 tsp. sugar in warm water. Add yeast and let stand 10 minutes, then stir well. Meanwhile, heat milk, margarine, 1/3 cup sugar, and salt until margarine melts. Cool to lukewarm. Add to dissolved yeast with 1 whole egg, 1 egg yolk, lemon rind, and 2 cups flour. Blend, then beat for 2 minutes at medium speed of electric mixer. Using a wooden spoon, stir in remaining flour until well blended. Cover and let rise until doubled in bulk, about 1 hour.

Meanwhile combine cream cheese, lemon juice, and 2 tbsp. sugar. Stir down dough with wooden spoon by beating 25 strokes. Turn out onto a well-floured board and roll with *floured* rolling pin to a 12-inch square. Spread evenly with cheese mixture, then cut into 16 squares. Fold each square to form a triangle, pressing edges together gently. Place on greased baking sheets. Let rise until doubled, about 30 minutes. Combine egg white and 2 tsp. water. Brush over surface of rolls and sprinkle with remaining 2 tbsp. sugar. Bake at 350°F for 20 to 25 minutes.

Makes 16 rolls.

Courtesy of Nabisco Brands Ltd

Sesame-Sour Cream Dinner Rolls

1 tsp. sugar
$^{1}/_{4}$ cup warm water (110°F)
1 envelope active dry yeast
$^{3}/_{4}$ cup sour cream (at room temperature)
2 tbsp. vegetable oil
2 tbsp. sugar
1 tsp. salt
1 egg
$2^{1}/_{4}$ cups all-purpose flour
2 tbsp. sesame seeds

Dissolve 1 tsp. sugar in warm water. Add yeast and let stand 10 minutes, then stir well. Add sour cream, oil, 2 tbsp. sugar, salt, egg, and 1 cup flour. Blend, then beat for 2 minutes at medium speed of electric mixer. Using a wooden spoon, stir in remaining flour until well blended.

Cover and let rise until doubled in bulk, about 35 minutes. Stir down dough with a wooden spoon by beating 25 strokes. Spoon evenly into 12 greased $2^{1}/_{2}$-inch muffin tins. Sprinkle with sesame seeds. Cover and let rise until doubled in bulk, about 45 minutes. Bake at 400°F for 25 to 30 minutes.

Makes 12 rolls.

Courtesy of Nabisco Brands Ltd

Whole-Wheat Bagels

These traditional Jewish delights are usually sliced in half, served plain or toasted, and spread with cream cheese, but use your imagination and top them with any other nutritious spread, or fill them, sandwich-style.

2 tsp. active dry yeast
1 tsp. sugar
¹/₂ cup warm water (110°F)
3 eggs
¹/₂ cup vegetable oil
¹/₂ tbsp. salt
1 cup warm water
3 tbsp. sugar *or* honey
3 cups all-purpose flour *or* unbleached hard flour
3 to 4 cups whole-wheat flour
1 egg, well beaten
poppy, sesame, *or* caraway seeds
cornmeal

Dissolve 1 tsp. sugar in ¹/₂ cup warm water. Add yeast. Stir once or twice and let sit 10 minutes, until foamy.

Meanwhile in a large bowl, beat 3 eggs. Add oil, salt, 1 cup warm water, and 3 tbsp. sugar or honey. Add dissolved yeast. Stir in all-purpose flour. Beat until smooth. Add whole-wheat flour, 1 cup at a time. Knead 5 minutes on floured board.

Place in a greased bowl (turn the dough over to grease both sides) in a warm spot, cover with a towel, and let rise for about 1 hour until dough has doubled in size. Punch dough down. Cut dough into 3 portions. While working with one, put the other two in a plastic bag in the refrigerator. Divide the portion into eight pieces. Roll each piece into a rope and form a bagel shape (like a doughnut). Do the same with the other 2 portions.

Drop each bagel into a large pot of rapidly boiling water for 10 to 20 seconds, turning once during boiling. Place on a cookie sheet that has been sprinkled with cornmeal. Brush each bagel with the beaten egg. Then sprinkle with seeds, if desired. Bake at 425°F for 20 minutes.

Makes 24 bagels.

Terry Knight, Cambridge, Ont

Pita Bread

This bread puffs up in the centre while baking, making a pocket that can be slit and filled as a sandwich. These are fun to make!

2¼ to 2¾ cups lukewarm water (110°F)
2 envelopes active dry yeast
1 tsp. sugar
8 cups all-purpose flour
2 tsp. salt
¼ cup vegetable oil
½ cup cornmeal

Pour ¼ cup of the water into a small bowl and dissolve sugar in it. Sprinkle yeast on top and jiggle to mix. Let rest 10 minutes, then stir foamy mixture with a fork.

Combine flour and salt; make a well in the centre and pour in the yeast mixture, oil, and 2 cups of lukewarm water.

Gently stir until well combined. Add more water, up to ½ cup, until dough forms a ball. Knead on a lightly-floured board for 20 minutes. Put dough in a greased bowl and turn it to grease all sides. Cover with a damp tea towel and place in a warm spot for 45 minutes or until doubled in volume.

Punch dough down on a board to remove all air bubbles and cut dough into 16 pieces. Roll into balls, cover with a damp tea towel, and let rest for 30 minutes.

Grease cookie sheets and sprinkle with cornmeal. With a rolling pin, roll balls into flat rounds about ⅛-inch thick. Arrange on cookie sheets about 2 inches apart, cover with a damp tea towel, and let rise 30 minutes longer.

Bake one sheet at a time in a very hot oven (500°F) on lower oven rack until pitas are lightly browned and puffy in the centre, about 10 minutes, but keep an eye on them! Cool slightly on wire racks and place in plastic bags to keep them moist and pliable. May be frozen.

Makes 16.

Ann Budge, Belfountain, Ont

Whole-Wheat Rolls

1 tsp. sugar
1¼ cups warm water (110°F)
1 envelope active dry yeast
1 egg
2 tbsp. margarine

¼ cup molasses
1 tsp. salt
2 cups all-purpose flour
1¼ cups whole-wheat flour

Dissolve sugar in warm water. Add yeast and let stand 10 minutes, then stir well. Add egg, margarine, molasses, salt, and all-purpose flour. Blend, then beat for 2 minutes at medium speed of electric mixer. Using a wooden spoon, stir in whole-wheat flour until well blended.

Cover and let rise until doubled in bulk, about 30 minutes. Stir down dough with a wooden spoon by beating 25 strokes. Spoon evenly into 15 greased 2½-inch muffin tins. Cover and let rise until doubled in bulk, about 30 minutes. Bake at 375°F for 25 to 30 minutes.

Makes 15 rolls.

Courtesy of Nabisco Brands Ltd

Quick Breads

Peanut Bread

This recipe is a find for peanut lovers. Team a slice with a glass of milk for a delicious, nutritious breakfast or snack.

1 cup all-purpose flour
⁷/₈ cup whole-wheat flour
4 tsp. baking powder
¹/₃ cup white *or* brown sugar
³/₄ cup smooth peanut butter
1¹/₄ cups milk
1 egg
³/₄ cup chopped unsalted peanuts

Mix flours, baking powder, and sugar. Add peanut butter and cut in with a pastry blender or 2 knives until mixture resembles coarse crumbs. Mix egg into milk with a fork, and stir lightly into the dough. Fold in peanuts. Turn into a greased loaf pan and bake at 350°F for 45 to 50 minutes.

Variation: Reduce milk to 1 cup and add 1 mashed ripe banana for that classic flavour combo!

Zucchini Bread

Grated cucumber or carrots could be used in place of zucchini.

1½ **cups grated unpeeled zucchini (A food processor will leave it less mushy.)**
2 **eggs**
¼ **cup Demerara** *or* **brown sugar**
¼ **cup white sugar**
½ **cup vegetable oil**
½ **cup raisins** *or* **coconut**
½ **cup chopped walnuts**
1 **cup all-purpose flour**
½ **cup whole-wheat flour**
½ **tsp. baking soda**
½ **tsp. baking powder**
¼ **tsp. salt**
½ **tsp. cinnamon**

Beat eggs, sugars, and vegetable oil. Stir in zucchini, raisins or coconut, and nuts. Mix well. Combine dry ingredients and stir into zucchini mixture just until blended. Pour into a greased loaf pan and bake at 350°F for about 1 hour. Bread is cooked when a toothpick inserted in the centre comes out clean.

Pumpkin Bread

This is our favourite bread. It usually comes in our picnic basket to autumn orienteering meets. Be sure to chop the raisins as they have more flavour that way.

⅔ **cup butter, melted**
1 **to 2 cups white** *or* **brown sugar**
4 **eggs**
2 **cups fresh cooked pumpkin purée** *or* **canned pumpkin**
⅔ **cup water (less if pumpkin purée is very moist)**
3 **tbsp. orange juice**
3 **cups whole-wheat flour**
½ **tsp. baking powder**
2 **tsp. baking soda**
½ **tsp. salt**
1 **tsp. cinnamon**
1 **tsp. ground cloves**
¾ **cup chopped raisins**

Cream butter with sugar. Add eggs, pumpkin, water, and orange juice. Mix well. Stir together the dry ingredients and add to pumpkin mixture. Add raisins, then stir several times to mix.

Grease 2 loaf pans well, or preferably line the bottoms with greased wax paper. Divide the batter between them and bake at 350°F for 50 minutes or so. Bread is cooked when springy to the touch and still a little moist (but not wet). Cool 10 minutes in pan before turning out on a rack to finish cooling. Wrap and store at room temperature for a day for flavours to mellow.

Ann Budge, Belfountain, Ont

Apricot Loaf

Be prepared for this tasty bread to disappear very quickly. Nancy once baked this loaf for her Ladies Ski School's bus trip home. It was a mjor hit, and not just because everyone was tired and hungry! It is indeed delicious.

$^1/_2$ **cup dried apricots**
$^1/_2$ **cup chopped walnuts** *or* **almonds**
1 cup white sugar
2 tbsp. butter
1 egg
2 cups all-purpose flour
$^1/_4$ **tsp. baking soda**
3 tsp. baking powder
$^1/_2$ **cup orange juice**
$^1/_4$ **tsp. salt**

Soak apricots in water for 3 hours. Drain, reserving $^1/_2$ cup of water. Chop very fine.

Cream butter and sugar. Add egg. Mix dry ingredients. Mix orange juice with the $^1/_2$ cup of soaking water and add to batter alternately with dry ingredients. Mix well. Stir in fruit and nuts. Pour into a greased 9 x 5-inch loaf pan. Bake at 350°F for 1 hour. Cool 10 minutes on a rack and turn out to finish cooling. Wrap and leave at room temperature overnight.

Nancy Roy, Pierrefonds, Qué

Cranberry and Walnut Loaf

Donna says that people are always asking her for this recipe!

2 cups all-purpose flour
1 cup white sugar
1½ tsp. baking powder
½ tsp. baking soda
½ tsp. salt
2 cups fresh cranberries
¼ cup vegetable shortening
¾ cup orange juice
1 tbsp. grated orange peel
1 egg
½ cup chopped nuts (preferably walnuts)

Cut cranberries in half and set aside.

Sift flour, sugar, baking powder, baking soda, and salt. Cut in shortening with 2 knives until mixture resembles coarse crumbs. Combine orange juice and peel with well-beaten egg. Pour all at once into crumb mixture, mixing just enough to moisten. Carefully fold in chopped nuts and cranberries. Spoon into greased and floured 9 x 5 x 3-inch loaf pan. Spread corners and sides slightly higher than centre.

Bake at 350°F for 1 hour, until crust is golden brown and toothpick inserted comes out clean. Cool in pan for 5 minutes, then remove from pan, cool, wrap, and leave overnight at room temperature for flavours to mellow. It will slice more easily the next day. This bread freezes very well.

Donna Grieve, Toronto, Ont

Fresh Coconut Bread

This unique bread will have a full coconut flavour if it is wrapped tightly and allowed to mellow for two or three days.

1 coconut
milk from coconut and enough
    water to make 1½ cups
¾ cup white sugar
2 tbsp. butter
2 eggs
1 tsp. pure vanilla extract
4 cups all-purpose flour
4 tsp. baking powder
¼ tsp. salt
1 cup golden raisins
½ tsp. grated orange peel
½ cup sliced almonds
1 tbsp. water
1 tbsp. white sugar

Puncture coconut and pour milk into a measuring cup. Add enough water to make 1½ cups of liquid. Crack coconut open and remove coconut meat from the shell. (You can leave the thin brown skin on the coconut meat.) Cut coconut into small pieces and place in a food processor or blender along with the 1½ cups of liquid. Process for about 3 minutes. There should be about 3 cups of coconut mixture.

Place coconut mixture in a large bowl and add ¾ cup sugar, eggs, butter, vanilla, and orange peel. Beat until batter is smooth.

Combine flour, baking powder, and salt. Add flour mixture, raisins, and almonds to coconut mixture. Mix well. Pour into 2 greased 9 x 5-inch loaf pans and bake at 350°F for 40 minutes. Loaves will be almost fully cooked. Brush quickly with a glaze of 1 tbsp. water mixed with 1 tbsp. white sugar. Bake another 10 minutes. Cool in pan on a rack for 10 minutes, then turn out on rack to cool completely. Wrap tightly and let sit 2 to 3 days for full coconut flavour. This bread freezes well.

Pineapple Loaf

3 eggs
½ cup liquid honey
½ cup vegetable oil
½ cup water *or* any fruit juice
1 cup canned crushed pineapple, undrained
2 cups whole-wheat flour
1 cup all-purpose flour
¾ tsp. baking soda
3 tsp. baking powder
½ tsp. salt
½ tsp. pure vanilla extract
½ tsp. almond extract
¾ cup chopped nuts, lightly toasted for additional flavour

Beat eggs well, then add honey, oil, water or fruit juice, and undrained pineapple. Mix well. Sift dry ingredients together and add to batter. Mix until just moistened. Fold in vanilla and almond flavourings and nuts. Pour into greased 9 x 5-inch loaf pan. Bake at 350°F for 1 hour or until a cake tester or toothpick comes out clean. Cool in pan on rack for 10 minutes, then turn out onto rack to cool completely. Wrap loaf and allow to mellow for 24 hours before slicing.

Blueberry Bread

A most delicious bread with a crumbly topping!

**2 cups all-purpose flour
2 tsp. baking powder
¹/₂ tsp. salt
¹/₄ cup butter
1 cup white sugar
1 egg
¹/₂ cup milk
1¹/₂ cups fresh blueberries**

Cream butter and sugar until light. Beat in egg. Mix well flour, baking powder, and salt. Add dry ingredients in three parts alternately with milk in two parts. Fold in berries gently. Spoon into a well-greased 9 x 5-inch loaf pan.

Topping

**¹/₂ cup brown sugar
¹/₄ cup all-purpose flour
¹/₄ cup butter
¹/₂ tsp. cinnamon**

Mix topping ingredients until crumbly and sprinkle on top of batter.

Bake at 375°F for 40 to 45 minutes. Cool 10 minutes in pan on rack, then turn out to finish cooling.

Nancy Roy, Pierrefonds, Qué

Banana-Oat Bran Bread

A loaf with excellent flavour and the nutritious addition of oat bran. Try it for breakfast as a change from the usual.

**¹/₂ cup butter *or* margarine
³/₄ cup sugar
2 eggs
4 to 5 mashed very ripe medium bananas
1 tsp. pure vanilla extract
1 cup oat bran *or* wheat bran
1¹/₂ cups all-purpose flour
2 tsp. baking powder
¹/₂ tsp. baking soda
¹/₄ tsp. salt**

Cream butter and sugar; add eggs, then bananas and vanilla. Mix well. Stir in oat bran and let stand for 5 minutes.

Combine dry ingredients and mix into banana mixture until just moistened. Pour into well-greased and floured 9 x 5 x 3-inch loaf pan. Bake in 350°F oven for 65 to 70 minutes. Test whether it is cooked through by inserting a toothpick or cake tester in centre; it will come out clean when bread is ready. Cool in pan for 10 minutes, then remove to wire rack to finish cooling.

Banana Bread

Everyone loves banana bread, and especially this one! A member of Canada's National Orienteering Team, Denise competed in the World Championships in Switzerland in 1981 and Australia in 1985.

3 very ripe bananas
4 tbsp. vegetable oil *or* melted margarine
1/2 cup white *or* brown sugar
1 1/2 cups whole-wheat flour
1 tsp. baking soda
1/4 tsp. salt
1 tsp. lemon juice
2 eggs, lightly beaten
1 cup walnuts (optional)

Mash bananas in a large bowl. Add vegetable oil and lemon juice. Stir in sugar. Add beaten eggs. Mix flour, soda, and salt, then add to batter. Stir in walnuts. Pour into a 9 x 5-inch greased loaf pan.

Bake at 325°F for 50 minutes or so. Cool 10 minutes in pan; then turn out onto wire rack to cool completely. Wrap tightly and let mellow 1 day before serving.

Denise Demonte, Hamilton, Ont

Seedy-Nutty Muffin Loaf

An excellent bread for any occasion.

1 egg
1 cup buttermilk *or* soured milk
¼ cup vegetable oil
1 cup all-purpose flour
1 cup whole-wheat flour
1 tsp. baking powder
1 tsp. baking soda
½ to 1 cup firmly-packed brown *or* Demerara sugar
2 tbsp. wheat germ *or* bran
½ cup chopped nuts
2 tbsp. sunflower seeds
2 tbsp. poppy seeds

Beat egg, then beat in milk and oil. Sift together flours, baking powder, and baking soda. Stir in sugar, wheat germ or bran, then nuts and seeds.

Make a well in dry ingredients and pour in liquid. Stir until dry ingredients are just moistened.

Bake in a greased loaf pan in a 350°F oven about 65 minutes.

Jeanette Sokol, Toronto, Ont

Cheese 'n' Apple Bread

The aroma from the oven is reward enough for making this bread.

2 red *or* green unpeeled apples, medium grated
¾ cup grated sharp Cheddar cheese
½ cup golden raisins
½ cup chopped walnuts *or* pecans
1¾ cups all-purpose flour
1 tsp. baking powder
½ tsp. baking soda
½ tsp. salt
½ tsp. nutmeg
1 tsp. cinnamon
½ cup butter
¾ cup white *or* brown sugar
2 eggs

Blend dry ingredients and set aside. Cream butter and sugar until light and fluffy. Add eggs and beat well. Mix in half the sifted ingredients. Stir apple, raisins, cheese, and nuts into remaining dry ingredients, then add to batter. Mix gently. Pour into a greased 9 x 5-inch loaf pan. Bake at 350°F for 1 hour. Cool 10 minutes in pan on rack before removing loaf from pan. Complete cooling on rack. Wrap and allow to mellow for a day.

Easy Brown Bread

1½ cups all-purpose flour
1½ cups whole-wheat flour
1 cup light rye flour
2 tsp. baking powder
1 tsp. baking soda
½ tsp. salt
¼ cup molasses *or* honey
1¼ to 1½ cups buttermilk (at room temperature)

Combine dry ingredients in a large bowl. Stir in molasses and 1¼ cups buttermilk. Add additional buttermilk if necessary to make a soft dough. Beat on high speed with electric mixer about 3 minutes, until mixture forms a ball. Knead vigorously for 2 minutes on a lightly-floured board to make a smooth dough.

Form into a round loaf 2 inches thick. Place on a greased baking sheet and cut a cross ½-inch deep on top of loaf. Bake at 375°F until loaf sounds hollow when tapped on the bottom, about 55 minutes. Cool on rack.

Jiffy Cheese Loaf

1 cup all-purpose flour
1 cup whole-wheat flour
1½ tsp. baking powder
½ tsp. baking soda
2 tsp. dry mustard
dash of cayenne pepper
½ tsp. salt
2 tbsp. grated onion
1 cup grated old Cheddar cheese
1 cup buttermilk *or* plain yogurt
¼ cup vegetable oil
2 eggs

Combine dry ingredients and stir in cheese and onion. Beat together eggs, buttermilk or yogurt, and oil. Add to the dry ingredients and stir just until moistened. Bake in a greased loaf pan at 375°F for 45 to 50 minutes. Cool on rack for 10 minutes before turning out of pan to cool completely.

Double-Cheese Bread

This fragrant bread can be sliced while very fresh and is good warm or cool.

1 cup whole-wheat flour
1 cup all-purpose flour
1 tbsp. baking powder
½ tsp. salt
1½ cups grated Cheddar cheese
¼ cup grated Parmesan cheese
2 eggs, beaten
¼ cup margarine, melted
1 cup milk
2 tbsp. grated Parmesan cheese

Combine flours, baking powder, salt, Cheddar cheese, and ¼ cup Parmesan cheese and set aside. Combine eggs, margarine, and milk; add to dry ingedients all at once, stirring only until moistened. *Do not overmix.* Turn into greased 9 x 5-inch loaf pan, smooth top with knife, and sprinkle with 2 tbsp. Parmesan cheese. Bake at 350°F about 45 minutes.

Courtesy of Nabisco Brands Ltd

Raisin, Oat, and Bran Bread

This bread has a heavy muffin-like texture and a nice molasses flavour.

2 eggs, lightly beaten
1¹/₃ cups buttermilk, soured milk, *or* plain yogurt
¹/₂ cup molasses
¹/₄ cup vegetable oil
1³/₄ cups whole-wheat flour
1 tsp. baking soda
¹/₂ tsp. salt
1¹/₂ cups quick-cooking rolled oats
1 cup natural bran
¹/₂ cup raisins

To sour milk, add 2 tbsp. lemon juice or 1³/₄ tbsp. vinegar to 1¹/₃ cups lukewarm milk. Let stand a few minutes, then stir.

To eggs add milk, molasses, and oil. Beat well. Sift flour, soda, and salt together, then stir into egg mixture.

Add oats, bran, and raisins. Stir to blend well and spoon into 2 greased 7¹/₂ x 3¹/₂-inch pans. Bake at 350°F for about 50 minutes, until a toothpick inserted in the centre comes out clean. Turn out onto a rack to cool. Makes 2 small loaves.

Erin's Soda Bread

4 cups all-purpose flour
¹/₂ tsp. salt
1 tsp. baking soda
³/₄ cup soured milk *or* buttermilk
raisins *or* currants (optional)

Mix flour, soda, and salt together in mixing bowl, then make a well in the centre. Add enough milk to make a thick dough. Add optional raisins or currants and stir with a wooden spoon. The mixture should be slack but not too wet, and the mixing done quickly. Add a little more milk if mixture is too stiff.

With floured hands put dough on floured board or counter and make into a circle about 1¹/₂ inches thick. Cut a line across the top with a floured knife. Bake on a greased baking sheet at 400°F for 35 to 40 minutes. Wrap in a clean tea towel to keep fresh.

Erin Day, Ottawa, Ont

Coffee Can Bread

Try this bread toasted and spread thinly with honey! The round shape is a conversation piece.

1 cup whole-wheat flour
1 cup quick-cooking rolled oats
1 cup wheat germ
2 tsp. baking soda
¹/₂ tsp. salt
1³/₄ cups milk
2 tbsp. liquid honey

Mix dry ingredients thoroughly. Stir in milk and honey, mixing completely. Grease a 450-gram (1-lb.) coffee can and spoon in the batter. Cover with greased foil and tie with string to secure. Let stand 5 minutes before placing in oven. Bake at 350°F for 1¹/₄ hours. Allow to cool 5 to 10 minutes and turn out onto a rack to cool completely.

Uffculme Fruit Loaf

"Fantastic!" says Margaret, who sent this recipe all the way from her temporary home in England.

2¹/₂ cups tightly-packed mixed dried fruit (golden raisins;
      chopped apricots, peaches, pears, apples, citron, *or* peel)
1¹/₄ cups sweet apple cider
1 cup firmly-packed brown sugar
2 cups all-purpose flour
2¹/₂ tsp. baking powder
2 small eggs
¹/₄ cup chopped walnuts

Bring dried fruit, sugar, and cider to boiling point in a saucepan. Remove from heat and leave to cool. Sift together flour and baking powder, then add walnuts. Add beaten eggs and cooled fruit mixture. Mix well. Pour into greased 9 x 5 x 3-inch loaf tin that has been lined with greased waxed paper.

Bake on centre rack of oven at 350°F for 30 minutes, then reduce heat to 325°F for about 45 minutes. Cool in pan for 5 minutes, then remove and cool on wire rack.

If you can keep your family away, let it sit for 2 or 3 days for flavours to mingle before cutting.

232

Variations

- Instead of cider, use apple, orange, or pineapple juice.
- Instead of all-purpose flour, use whole-wheat flour.
- Instead of walnuts, use wheat germ, or wheat germ and bran mixed.
- Instead of brown sugar, use Demerara sugar.
- Instead of 2 eggs, use 1 egg.

Margaret Gaunt, Winnipeg, Man

Boston Brown Bread

Traditionally served with baked beans.

1 cup whole-wheat flour
1 cup light rye flour
1 cup yellow cornmeal
$^1/_2$ tsp. salt
1 tbsp. water
1 tsp. baking soda
$^1/_2$ cup molasses
2 tbsp. vinegar *or* lemon juice
$1^7/_8$ cups milk
1 cup raisins
2 tbsp. all-purpose flour

Combine flours, cornmeal, and salt in a large bowl. In another bowl, mix baking soda with 1 tbsp. water, then add molasses. Stir vinegar or lemon juice into the milk. Add the milk mixture to the molasses mixture.

Stir liquid mixture into the flours and cornmeal, and mix well. Dredge raisins with 2 tbsp. flour and add. Pour into a well-greased covered 2-quart mould (one made for steaming). Cover, then put on a rack in a deep, covered roasting pan and fill the pan with boiling water to half-way up the mould. Cover the roasting pan and steam on top of the stove for 3 hours; add water when necessary to maintain depth. Unmould the bread, place on a baking sheet, and bake at 325°F for 10 minutes. Allow to cool before slicing.

Olympic Bread

A bread packed with nutritious ingredients is surely an athlete's dream!

2 cups whole-wheat flour
$\frac{1}{2}$ cup brown *or* Demerara sugar
$\frac{2}{3}$ cup instant skim milk powder
$\frac{1}{3}$ cup wheat germ
$\frac{1}{3}$ cup oat bran *or* wheat bran
$\frac{1}{2}$ tsp. baking soda
1 tbsp. baking powder
$\frac{1}{4}$ tsp. salt
$\frac{1}{2}$ cup unsalted peanuts
$\frac{1}{4}$ cup walnuts, almonds, *or* pecans
$\frac{1}{2}$ cup chopped dried apricots *or* dates
$\frac{1}{2}$ cup raisins
3 eggs
$\frac{1}{3}$ cup vegetable oil
1 cup orange *or* other fruit juice
$\frac{1}{2}$ cup blackstrap molasses
1 cup mashed bananas *or* $1\frac{1}{4}$ cup grated zucchini *or* chopped
    apple

Grind nuts finely. In a large bowl, mix dry ingredients well. Add nuts, apricots or dates, and raisins. In another bowl, beat eggs for 2 minutes. Beat in oil, then juice, molasses, and bananas, zucchini, or apples. Blend well.

Pour liquid mixture into dry ingredients and stir until the dry ingredients are just moistened. Grease and flour two 8 x 4-inch loaf pans and divide the batter between them. Bake at 325°F for 55 minutes or until cake tester comes out clean. Cool in pans for 20 minutes, then turn out onto wire rack to finish cooling. Wrap in foil and allow loaves to age 24 hours. This bread freezes well.

Essene Bread

A popular item in many natural food stores. Here's how to duplicate that old-time goodness at home!

$1\frac{1}{2}$ cups wheat berries
$\frac{1}{4}$ cup sesame seeds, sunflower seeds, raisins, *or* chopped nuts

Soak wheat berries covered with water for 8 hours in a large seed sprouter or in a quart bottle topped with cheesecloth held in place with an elastic band. Drain off water. Place upside down jar or sprouter in a dark cupboard, taking it out to rinse the wheat berries with fresh water and drain at least once a day.

When the sprouts are about 1/4 inch long, which should be in about 3 days, grind the drained berries in a food processor or grain mill (do not use a food chopper) until they are doughy. Mix in seeds, nuts, or raisins. Shape the sticky dough (oil your hands if necessary) into a round loaf. Flatten it slightly and place it on a greased baking sheet. Let rise in a warm place for about 4 hours. Do not expect this bread to double in bulk as it rises; it will rise only a very small amount.

Bake in a 350°F oven about 1 1/4 hours or until the outer crust is brown and crispy. Allow to cool completely on a rack before attempting to slice it, otherwise it will be extremely sticky. Refrigerate, and it will keep for a week or so.

Barmbrack

A hearty bread, especially good served warm with butter. Be sure to begin preparation 12 hours or the night before, as the instructions indicate.

1 cup hot strong tea
3/4 cup firmly-packed brown sugar
1/2 cup chopped dates
1 cup raisins *or* currants
1/2 cup chopped mixed peel
1 egg
1 3/4 cups whole-wheat flour
1/4 tsp. baking soda
1 tsp. baking powder
1/4 tsp. salt

Pour tea over dates, peel, raisins, and sugar, then let sit 12 hours or overnight. The next day, stir in beaten egg, then flour blended with baking powder, baking soda, and salt. Spoon into 9 x 5 x 3-inch greased loaf pan. Bake in a 300°F oven for 1 1/2 hours. Remove from pan and cool on wire rack.

Mock Pumpernickel Bread

Easy and just like the real thing. Well, almost!

3 tbsp. molasses
3 cups hot water (almost boiling)
3 cups uncooked Red River Cereal®
1 cup whole-wheat flour
2 tsp. baking soda
½ tsp. salt

Combine water and molasses in a large bowl. Blend flour, baking soda, and salt. Add flour mixture to molasses mixture and beat for 2 minutes on high speed of electric mixer. Cover bowl tightly and let stand for at least 4 hours or overnight. Spoon into a greased loaf pan, smooth the top, and cover tightly with foil.

Bake at 275°F for 1 hour. Reduce heat to 250°F and bake 2 more hours. Remove foil for last 20 minutes. Cool in pan for 10 minutes, then remove from pan and cool completely on a rack. Wrap tightly. Store in refrigerator for a day before slicing.

Andy's Bread

This is a moist, heavy, and nutritious bread. It is very easy to make, but it turns out differently each time!

1 qt. *or* 1 l buttermilk
1 cup molasses
2 tsp. baking soda
flour

Mix buttermilk, molasses, and baking soda, then add *small* amounts (about ¼ cup) of some of the following ingredients: rolled oats, wheat germ, bran, sunflower seeds, coconut, brewer's yeast (not more than 1 tbsp.), nuts, cinnamon (1 tsp.), or other bulky ingredients or spices.

Now add enough flour (any combination of whole-wheat, graham, or rye) to make a batter the consistency of muffin batter.

Divide batter between 2 greased loaf pans. Bake at 350°F for one hour or so. Be careful not to underbake.

Andy de St. Croix, Vineland, Ont

Red River Cereal® is a registered trademark of Maple Leaf Mills Limited.

Cottage Cheese Rolls

These delicious yeast-like rolls are a particularly nice accompaniment to a hearty soup. They are quick and easy to prepare.

1 cup cottage cheese
1 egg
¼ cup milk
5 tbsp. vegetable oil
2 cups sifted all-purpose flour *or* ⅞ cup whole-wheat flour and
    1 cup all-purpose flour
1 tbsp. baking powder
½ tsp. salt
1 egg yolk, beaten, for brushing rolls
poppy seeds, sesame seeds, *or* caraway seeds, for topping

Combine cottage cheese, egg, milk, and oil in a blender or food processor. Sift flour, baking powder, and salt together. Stir in cottage cheese mixture to form a firm dough. Knead dough on a floured board until smooth, adding a little flour if dough is too sticky. Cut into 10 pieces and shape into rolls. Place on a greased baking sheet. For a nice brown crust, brush each roll with beaten egg yolk. With a sharp knife, make a cut across the top of each roll. Sprinkle with one of the topping seeds. Bake at 400°F until golden brown, about 20 minutes. Best served warm.

Oat Scones

Wonderful with tea or hot lemon drink after a brisk cold-weather walk! Brushing these with beaten egg yolk before they are baked gives them a nice golden colour.

1½ cups rolled oats (*not* quick-cooking)
1½ cups all-purpose flour
1 tbsp. baking powder
½ tsp. salt
¼ cup white sugar
⅔ cup butter, chilled
½ cup raisins *or* currants
¾ cup milk
1 egg
1 egg yolk

Combine oats, flour, baking powder, salt, and sugar. Using a pastry blender or 2 knives, cut in butter until mixture resembles coarse crumbs. Stir in raisins or currants.

Beat whole egg with milk and stir into dry ingredients with a fork until ingredients are just moistened.

Knead dough gently about 15 times on a lightly-floured board or counter top. Place dough on an ungreased baking sheet and pat with hands or roll lightly with a rolling pin into a round loaf ¾-inch thick. Score into 8 wedges (as if cutting a pie) but do *not* separate pieces. Brush top with beaten egg yolk. Bake at 425°F for 15 to 20 minutes. Scones should be golden brown. Cool slightly and cut wedges through. Serve with butter and home-made jam, marmalade, or honey.

Whole-Wheat Cheese Scones

If you prefer, omit the cheese and herbs and add ½ cup raisins or currants for classic scones.

2 cups whole-wheat flour
2 tbsp. brown sugar
2 tsp. baking powder
¼ tsp. salt
1 tbsp. butter
1 egg, beaten
¾ cup grated old Cheddar cheese
¾ cup yogurt
2 to 3 tbsp. milk
sesame seeds
dill weed *or* seed, *or* tarragon (optional)

Mix together dry ingredients; cut in butter with pastry blender or two knives until mixture resembles crumbs. Stir in cheese. Mix in the beaten egg. Stir in yogurt gradually until a thick dough is formed. Knead lightly with hands on a floured surface. Roll out to ³/₄-inch thickness. Cut with a round floured biscuit cutter. Place rounds on a greased baking sheet. Brush tops with milk and sprinkle with sesame seeds, or if you plan to serve these with soup or a main course, try sprinkling tops with dill weed or seed, or tarragon. Bake at 450°F for 10 to 15 minutes.

Makes 14 to 16 scones.

Cheese-Filled Biscuits

2 cups all-purpose flour
4 tsp. baking powder
¹/₄ tsp. salt
¹/₂ cup vegetable shortening
²/₃ cup milk
1 cup grated old Cheddar cheese
1 tbsp. mayonnaise
1 tsp. prepared mustard
poppy seeds *or* sesame seeds, for topping
3 tbsp. milk

In a large bowl mix flour, baking powder, and salt. Cut in shortening with a pastry blender or 2 knives until mixture resembles coarse crumbs. Make a well in the centre and pour in milk all at once, stirring just until dough comes away from the sides of the bowl.

Knead gently on a floured surface 10 to 12 times. Roll out dough to ¹/₄ inch thick. With a floured 2¹/₂-inch biscuit cutter, cut dough into 20 biscuits.

Blend cheese, mayonnaise, and mustard together. Spoon 1 tbsp. of mixture onto 10 of the biscuits. Brush edges with a little milk and top with remaining biscuits. Lightly press edges together to enclose filling. Place on an ungreased baking sheet and brush tops lightly with milk. Sprinkle with poppy or sesame seeds. Bake at 450°F for 10 to 12 minutes. Serve warm. These freeze well.

Quick 'n' Easy Pizza Crust

It isn't absolutely necessary to have a yeast-dough crust for pizza. This one is excellent, and much quicker and easier to prepare.

1 cup cottage cheese
2¼ cups all-purpose flour
2 tsp. baking powder
4 tbsp. milk
4 tbsp. vegetable oil
1 egg, beaten

Sift flour with baking powder. Combine cottage cheese and flour mixture with pastry cutter or 2 knives until crumbly. Beat milk, oil, and egg, then add to dry ingredients. Stir until well mixed. Divide dough into 2 equal parts. Roll out with a rolling pin on a floured surface to fit two 12-inch pizza pans.

At this point, refrigerate crusts until later in the day, freeze them, or add your favourite toppings and bake them at 400°F for 35 to 40 minutes. Toppings might include **Tomato Sauce (Italian Style)** (see page 41), grated Mozzarella cheese, sliced pepperoni, ham, crisp bacon, sliced tomatoes, pineapple tidbits, sliced olives, mushrooms, or whatever your heart desires!

Makes two 12-inch crusts.

Day Starters

Jogger's Nog

The early-morning jogger's delight! Have a muffin or whole-wheat toast and an orange after your run for a complete breakfast. Actually, this is great for athletes such as swimmers, figure skaters, and hockey players, who frequently train early in the morning, as liquids digest more quickly than solids.

1 cup canned undrained unsweetened crushed pineapple *or*
  1 very ripe banana
1 egg
1 tsp. vegetable oil
1 cup cold milk
3 ice cubes

Combine pineapple or banana, vegetable oil, and egg in blender until smooth and creamy, about 30 seconds. Add milk and ice cubes and whirl about 30 seconds, until drink is foamy. Down the hatch!

Orange Breakfast Shake

A shake for breakfast? Why not! Needless to say, this is popular with the younger generations. A quick and complete breakfast for those in a hurry.

³/₄ cup orange juice
1 cup plain yogurt
1 egg
1 tsp. liquid honey
1 pinch of nutmeg *or* **cinnamon**
2 ice cubes *or* **1 small scoop of vanilla ice cream**

Combine all ingredients in a blender or food processor. If you use the ice cream, you may wish to omit the honey. Blend until smooth, pour into a tall glass, and serve immediately.

Early-to-Rise Apple Nog

A nourishing way to start the day!

1 19-oz. can apple juice *or* pineapple juice
2 eggs
1 tbsp. fresh lemon juice
¼ tsp. grated lemon peel
small pinch *each* of cinnamon and nutmeg
6 ice cubes
½ cup milk

Combine all ingredients in a blender and whirl until the ice is ground into tiny pieces and the drink is foamy. Pour into 3 tall glasses.

Tofu-Berry Shake

This complete breakfast or wholesome snack is filling and tasty.

2 cups frozen *or* fresh whole strawberries, blueberries *or*
    raspberries
1 cup soft tofu
2 tbsp. liquid honey *or* brown sugar
¾ cup skim milk powder
1 tsp. pure vanilla extract *or* almond extract
1½ cups very cold water

Blend all ingredients together in a blender or food processor. Pour into 2 or 3 tall glasses.

Isabelle Swales, Calgary, Alta

Wholesome Hot Cereal Mix

Quick to cook before a day of hard skiing or a cold-weather orienteering competition. Hot cereal haters usually love *this* cereal! It is of the chewy variety rather than the smooth type, and is exceptionally delicious!

1 cup large-flake oats
½ cup wheat flakes
1 cup barley (Use more nutritious pot barley for a crunchy
    texture or pearl barley for a softer texture.)

½ cup millet
½ cup cracked wheat
1 cup sunflower seeds
1 cup raisins *or* currants

Mix all ingredients and store in a large airtight jar. The night before serving, put 1 part cereal in a pot and cover with 2 parts water. Next morning at breakfast time, heat to boiling. Boil gently, uncovered, for 5 minutes or until cereal is of desired consistency. Stir occasionally just to prevent sticking. Overstirring will make the cereal pasty. Serve with milk, or a little pure maple syrup, Demerara sugar, or honey.

Apple-Oatmeal Porridge

1¼ cups rolled oats
1½ cups skim milk
1¼ cups water
¼ tsp. salt
1 or 2 unpeeled apples, diced *or* grated
2 tbsp. liquid honey
1 tsp. pure vanilla extract
½ tsp. cinnamon
2 tbsp. wheat germ

Mix oats, milk, water, and salt in a saucepan and let stand 10 minutes. Bring to a boil. Reduce heat and simmer uncovered 10 to 15 minutes, stirring gently only once or twice, until oatmeal is thick and creamy. Stir in apples, honey, wheat germ, vanilla, and cinnamon. Serve immediately.

Makes 4 servings.

Variation: Dried chopped apricots or raisins could be added instead of, or as well as, the apples.

Spiced Oatmeal Porridge

Top this tasty porridge with milk and brown sugar and a small handful of nuts, granola-type cereal, dates, or chopped dried fruit of your choice.

3 cups water
1¹/₂ cups rolled oats
¹/₄ tsp. salt
¹/₂ tsp. grated orange peel (optional)
¹/₂ to ³/₄ tsp. nutmeg (preferably freshly ground)
1 2-inch cinnamon stick

Bring 3 cups of water to the boil in a medium saucepan. Add orange peel, nutmeg, cinnamon stick, and salt. Turn heat to high and slowly add oats, stirring *constantly* to prevent lumps from forming. When porridge comes to the boil, reduce heat and allow to simmer, uncovered, for 15 minutes or until thickened to your liking. Be sure to stir just enough to keep it from sticking. Should it become too thick, thin with a little water.

Makes 4 active-people's servings! Top it with whatever you wish.

Porridge

No better way to start the day — no matter what your activity will be — especially in the depths of winter! We usually think only of oatmeal or cream of wheat when porridge is mentioned, but almost any grain can be cooked for breakfast. Here are some guidelines for 4 servings.

To 4 cups of cold water and ¹/₂ tsp. salt, add the following quantities for your particular grain and cook for approximately the given time. Cooking times may vary because size of grains and starch content vary.

Grain	Quantity	Cooking Time
rolled oats	1¹/₂ cups	15 minutes
steel-cut oats	1 cup	45 minutes
cracked wheat	1¹/₄ cups	25 minutes
wheat flakes	1¹/₄ cups	15 minutes
bulgur	2 cups	20 minutes
cornmeal	1 cup	5 minutes
millet	1¹/₂ cups	20 minutes

Use a *heavy-bottomed* pot. Bring grain of your choice, uncovered, to a gentle boil. Stir once and turn heat to low. Cover pot and do not stir again. When cooking time is up, check that water is completely absorbed and turn off the burner. For peak flavour, let the porridge sit for 10 minutes. Serve with milk, buttermilk, yogurt, dried fruit, fresh fruit, nuts, maple syrup, honey, Demerara sugar, nutritional yeast, or whatever else you could possibly fancy!

Granola Cereal

We have tried many granola mixtures, but we like this one best.

4 cups large-flake rolled oats
2 cups wheat germ
1 cup flaked unsweetened coconut
1 cup sunflower seeds
¹/₂ cup sesame seeds
1 cup walnuts *or* peanuts
³/₄ cup Demerara *or* brown sugar
2 tsp. pure vanilla extract
³/₄ cup vegetable oil
¹/₃ cup water
raisins *and/or* other chopped dried fruits (optional)

Mix oats, coconut, seeds, nuts, and wheat germ. Combine by beating with a wire whisk sugar, water, vegetable oil, and vanilla, and pour over oat mixture. Mix until all dry ingredients are coated.

Pour into a large roasting pan or 2 smaller ones and bake at 300°F for 1 hour or until just barely browned, stirring well every 10 minutes. Remove from oven. Stir 4 or 5 times while cooling. When cool, add optional raisins or other dried fruits. Put in jars with tight lids and store in refrigerator.

Julie DePass, Oakville, Ont

Homemade Cereal Flakes

Make your own nutritious dry cereal quickly and easily! You may wish to vary the ingredients according to what you like or what you have on hand. Two basic recipes follow.

Whole-Wheat Cereal

1³/₄ cups whole-wheat flour
¹/₄ cup wheat germ
¹/₄ tsp. salt
²/₃ cup water
¹/₄ cup smooth peanut butter

Mix dry ingredients. Blend water and peanut butter; stir into dry ingredients.

Bran Cereal

2 cups natural bran
2 cups whole-wheat flour
¹/₂ cup skim milk powder
¹/₄ tsp. salt
³/₄ cup water
¹/₄ cup vegetable oil
1 tbsp. molasses

Mix dry ingredients. Blend water, oil, and molasses; stir into dry ingredients.

For both **Whole-Wheat Cereal** and **Bran Cereal,** mix together well, using hands if necessary to knead. Divide dough into 4 pieces. To roll out, sprinkle a little whole-wheat flour onto a piece of waxed paper. Place ¹/₄ of the dough on it and cover with a second piece of waxed paper. Roll with rolling pin as thin as possible (paper thin). Remove top piece of paper; invert dough onto a wire cake-cooling rack or onto a greased cookie sheet. Peel off second sheet of waxed paper. Repeat with other pieces of dough.

Bake **Whole-Wheat Cereal** at 350°F for 18 to 20 minutes. Bake **Bran Cereal** for 15 to 16 minutes. The sheets of dough should be lightly browned and crispy. Cool. Place sheets in a plastic bag and crush with fingers or a wooden mallet until the pieces are the size of cereal flakes. Serve in a bowl with milk and/or yogurt and whatever fruit you like to add to your morning cereal!

Store cereal in an airtight container.

Swiss Muesli

Muesli is the traditional Swiss breakfast cereal.

2²/₃ **cups large-flake rolled oats**
2²/₃ **cups wheat flakes**
2 cups wheat germ
1 cup chopped dried apple
1 cup sunflower seeds
1 cup chopped almonds, hazelnuts, *or* **peanuts**
1 cup raisins

Mix all ingredients together and store in a tightly covered container in the refrigerator. Serve with milk, buttermilk, yogurt, or filmjölk.

Variation: Traditionally muesli is made with almonds and hazelnuts. I prefer to substitute peanuts to provide added protein. Sesame seeds may be used in place of sunflower seeds. Chopped dried apple is traditional, but chopped dried apricots or dates are good. Fresh fruit in season may be added at serving time.
   When camping, add ¹/₃ cup instant milk powder per cup of muesli. Stir in hot or cold water and you have a bowl of cereal and milk!

Christine Kennedy, Downsview, Ont

Heidi's Special

Heidi was seven when she offered *Fit to Eat* this recipe that children can make for themselves.

glob of butter
1 egg
2 slices of toast

Put a small glob of butter in a pan and melt it. Break one egg in the pan and mix it. Cook it until egg is set.
   Put cooked egg between two slices of toast. *Eat it!*

Heidi Pearson, Hamilton, Ont

Breakfast Pudding

Good hot or cold, for breakfast or as a dessert.

³/₄ **cup butter**
1 tsp. cardamon
2 tsp. cinnamon
1 cup semolina flour *or* **wheat hearts**
2 cups water
1 6-oz. can evaporated milk
¹/₂ **cup honey**
¹/₄ **cup raisins** *or* **currants**
¹/₄ **cup slivered** *or* **sliced almonds, lightly toasted**
¹/₄ **tsp. nutmeg, freshly grated**

Melt butter in a heavy saucepan, then stir in cardamon and cinnamon. Blend in flour or wheat hearts, water, milk, honey, and raisins or currants. Cook over low heat until water is absorbed, stirring lightly to prevent lumps from forming. Add toasted almonds and nutmeg. Stir and cook for 5 more minutes.

Serves 4.

Jennifer Hamilton, Winnipeg, Man

LSD Runner's Special

LSD (runner's language for *Long Slow Distance*) runner's breakfast-lunch special.

1 cup milk
2 eggs
100 g cheese
2 slices of whole-wheat toast
¹/₄ **tomato (optional)**

Pour milk into pan and heat to the boil. Add 2 mixed-up eggs. (Steve means 'lightly beaten'!) Stir occasionally with spoon. Add 100 g of cheese that has been chopped into 1-cm cubes.

Continue to heat and stir until you have a mess, and then pour it onto 2 slices of whole-wheat toast. You can add ¹/₄ tomato, chopped, to enhance flavour.

The concoction brewed appears gross but tastes delicious.

Steve Pearson, Hamilton, Ont

French Toast

Old-fashioned goodness for a hearty breakfast or brunch. Try a French toast sandwich!

2 eggs
$^1/_2$ cup milk
$^1/_2$ tsp. vanilla
$^1/_2$ tsp. cinnamon (optional)
8 slices of whole-wheat bread *or* sour dough bread (best!)

Beat eggs lightly. Add milk and flavourings and mix well. Pour into a shallow bowl and dip in bread slices, turning to coat both sides. Brown in a hot, well-greased frying pan. Turn and brown other side. Outside should be crispy with inside creamy. Serve with warm maple syrup, **Honey-Orange Sauce,** or whatever you fancy.

Note: For a heartier meal, make a sandwich with two slices of French toast. Between the slices put a layer of sliced apples or bananas, warm spiced applesauce, crisp bacon, thin slices of cheese, or any combination of the above. Top with maple syrup. Delicious!

Honey-Orange Sauce

2 tbsp. butter
$^1/_4$ cup sesame seeds
$^1/_2$ cup honey
2 tbsp. orange juice
1 tsp. grated orange peel

Heat butter in a small heavy pot. Add sesame seeds and cook, stirring, until seeds are golden brown. Add honey, orange juice, and grated orange peel.

Oatmeal Pancakes

The addition of fresh blueberries or finely chopped apple makes these extra special.

1 cup milk	1 tbsp. brown sugar
1 cup quick-cooking oats	1 tsp. baking powder
2 eggs	1/4 tsp. salt
2 tbsp. vegetable oil	fresh blueberries *or* finely
1/2 cup whole-wheat flour	chopped apple

Preheat griddle or electric frying pan. Combine milk and oats and let stand 5 minutes. Add oil and beaten eggs to oat mixture, mixing well. Combine flour, brown sugar, baking powder, and salt, and stir into oat mixture just until dry ingredients are moistened.

If using chopped apple, add to batter now. Spoon batter onto hot griddle greased with vegetable oil, using 1/4 cup of batter for each pancake. After a minute or so, sprinkle a small handful of fresh blueberries over the batter on the griddle. Turn when top is bubbly and edges are slightly dry.

Makes 10 to 12 delicious 4-inch pancakes! Serve with pure maple syrup, which may be warmed slightly.

Three-Grain Pancakes

Serve with whipped sweet butter and warm home-produced maple syrup if you are lucky enough to have a few maple trees!

1/2 cup whole-wheat flour	1/2 tsp. salt
1/2 cup rye flour	1/4 tsp. baking soda
1/4 cup all-purpose flour	3 large eggs
1/4 cup cornmeal	1 1/4 to 1 1/2 cups milk
1 1/2 tbsp. brown sugar	3 tbsp. butter, melted
1 tbsp. baking powder	

Mix flours, cornmeal, sugar, baking powder and soda, and salt. Beat together eggs, 1 1/4 cup milk, and melted butter. Stir liquid ingredients into dry ones until mixed but still slightly lumpy. Let batter stand 20 to 30 minutes. Add a little of the remaining 1/4 cup milk if batter is too thick. Drop by 1/4-cupfuls onto hot, lightly-greased griddle or frying pan. Turn when first side has formed bubbles and is lightly browned on bottom. If you must keep pancakes warm in the oven, prevent them from becoming soggy by putting them on a cake-cooling rack and avoiding stacking them.

Makes a dozen medium-sized pancakes

Whipped Sweet Butter

sweet butter
sunflower oil

A great idea for those concerned about their cholesterol and salt intake! We use whipped sweet (unsalted) butter all the time.

Beat sweet butter with an electric mixer until very soft and creamy. Add a little sunflower oil. (A good guide is 1 tbsp. of oil to ⅓ cup of butter.) Continue beating for several minutes. Spoon into a small crock and store in the refrigerator.

Ann Budge, Belfountain, Ont

Whole-Grain Pancake Mix

8 cups whole-wheat flour
3 cups rolled oats (*not* quick-cooking)
2 cups skim milk powder
3 tbsp. baking powder
1 cup wheat germ
1 tsp. salt (optional)
2 tsp. sugar (optional)

Combine ingredients in a large bowl. Store in a tightly-covered jar in refrigerator and use to make the following pancakes.

Whole-Wheat Oatmeal Pancakes

1 egg, beaten
1¼ cups milk
1 tbsp. vegetable oil
1½ cups Whole-Grain Pancake Mix

Stir ingredients together until blended but still lumpy; do not overmix. Drop by ¼-cupfuls onto a lightly-greased hot griddle or electric frying pan. Turn when top is bubbly and edges are slightly dry. Serve with your favourite topping.

Makes 8 pancakes.

Lynda Sidney, Sudbury, Ont

Banana Pancakes

Puffy pancakes with unbeatable flavour. These should get you through your mid-morning aerobics class, 10-km run, or cross-country ski!

2 eggs
2 cups buttermilk *or* yogurt
2 tsp. baking soda
2 tsp. baking powder

1 cup all-purpose flour
1 cup whole-wheat flour
5 tbsp. vegetable oil
1 cup mashed very ripe bananas

Mix eggs, buttermilk or yogurt, baking powder, and baking soda. Stir in flour, then oil, but stir *only* until blended. Fold in bananas carefully. Heat griddle or electric frying pan to a fairly high temperature. Oil griddle well with vegetable oil and drop batter by large spoonfuls. Turn when bubbles form and edges are slightly dry.

Makes 12 pancakes. Maple syrup is great on these.

Apple-Cottage Cheese Pancakes

A filling breakfast or brunch pancake. Should last you through a morning of activity!

1 cup cottage *or* ricotta cheese
4 eggs
½ cup all-purpose flour
¼ cup whole-wheat flour
1½ cups grated unpeeled apples, preferably cooking
1 tbsp. liquid honey
1 tsp. lemon juice
1 tbsp. sesame seeds
½ tsp. cinnamon
pinch of nutmeg *or* ground allspice
pinch of salt

Press cottage or ricotta cheese through a sieve. Separate eggs, putting yolks into one bowl and whites into another.

Mix all ingredients together except egg whites. Beat egg whites until stiff but not dry and fold into batter.

Drop by ¼-cupfuls onto a hot griddle or frying pan that has been greased with vegetable oil. Cook, turning once, until golden brown, being sure pancakes are cooked in the centre.

Makes twelve 4-inch pancakes. Serve with maple syrup, **Apple or Peach Butter** (see page 256), yogurt mixed with cinnamon sugar, or the following syrup.

Apple Syrup

³/₄ **cup firmly-packed brown sugar**
³/₄ **cup apple juice** *or* **apple cider**
1 cup applesauce (unsweetened)
¹/₂ **tsp. cinnamon**
2 tbsp. butter

Simmer sugar, juice, and applesauce for about 5 minutes in a heavy saucepan. It should be at the thick syrup stage. Stir in butter and cinnamon.

Makes about 2 cups. Halve the recipe to make a smaller quantity.

Berry Puff Pancakes

An unusual brunch dish to supply down-to-earth nutrition.

4 eggs, separated
1 cup milk
3 tbsp. butter, melted
1 cup all-purpose flour
¹/₄ **tsp. salt**
1 tbsp. honey
2 cups fresh berries such as raspberries, blueberries, *or* **pitted cherries**
icing sugar

Combine egg yolks, milk, 1 tbsp. butter, flour, salt, and honey. Beat egg whites until stiff but not dry; fold into milk mixture.

Heat 1 tbsp. butter in a 9-inch or 10-inch frying pan. Pour half of mixture into pan; cook over low heat 3 to 5 minutes or until bubbles appear on the surface. Spoon 1 cup of berries over top.

Cover handle of frying pan with foil; place under hot broiler until pancake is puffed and golden brown, about 2 to 3 minutes. Remove from pan and keep warm. Repeat with remaining mixture. Sprinkle pancakes with icing sugar and serve in wedges.

Makes 2 pancakes, 2 to 4 servings. Accompany with maple syrup

Courtesy of The Ontario Milk Marketing Board

Blueberry Sauce

Superb on pancakes, waffles, ice cream, or yogurt.

2 cups blueberries
¼ to ½ cup honey
¼ cup water
1 tsp. lemon juice
pinch of cinnamon *or* ground allspice
1 cup additional blueberries (optional)

Place all ingredients in a heavy saucepan. Stir and cook over low heat until blueberries are tender. Cool slightly. Purée in a blender until sauce is very smooth. Store in refrigerator. One additional cup of whole blueberries may be added to the sauce before serving. Serve warm or at room temperature over pancakes, waffles, ice cream, or plain yogurt.

Hot Apple Topping

Great on pancakes or on gingerbread.

6 large apples, preferably cooking
¼ cup water *or* apple juice
¼ cup raisins (optional)
⅓ cup firmly-packed brown sugar
1 tsp. cinnamon

Peel apples, core, and cut in half. Slice each half into eighths. Place apples, along with raisins, sugar, water, and cinnamon, into a heavy-bottomed saucepan. Cover and simmer gently for about 20 minutes until apples are soft but not really broken up. If topping is too thick, add a little water. Serve warm over pancakes or gingerbread. Topping may be made in advance and reheated at serving time.

Date Butter

Wonderful spread on whole-wheat toast!

²/₃ **cup whole dates**
¹/₄ **cup water**
¹/₂ **tsp. fresh lemon juice**
pinch of salt
¹/₂ **cup soft butter**

Cut dates with scissors. (If dates are very sticky, dip scissors into hot water.) Into a small heavy pot place dates, water, lemon juice, and salt. Cook uncovered over medium heat, stirring occasionally, until mixture is thick and dates are very soft and mushy. Allow to cool. Whip butter with electric mixer until light and fluffy. Gradually beat in date mixture. Store covered in the refrigerator. Allow to come to room temperature before serving.

Shirley Pommier, Sudbury, Ont

Molasses Butter

Pioneers sometimes extended their butter this way. It is delicious on whole-wheat toast.

1 cup molasses
3 to 4 tbsp. unsalted butter
¹/₄ **tsp. nutmeg**
pinch of baking soda
pinch of salt
2 eggs, well beaten

Use blackstrap molasses if you like it; otherwise use Barbados molasses, which is next in line as far as nutrition goes.

In a heavy pot, combine molasses, butter, nutmeg, soda, and salt. Bring to a boil while stirring over low heat. Gradually stir half of hot mixture into well-beaten eggs. Return egg mixture to pot. Cook and stir till thick, about 1 minute. Chill.

Makes 1¹/₂ cups.

Apple or Peach Butter

Spread on homemade bread or toast, or generously on pancakes.

apples *or* **peaches**
apple cider *or* **juice for apple butter**
orange juice for peach butter
honey (very little because the fruit is naturally sweet)
cinnamon
pinch of ginger, cloves, *and/or* **allspice**

Core unpeeled apples, or peel and pit peaches, and cut into pieces. Place in a heavy-bottomed saucepan with just enough apple cider or orange juice to cover the bottom of the pan. Cover and cook over low heat, stirring occasionally, until fruit is very tender. Press fruit through a sieve or food mill and return purée to saucepan. Add honey, cinnamon, and other spices to taste. Cook over low heat, uncovered, until very thick. Stir often to prevent scorching.

Pour hot apple or peach butter into hot sterilized jars, or cool and pour into small containers and freeze.

Prune Jam

A little different, but very good!

2 cups pitted prunes
4 cups water
1 small orange
2 cups white sugar
$^{1}/_{2}$ tsp. salt

Place prunes in a heavy saucepan. Add 3 cups water. Cover and bring to the boil. Boil 15 minutes. Drain, reserving liquid.

Put whole orange through fine blade of food chopper. Add to 1 cup water in small saucepan. Boil 10 minutes. Meanwhile put drained prunes through coarse blade of food chopper.

Combine orange, prunes, and reserved liquid in heavy pot. Boil, uncovered, 15 minutes or until jam is thick. Stir occasionally to prevent sticking and scorching.

Makes about 2$^{1}/_{2}$ cups.

Carrot Marmalade

This beautiful, richly-coloured marmalade is excellent on sourdough bread or toast.

16 to 18 carrots
2 lemons
1 orange
6 cups white sugar
chopped almonds (optional)

Peel carrots and grate coarsely. Cut up lemons and orange, discard seeds, and put peel and pulp through fine blade of food chopper.

Combine ingredients in a heavy-bottomed saucepan and stir over medium heat until sugar is dissolved. Cook over low heat about 40 minutes. Add a tablespoon of orange juice or water after 20 minutes or so, if it seems too thick. Chopped almonds, an interesting addition, could be included at this point.

Pour into hot sterilized jars, or cool and freeze in small containers.

Spiced Banana Jam

An interesting new taste for toast! Team it with peanut butter for the classic sandwich.

3 cups white sugar
²/₃ cup water
10 ripe bananas
2 tbsp. ascorbic acid (from drugstore)
¹/₄ tsp. cinnamon
pinch of freshly-grated nutmeg

Combine sugar and water in a heavy-bottomed saucepan. Boil uncovered for 10 minutes, stirring frequently. Chop bananas and add to syrup in saucepan. Stir in ascorbic acid. Simmer, uncovered, for 20 minutes, stirring occasionally. Stir in cinnamon and nutmeg; simmer 10 to 15 minutes longer. Cool slightly and spoon into sterilized jars. Store in refrigerator.

Overnight Breakfast Sandwich Casserole

A hearty, filling breakfast, easily put together the night before. In the morning, all you have to do is get up and pop it in the oven; then you can go back to bed for an hour or so. (Don't forget to reset your alarm!) This is an excellent dish for an informal brunch.

½ lb. lean bacon *or* cooked ham
12 to 16 slices whole-wheat bread (depending on size of loaf)
4 eggs
¼ tsp. salt
⅛ tsp. pepper
½ tsp. dry mustard
2 cups milk (2% or skim)
1½ cups grated old Cheddar *or* Swiss cheese
1½ cups crushed breakfast cereal flakes (unsweetened variety)
¼ cup butter, melted

If using bacon, cook until crispy and drain well on paper towels. Cut bacon or ham into bite-sized pieces.

Grease a 9 x 13-inch low glass baking dish. Cut crusts off bread. Place 6 to 8 slices of bread on bottom of baking dish. Cover with a layer of bacon or ham, then cheese. Top with another layer of bread slices.

Beat eggs until foamy. Beat in milk and seasonings. Pour evenly over top of casserole. Cover and place in refrigerator overnight.

In the morning, uncover, sprinkle cereal flakes over top, and drizzle melted butter evenly over all. Bake in 350°F oven for 1 to 1½ hours, until set, bubbly, and browned on top. Let stand 5 to 10 minutes before cutting into squares to serve.

Makes 6 to 8 hearty servings.

Variation: If serving as a brunch dish, a layer of cooked green peas, thinly sliced dill pickles, sautéed sliced mushrooms, or chopped green onion and green pepper could be added.

Drinks

Tomato-Vegetable Juice

Easy to make; more flavourful and less expensive than commercial tomato or vegetable juice.

16 large ripe tomatoes
1¹/₂ cups finely chopped vegetables such as carrots, celery, onions, zucchini, *or* potatoes
¹/₂ tsp. salt
2 tbsp. fresh lemon juice
1 tsp. Worcestershire sauce
dash of Tabasco sauce
pinch of any spice you like, such as basil, marjoram, thyme, *or* dill weed
celery sticks, for garnish

Peel and chop tomatoes. Combine all vegetables and seasonings in a heavy saucepan. Bring to a boil, lower heat slightly, and simmer until vegetables are *very* tender. Put through a food mill, or purée in a blender or food processor. Stir well and refrigerate purée. Add water to thin to desired consistency. Serve garnished with a stick of celery.

Old-Fashioned Lemonade

juice of 6 lemons (1 cup)
³/₄ cup white sugar, or to taste
4 cups cold water
1 whole lemon
ice cubes

Wash whole lemon and slice thinly. In a large jug, combine lemon juice and sugar. Stir to dissolve sugar. Add remaining ingredients and mix well.

Makes 6 cups. Add a sprig of mint for a festive look!

Lemon Syrup Concentrate

An old family recipe. Very economical and really thirst-quenching after running. Susan should know! She is a five-time Canadian orienteering champion and a member of Canada's team to the World Championships from 1976 to 1983. Susan's mom drinks "hot lemon" in place of tea or coffee, and always takes a thermos of it for after her cross-country ski races and cold-weather orienteering events.

6 lemons
4 oranges
1 oz. tartaric acid (from drugstore)
2 oz. citric acid (from drugstore)
8 cups white sugar
8 cups boiling water

Squeeze lemons and oranges and set juice aside. Grate rind. Add sugar, acids, and water. Stir until dissolved. When cool, add juice of lemons and oranges. Let stand 24 hours in a non-metal bowl or enamelled pot. Strain and store in sterilized bottles. Keeps for months in the refrigerator. Add a small quantity to a glass of cold water. Stir and add ice. May also be added to hot water to make a hot drink for winter. Add a slice of lemon or orange or a sprig of mint for garnish.

Susan Budge, Waterloo, Ont

Old-Fashioned Raspberry Vinegar

This is a delicious raspberry syrup that does not taste like vinegar at all. The recipe comes from my great-grandmother. It makes an unbelievably great drink, especially for after orienteering!

3 qts. raspberries
1 qt. white vinegar
sugar

Put raspberries in a non-metal bowl. Pour vinegar over berries and let sit 24 hours. Press through a fine sieve to remove seeds. Add 1 cup of sugar for each cup of purée. Place in a large pot and simmer 15 to 20 minutes. Skim the surface and put the remaining liquid in sterilized bottles. Store in refrigerator.

Raspberry vinegar keeps for months. I've kept some for a year. To serve, add 1 to 2 tbsp. to a glass of water, soda water, or mineral water. May also be added to a cup of hot water for a warm drink.

Susan Budge, Waterloo, Ont

Swedish Saft

My Swedish friend, Anna Lena Tynong, and her family prepare this delicious berry syrup every summer to take to orienteering meets, including the famous Swedish *5-Day O-Ringen*, where up to 25,000 orienteers compete each day for a 5-day total time. *O'Ringen* is said to be the largest sporting event in the world!

1.5 l berries
1.5 l boiling water
2 kg sugar
20 g tartaric acid (from drugstore)

Put berries in a bowl and pour boiling water over them. Stir in tartaric acid. Let stand 24 hours. Strain through cheese cloth. Add sugar and bring to a boil. Cool and bottle. Serve 1 part syrup to 5 parts warm or cold water.

Susan Budge, Waterloo, Ont

Hot Fruit Drink

The Laurentian University cross-country ski team drinks copious amounts of this mixture! For ten or twelve thirsty ski racers, triple this recipe.

1 64-oz. jar cranberry cocktail juice
1 48-oz. can apple juice
1 48-oz. can pineapple juice
1 cup orange juice
$^1/_2$ cup lemon juice
$^1/_4$ cup sugar (optional)
2 6-inch cinnamon sticks
1 tbsp. whole cloves
1 tbsp. whole allspice

Place whole cloves and allspice in a tea ball or spice bag, or tie them in several layers of cheese cloth. Pour juices into a very large pot and add cinammon sticks and sugar, as well as the cloves and allspice. Stir to dissolve sugar. Heat slowly until hot but do not boil. Remove spices and serve.

Lynda Sidney, Sudbury, Ont

Hot Mulled Cider

Take along a thermos of this tasty drink for after any cold-weather activity. Or fill the house with a wonderful spicy aroma by keeping cider hot all day in an electric slow cooker! Cold snowy arrivals will really appreciate a mugful!

4 cups sweet apple cider (non-alcoholic)
$^1/_4$ cup brown sugar
1 cinnamon stick
2 whole cloves
2 whole allspice
$^1/_4$ tsp. cinnamon
$^1/_4$ tsp. freshly-grated nutmeg (optional)
$^1/_4$ tsp. ground ginger (optional)
$^1/_2$ lemon, thinly sliced

Combine all ingredients in a large pot. Heat slowly and stir until sugar is dissolved. Cover and simmer for 30 minutes. Serve hot in mugs. (Pottery ones seem most appropriate!)

Winter Comfort Tea

A wonderful aromatic welcome for cold-weather guests, particularly in the country or at the cottage.

4 cups cold water
1 cup sugar
2 cinnamon sticks
2 tbsp. whole cloves
4 oranges

4 lemons
1 cup unsweetened
  pineapple juice
6 cups cold water
6 tea bags

Combine 4 cups water with sugar, cloves, and cinnamon stick in a saucepan. Stir to dissolve sugar. Bring to a boil, and boil 10 minutes. Remove spices and allow to cool. Squeeze oranges and lemons and add along with pineapple juice.

Bring 6 cups water to a boil. Add tea bags and steep for *exactly* 5 minutes. Remove tea bags and add fruit juice mixture. Bring to simmer before pouring into mugs.

Currant Tea

More nutritious and tastier than the artificially-flavoured drinks usually served at orienteering meets and cross-country ski races. May be served hot or cold. Currants may be replaced with dried apricots, pineapple, peaches, or pears.

This recipe comes from *The Little Cookbook for the Great Outdoors*, of which Suat Tuzlak is co-author, and is reprinted here with the kind permission of Rocky Mountain Books, Calgary, Alberta.

0.5 kg (1 lb.) currants (dried variety)
2 l (8 cups) water
5 oranges
2 lemons
spices (cinnamon stick, clove, allspice, *and/or* nutmeg)
sweetener (honey *or* brown sugar)

Soak currants for a couple of hours, or if possible overnight. (A canning pot is good for larger quantities.) Add unpeeled lemon and orange slices, spices, and sweetener. Simmer for 15 to 30 minutes. Strain and serve hot or chilled. The currants may be eaten separately as a snack or with porridge. The above quantities serve 10.

Suat Tuzlak, Calgary, Alta

Cranberry Tea

Refreshing whether served hot or cold. Should you wish a pure cranberry drink, omit the citrus fruit juice and increase the amount of cranberries.

4 cups fresh cranberries
4 cups water
1 or 2 cinnamon sticks
2 whole allspice
4 oranges
2 lemons
³/₄ to 1 cup white sugar

Squeeze oranges and lemons and set juice aside. Place cranberries, water, allspice, and cinnamon stick(s) in a saucepan. Cook over low heat until berries are very soft. Mash and put through a sieve to remove skins. Add sugar and citrus juices to cranberry purée, stirring until sugar is dissolved. Strain again through sieve to remove any cranberry seeds. Heat and serve, or chill in refrigerator for a cold drink. Serve in glass mugs with a slice of lemon or orange and perhaps a few whole cranberries on top.

Ginger Tea

A wonderful tea anytime, but try it when you have a stuffy head cold. It is most soothing!

4 cups water
2 inches fresh ginger root
2 tsp. lemon juice
2 tsp. honey

Peel ginger root and slice thinly. Simmer water and ginger for 5 minutes. Remove ginger slices and stir in lemon juice and honey. Serve hot in mugs.

Makes 4 servings.

Chilled Orange-Mint Tea

A most refreshing summer cooler!

4 tea bags
1 cup tightly-packed mint leaves
8 cups boiling water
2 cups fresh orange juice
white sugar
mint sprigs for garnish

Place tea bags and mint leaves in a large enamelled pot. Pour boiling water over tea bags and mint and allow to steep for 5 minutes. Strain out tea bags and mint leaves. Add orange juice and sugar to taste, then stir to dissolve sugar. Chill well. To serve, fill six tall glasses with ice cubes and pour the tea over the ice. Garnish with mint springs

Buttermilk-Fruit Frappé

Almost any fruit will be good. Try some interesting combinations.

$^1/_2$ cup buttermilk
$^1/_2$ cup cut-up fruit *or* berries of your choice
1 to 2 tsp. liquid honey
pinch of nutmeg
2 ice cubes, crushed

Blend all ingredients in a blender or food processor. Pour into a glass and enjoy!

Eggnog

2 eggs
4 tbsp. sugar
1 tsp. pure vanilla extract
2 cups cold milk

Beat all ingredients together thoroughly in a deep bowl. Pour into glasses. Sprinkle with nutmeg or cinnamon.

Barb Pearson, Hamilton, Ont

Bunny's Milk

Good for the little folk! The colour is attractive and, believe it or not, the drink has a slight coconut flavour.

1 cup milk
2 medium carrots

Scrub carrots and cut into small pieces. Place carrots and milk in a food processor or blender and process until liquified. Strain through a clean tea towel for a smoother drink.

Cocoa (with Optional Mocha Flavour)

A simple way to make this all-time classic tummy warmer! A basic chocolate syrup is prepared and added to warm milk. A little instant coffee gives the mocha flavour.

1 cup cocoa powder
2 cups white sugar
pinch of salt
$^1\!/_2$ tsp. cinnamon
2 cups boiling water
2 tsp. pure vanilla extract
milk
instant coffee (optional)

To make syrup, blend in a medium pot sugar, cocoa, salt, and cinnamon. With a wire whisk, beat in boiling water. Bring to a boil over high heat. Reduce heat and allow syrup to simmer for 10 minutes, stirring frequently. Remove from heat. When cool, stir in vanilla. Pour into a sterilized bottle that will hold the 3 cups of syrup. Store in refrigerator for future use.

To serve, add 1 to 2 tbsp. of syrup to a mug of hot milk and stir. For a mocha flavour, add $^1\!/_2$ tsp. instant coffee. Stir well. Add a cinnamon stick and perhaps a few gratings of orange peel.

Choco-Peanut Sipper

Good on a cold night!

2 cups skim *or* whole milk
2 tbsp. smooth peanut butter
2 tbsp. chocolate syrup

Combine all ingredients in a blender and whirl until smooth.
Heat *just* to boiling point in a saucepan, stirring occasionally.

Makes 4 mugfuls.

Lynda Sidney, Sudbury, Ont

Gluhwein

This is a favourite after-orienteering hot drink of the Guelph
Gators Orienteering Club.

500 ml red wine
250 ml water
1 cinnamon stick
4 whole cloves
3 tbsp. honey
1 orange *or* lemon slice

Insert cloves into fruit slice. Make a syrup by combining water
and honey. Add fruit slice and cinnamon stick. Heat syrup
without letting it boil, then add wine and gently heat again.
Serve in mugs; glass ones are nice if you have them!

Mulled Golden Wine

Excellent to serve when entertaining *après-ski!*

1 48-oz. can unsweetened pineapple juice
1½ cups Moselle *or* other medium dry white wine
⅛ tsp. ground cloves
⅛ tsp. ground allspice
dash of salt
1 tbsp. granulated sugar (optional)

Combine all ingredients and heat slowly to just below the boiling
point. Serve hot in mugs.

Summertime Sangria

Traditional Sangria is made with red wine, but this version with white wine is light and refreshing. Add whatever fresh fruits are in season and you have available. Other fruit juice may be substituted for the cranapple juice.

2 cups white wine
1 cup cranapple juice
1 cup soda water
2 whole cloves
piece of cinnamon stick
1 cup diced *or* **sliced fresh fruit**
1 orange *or* **lemon, sliced**

Combine wine, cranapple juice, cloves, cinnamon stick, and fruit in a large glass jug. Refrigerate for several hours. At serving time add chilled soda water. Pour into large-diameter glasses, allowing some of the fruit to be poured in as well. (Spoon some fruit in if necessary.) Serve with a small teaspoon in each glass for enjoying the fruit!

Light Lunches & Snacks

Liver Pâté

Another recipe for people who think they hate liver! This comes from my sister-in-law, Ruth McNally. While not a true pâté, it is easy to prepare.

1 lb. beef liver
1 large carrot
1 large onion
1 tbsp. vegetable oil
$^1/_2$ to 1 clove garlic
$^1/_2$ to 1 tsp. salt
freshly-ground black pepper
$^1/_4$ tsp. ground sage *or* savory
1 tbsp. dry sherry (optional)
3 tbsp. butter (at room temperature)
$^1/_3$ cup skim milk powder
fresh parsley, chopped

Trim off membranes and slice liver into strips. This is best accomplished when liver is almost frozen. Thinly slice carrot and onion. Heat oil in a large skillet, add carrot, and sauté over medium heat for 5 minutes. Add onion and sauté until soft. Reduce heat. Place liver strips on top of vegetables, cover pan, and cook about 10 minutes, until liver is cooked through. Grind liver, vegetables, and garlic in a food chopper, then add seasonings. Stir butter and milk powder into mixture. Add sherry. Mix thoroughly. Form into a ball or fill a small crock and chill. Sprinkle parsley on top at serving time. Serve with rye bread.

Ann Budge, Belfountain, Ont

Cheese Snack Spread

A bagel, sliced thinly, is an interesting substitute for crackers and is excellent with this spread. The bagel slices may be lightly toasted.

1 cup grated old Cheddar cheese
1 hard-cooked egg
½ green pepper
1 medium-sized dill pickle
½ small onion
salt and pepper
2 tbsp. mayonnaise

Remove cheese from refrigerator, grate it finely, and allow it to come to room temperature. Chop egg finely. Mince onion, green pepper, and dill pickle. Combine cheese, egg, vegetables, salt, and pepper. Stir in about 2 tbps. mayonnaise to moisten. Spoon into a crock or small pottery bowl. Spread on thin slices of bagel or crackers.

Scottish Baloney

Also called poloni or polony, both of which are slang for bologna! This roll is a little bland-looking, but recently won the stamp of approval of the University of Waterloo Cross-Country Ski Team when they were served it with homemade crackers and French bread. I should add that they were starving, having been stranded for six hours in a snow storm returning from the Muskoka Cross-Country Ski Loppet!

1½ lb. lean ground beef
1 large onion
½ tsp. sage *or* savory (more if desired)
½ tsp. thyme (more if desired)
salt and pepper
2 eggs, lightly beaten
1½ cups bread-crumbs

Chop onions finely. Mix all ingredients as if preparing a meat loaf. Shape into 1 or 2 rolls about 1½-inches in diameter. Wrap each tightly in a piece of white cotton and tie the ends with string as a sausage. Simmer in a large pot for 1½ hours in enough water to cover. Chill; then unwrap and serve thinly sliced with crackers or French bread.

Ann Budge, Belfountain, Ont

Avocado Dip

A dip that everyone always likes.

1 large ripe avocado
1 4-oz. package cream cheese, at room temperature
1 tbsp. mayonnaise
1 tbsp. lemon juice
salt and pepper
1 tsp. grated onion
milk (optional)

Cut avocado in half, remove stone, and spoon out fruit into a bowl. Add softened cream cheese and mayonnaise. Beat together well.

Add lemon juice, salt, pepper, and onion. Mix well. Add a little milk if necessary to make a smoother consistency. Refrigerate in several small crocks or bowls. Great with crackers or fresh cut-up vegetables!

Bruce Rennie, Vancouver, BC

Guacamole

An avocado dip that is traditionally served with corn chips or corn crackers.

1 very ripe but not over-ripe avocado
1 small tomato
1 small onion
1 clove garlic, minced
1 tbsp. lemon juice
¼ tsp. salt
freshly-ground black pepper

Mash avocado. Chop onion finely. Peel, seed, and chop tomato.

Combine all ingredients in blender or food processor and blend until smooth, adding additional lemon juice if necessary to thin mixture. Serve at room temperature or chilled with corn chips or corn crackers.

Tofu Dip

A nutritious dip for fresh cut-up vegetables.

1 cube of tofu
1½ tbsp. cider vinegar
3 tbsp. vegetable oil
1 to 2 tbsp. Tamari sauce
dash of Tabasco sauce (optional)
garlic powder, grated cheese, minced onion, *or* fresh or dried
    herbs of your choice
milk *or* lemon juice (optional)

Blend ingredients and seasonings with electric mixer until smooth. Thin mixture with a little milk or lemon juice if necessary. Refrigerate for at least 1 hour to allow flavours to mellow. Serve with cool, crisp raw vegetables.

Hot Crunchy Crab Dip

1 6-oz. can crab meat
1 8-oz. package plain cream cheese
1 tbsp. chopped green onion tops *or* chives
1 cup finely-chopped pecans, walnuts, *or* almonds
1 tsp. horseradish (optional)

Drain crab, reserving liquid. Cream the cheese, crab meat, and enough crab liquid to make creaming easy. Add horseradish, onions, and ¾ cup nuts. Combine thoroughly. Age in the fridge for 3 hours. Sprinkle ¼ cup nuts on top and bake in a small, shallow oven-proof dish such as a French onion soup bowl for 15 minutes at 350°F. Serve with crackers or fresh vegetables cut for dipping.

Lee Wisener, Eden Mills, Ont

Calorie-Counter's Dip

Serve this dip with raw, crispy vegetables.

2 cups plain low-fat yogurt
4 oz. Roquefort or other blue cheese
1 tsp. Worcestershire sauce
1 tbsp. minced chives
1/8 tsp. pepper

Crumble cheese and combine with the other ingredients by beating with an electric mixer. Chill before serving.

Lemon Yogurt Dip for Fruit

This tangy dip for fresh fruit is nice to serve in the summertime.

1 cup cottage cheese
1 cup lemon-flavoured yogurt *or* **other flavour if lemon is not**
   available
1/3 cup chopped almonds *or* **cashews**
2 tsp. grated lemon peel

Lightly toast nuts. With an electric mixer, beat cottage cheese until smooth. Stir in yogurt, nuts, and lemon peel. Cover and refrigerate 1 to 2 hours for flavours to blend. Serve with banana, melon, or pineapple spears; or strawberries, grapes, apple wedges, or kiwi wheels.

Tasty Sunflower Seeds

1 lb. raw, unsalted, hulled sunflower seeds
2 tbsp. margarine
2 tbsp. grated Parmesan cheese
2 tbsp. soy sauce (I prefer the less salty Indonesian type to the
   usual Chinese type. It is found in specialty shops or Dutch
   stores.)

Combine margarine, cheese, and soy sauce. Add to sunflower seeds in a large bowl. Mix well and spread on a cookie sheet. Bake at 350 to 375°F for 15 minutes.

Gloria Charlow, Montreal, Qué

Nuts 'n' Bolts

An old standby!

1 525-g pkg. Shreddies®
1 300-g pkg. Cheerios®
1 pkg. very thin pretzels
1 lb. cashews (Use soynuts if you are on a budget.)
1 lb. unsalted peanuts
1/2 to 2/3 lb. butter *or* margarine
1/4 cup Worcestershire sauce
1 tbsp. garlic salt
1 tbsp. celery salt

Mix cereals and nuts in a large roasting pan. Melt butter over low heat, then add Worcestershire sauce and seasonings. Pour butter mixture over contents of roasting pan. Stir well to mix thoroughly. Bake in 250°F oven for 2 hours, stirring frequently. Cool, then store in airtight jars.

Popcorn au Parmesan

Curl up in your favourite chair with a book and a bowl of popcorn to rest your weary but well-stretched muscles!

10 cups popped popcorn (unsalted)
3 tbsp. unsalted butter
1/2 tsp. fresh lemon juice
1/2 cup freshly-grated Parmesan cheese
salt (optional)

Melt butter in a tiny pot. Stir in lemon juice and remove from heat. Place popcorn in a large roasting pan. Drizzle the butter mixture over popcorn; stir and toss well. Bake in a 300°F oven until crispy and very hot, stirring a couple of times. Remove from oven and sprinkle with cheese and possibly a little salt. Toss well.

Variation: A dried herb of your choice could be sprinkled on at the same time as the cheese. Try oregano for pizza-flavoured popcorn!

Shreddies® is a registered trademark of Nabisco Brands Ltd.
Cheerios® is a registered trademark of General Mills Canada, Inc.

Crispy Potato Skins

A very popular snack, especially with the younger generations. There's an abundance of nutrients just under the skins of potatoes!

6 medium baking potatoes
3 tbsp. freshly-grated Parmesan, Swiss, *or* Cheddar cheese
1 clove garlic
1 tbsp. sesame seeds
1 tbsp. chopped chives *or* green onion tops
2 tsp. chopped parsley
1 tsp. paprika
¹/₂ tsp. celery seeds
¹/₄ tsp. *each* salt and pepper
¹/₃ cup vegetable oil

Scrub potatoes with a brush, dry them, prick once with a fork, and place in a hot oven (425°F). Bake potatoes until tender, 40 to 50 minutes.

In a small bowl put the following ingredients: 1 tbsp. Parmesan cheese, minced garlic clove, sesame seeds, chives or green onions, parsley, paprika, celery seeds, salt, and pepper. Mash and combine well with a fork to form paste. Add vegetable oil and combine thoroughly.

When potatoes are cool enough to handle, cut in half lengthwise, and then each piece in half again crosswise. Carefully scoop out most of the potato, but leave a thin layer attached to each skin. (Save the scooped-out potato for potato patties or hash-browns.) Once again cut each piece of potato in half. Place skins skin-side-down on a lightly-greased baking sheet. Brush inside of each skin generously with the cheese, spice, and oil mixture.

Bake at 350°F for 15 minutes or until skins are crispy. Sprinkle with the additional 2 tbsp. of Parmesan cheese and cook another 5 to 10 minutes until skins are lightly browned.

Serve as a finger food. Some people serve sour cream to dip skins into, but this is not necessary; they are delicious just as they are.

Makes 48 skins.

Banana-Orange Yogurt Popsicles

These popsicles are a refreshing, nutritious substitute for the commercial ones. About 55 calories each.

2 large bananas, mashed
2 to 3 tbsp. liquid honey
1 tbsp. fresh lemon juice
2 cups plain skim milk yogurt
1 cup fresh orange juice

In a large bowl, combine bananas, honey, and lemon juice. Add yogurt and orange juice, beating until blended and smooth. Spoon into small paper cups or moulds. Cover with foil. Freeze until mixture is slushy, about 1 hour. Insert a wooden stick through the foil into the centre of each cup. Freeze until firm, about 2 hours. To unmould at serving time, dip cup quickly into a bowl of hot water.

Makes 12 popsicles.

Apple Wheels

A favourite snack or dessert for children.

8 medium apples, unpeeled
¹/₂ cup semi-sweet pure chocolate chips
¹/₂ cup smooth peanut butter
¹/₄ cup raisins, chopped
1 tbsp.liquid honey

Remove from each apple a core about 1¹/₄-inch in diameter. Crush chocolate chips quickly in a blender or food processor. In a bowl mix chocolate, peanut butter, raisins, and honey. Stuff hole in apples with mixture. Wrap each apple tightly in plastic wrap. Refrigerate for at least an hour. At serving time, slice apples into ¹/₂-inch-thick "wheels."

Frozen Fruit Snacks

This dessert, popular with young children, is welcomed by everyone when a refreshing snack is called for.

thick slices of banana
wedges of apple
liquid honey
finely chopped pecans *or* **almonds**

Dip pieces of fruit into honey, then roll in nuts. Place on a tray in the freezer and freeze until firm, about 2 hours. Eat while frozen for a hot-weather snack.

Apple-Cheese Dreams

This new version of an old favourite makes a good light lunch, especially for children.

2 apples
1 tbsp. unsalted butter
1 tsp. fresh lemon juice
1 cup grated medium Cheddar cheese
freshly-ground black pepper
8 slices whole-wheat bread, toasted

Peel apples and slice thinly. Heat butter in a small pot and stir in lemon juice and apple slices. Cook over medium heat until apples are barely soft. Turn heat to low. Add cheese and pepper, then stir just enough to mix. Heat over low heat until cheese melts. Spread on toast. Broil 3 inches from heat until brown. These may be prepared in advance, covered, and refrigerated, then broiled just before serving.

Makes 8.

Swiss-and-English Muffins

1 7-oz. can tuna fish
1 cup finely-grated Swiss cheese
$^1\!/_2$ cup mayonnaise
1 tbsp. fresh lemon juice

$^1\!/_4$ tsp. Worcestershire sauce
3 drops Tabasco sauce
6 English muffins

Split muffins, toast lightly, and set aside.

Drain and flake tuna. Mix tuna and cheese. Combine mayonnaise with lemon juice, Worcestershire sauce, and Tabasco sauce; then stir into tuna-cheese mixture. Spread on muffins. Place on cookie sheet. Broil until cheese is melted.

Barb Pearson, Hamilton, Ont

Ham-Pineapple Mini-Pizzas

A quick-and-easy lunch or late-night snack. These may be put together in advance.

English muffins
mustard *or* cream cheese
pineapple juice and cinnamon if cream cheese is used
thin slices of cooked ham
pineapple rings, drained
Mozzarella cheese, sliced *or* grated

Add a little cinnamon to cream cheese and thin with a little pineapple juice. Halve the English muffins and spread with mustard or cream cheese. Next comes a slice of ham, then a pineapple ring. Top it off with the sliced or grated cheese. At this point the mini-pizza may be covered and refrigerated. At serving time, uncover and broil until bubbly.

Lee's Sandwich Spread

Tahini and miso are available at most natural food stores. Miso is also obtainable at Oriental food stores.

tahini (sesame seed butter)
miso paste (soybean paste)
lemon juice

Combine equal parts of tahini and miso paste. Add a squirt of lemon juice, to taste. Spread on hearty bread of your choice!

Variation: Add lightly-toasted sunflower seeds for more crunch!

Lee Wisener, Eden Mills, Ont

278

Soft Pretzels

Soft pretzels have become a popular snack. They are easy to make. The process is similar to that for making bagels. These are not nearly as salty as the commercial ones.

1 envelope active dry yeast
¼ cup warm water (110°F)
1 tsp. white sugar
2½ to 3 cups all-purpose flour
1 tsp. salt
¾ cup warm water (110°F)
1½ to 2 quarts boiling water
¼ cup baking soda
1 egg white
poppy seeds *or* sesame seeds

Dissolve 1 teaspoon sugar in ¼ cup warm water. Sprinkle yeast over top and allow to stand 10 minutes. When foamy, stir yeast and add remaining ¾ cup warm water.

Place 2½ cups flour in a large bowl and mix in salt. Mix yeast and water into flour. If dough is too sticky, add additional flour until it is firm yet elastic and can be handled easily. Knead on a floured surface for 7 or 8 minutes.

Allow dough to sit 10 minutes. Cut into 12 equal pieces. Roll each into a rope 18 to 22 inches long. Shape into a pretzel. Place on a well-greased cookie sheet and let rise 30 minutes.

Bring 1½ to 2 quarts water and baking soda to a boil in a large pot (*not* an aluminum pot). Water should be 3 to 4 inches deep. Carefully drop in one pretzel at a time and cook for 30 seconds, turn, and cook 30 seconds on the other side. Pretzel should be slightly puffed. Remove with a slotted spoon, drain well, and place on a greased cookie sheet.

Beat egg white slightly and brush top of pretzels. Sprinkle lightly with poppy seeds or toasted sesame seeds. Bake at 375°F for 20 to 25 minutes until golden.

Makes 12 large pretzels.

Sesame-Oat Crackers

Homemade crackers are truly a delightful treat. There's just no comparison with bought ones! This recipe makes about 5 dozen crackers.

1 cup rolled oats
2 tbsp. sesame seeds
1½ cups all-purpose flour
2 tsp. baking powder
¼ tsp. salt
1 tsp. white sugar
½ cup butter
1 egg
½ cup milk

In a large bowl, stir together oats, sesame seeds, flour, baking powder, salt, and sugar. Melt butter over low heat, then place in a small bowl. Add egg and milk, then beat gently. Stir liquid ingredients into dry ones, mixing well to form a dough.

Lightly flour a baking board or counter top and a rolling pin. Divide dough into 2 or 3 portions. Roll one portion at a time to ⅛-inch to ¼-inch thickness. Cut into squares with a sharp knife or a pastry-cutting wheel, or cut into rounds with a floured 2-inch cookie cutter. Lightly grease baking sheets and place crackers on them. Bake at 400°F for 10 to 15 minutes or until crackers have browned lightly. Remove from oven and allow to cool completely. Store in airtight containers. Crackers may be crisped by heating briefly in a hot oven.

Trail Foods

Expedition Bread

This recipe comes to us from the Bruce Trail Association. They found it in a newsletter of the Federation of Ontario Hiking Trails Association.

The recipe was devised for an expedition up Mt. Logan. It is supposed to sustain two people for sixteen days; a two-inch square will sustain a person for a day. The recipe may be halved or quartered.

4 cups water
16 cups whole-wheat flour
3½ cups firmly-packed raw *or* brown sugar
1½ cups skim milk powder
2 tbsp. baking powder
2 tbsp. salt
1¼ cups vegetable oil
1 cup sesame seeds
2 cups honey
1½ cups wheat germ
1 cup blackstrap molasses

Beginning with liquids, mix all ingredients well in a huge bowl. Then pour into a large roasting pan, pressing it to fit the pan. Bake in a 300°F oven for about 1 hour or until a knife comes out clean. Cut into squares and air-dry until semi-dry. Then wrap tightly in foil or heavy plastic wrap. Bread may be stored in a metal tin for 6 months or frozen for a longer period.

Dried Fruit Bars

A quick trail snack that does not require baking. This recipe comes courtesy of *Cross-Country Skiing on the Bruce Trail,* a little booklet published by the Bruce Trail Association.

1 lb. dried apricots
$^{1}/_{2}$ lb. dried figs
$^{1}/_{2}$ lb. pitted dates
1 tbsp. grated orange rind
$^{1}/_{2}$ lb. currants
2 cups chopped nuts
$^{1}/_{2}$ cup unsweetened shredded coconut

Put apricots, figs, and dates through a food chopper (*not* a blender). Add remaining ingredients and mix well. Press into a greased 9 x 13-inch baking dish or a smaller one if you wish thicker squares. Chill several hours before cutting into bars. Wrap individually and place in your pack.

Bannock Bread

A traditional backpacker's bread. Can be prepared on a small backpacking stove or over an open fire.

4 cups all-purpose flour
6 tbsp. sugar
1 tsp. salt
4 tsp. baking powder
$^{1}/_{4}$ cup instant skim milk powder
$^{1}/_{3}$ cup shortening
water

Measure and package flour, sugar, salt, baking powder, and milk powder. Package shortening separately.

When ready to cook, cream shortening and dry ingredients with a fork. Gradually stir in water until dough has no dry spots but is not soggy. Press into a round cake about 1 inch thick and lay in a *hot*, greased skillet. Cook until bottom is brown, then turn and cook the other side. If an open fire is used, tip the skillet and let the direct heat warm and brown the top when the second side is browned. Delicious with butter, honey, jam, or whatever you fancy!

Variation: Grated cheese could be added to the batter.

Skiers' Pancakes

These are filling and delicious on the ski trail. They don't require any utensils except a frying pan — use it to melt the snow.

1 cup pancake mix of a variety that requires only water to be added
¹/₂ tsp. cinnamon
¹/₄ tsp. nutmeg
¹/₂ cup chopped dried apples, dates, *or* apricots
¹/₃ cup raisins *or* currants
¹/₃ cup finely-chopped nuts

Mix pancake mix, spices, fruits, and nuts in a strong plastic bag. Tie bag securely. Fill a small plastic bottle with a little vegetable oil for the frying pan.

When fire or cook stove is ready, add 1¹/₂ cups water (clean snow melted) to the plastic bag and mix lightly. Grease frying pan and drop large globs of batter onto the hot pan. Turn when first side is browned and brown the second side, cooking until pancake is cooked through.

Spread cooked pancakes with honey or jam (from squeeze tubes), roll up, and enjoy!

Shreddies® Trail Mix

3 cups Shreddies®
1 cup salted peanuts
1 cup (175-g pkg.) semi-sweet Chocolate Chipits®
1 cup shredded coconut
1 cup raisins
1 cup banana chips (optional)

Combine all ingredients and toss well. Store in an airtight container. Serve as a snack or pack small bags of mixture for lunches or picnics.

Makes 8 cups.

Courtesy of Nabisco Brands Ltd

Shreddies® and Chipits® are registered trademarks of Nabisco Brands Ltd.

Hot Blueberry Tea

These are recipes for the traditional warm drink called "Blueberry Soup" that is served on the cross-country ski trails of Scandinavia. It awaits finishers of the 55-km American Birkebeiner Ski Race of the World Loppet Series. The thought of it makes a skier push on! Multiply the ingredients according to the number you have to satisfy.

Recipe I

1 cup blueberries, frozen, fresh *or* canned, drained
3 cups water
1 cup sugar
**1 or 2 tbsp. cornstarch (vary according to how thick or thin you
    wish the tea to be)**

Purée blueberries in a blender. Bring blueberries, water, and sugar to the boiling point in a saucepan. Add cornstarch that has been mixed with 2 to 3 tbsp. water. Cook, stirring, until mixture has thickened a little. Serve warm.

Makes 3 servings.

Recipe II

1 cup blueberries, frozen, fresh *or* canned, drained
2 cups water
$^2/_3$ cup instant mashed potatoes
$^1/_2$ cup sugar

Bring water to the boil and stir in potatoes. Add blueberries and sugar. Stir well, heat through, and serve.

Makes 3 servings

Acknowledgements

The author is grateful to the following publications for permission to use or adapt their recipes:

The Athlete's Kitchen by Nancy Clark (Englewood Cliffs, N.J., Prentice-Hall, 1981) for **Egg Drop Soup** and **Egg and Potato Supper**

The Best of the Farmhouse Kitchen by Betty Aldridge (Tottenham, Ont., 1984) for **Country Vegetable Casserole**

Caledon Citizen (Simcoe-York Printing and Publishing, Beeton, Ont.) for **Herbed Meat and Spinach Loaf**

Canadian Living Everyday Cookbook Special (Toronto, TV Guide, 1982) for **Triple-Cheese Macaroni**

Canadian Living Harvest-Time Cookbook Special (Toronto, Telemedia Publishing, 1984) for **Cabbage Pie**

Cornel Bread Book by Jeanette and Clive McCay (Mineola, N.Y., Dover, 1980) for **Cornell Triple Rich Mixture**

Cross-Country Skiing on the Bruce Trail (Bruce Trail Association, Burlington, Ont., 1981) for **Dried Fruit Bars**

The Little Cookbook for the Great Outdoors by Linda Darling and Suat Tuzlak (Calgary, Rocky Mountain Books, 1984) for **Currant Tea**

The Milk Calendars (The Ontario Milk Marketing Board, Belleville, Ont.) for **Moussaka**, **Berry Puff Pancakes**, **Poached Fish Parmesan**, and **Scalloped Potatoes with Cheese and Herbs**

Ontario Salads (Foodland Ontario, Toronto, 1981) for **Overnight Macaroni Salad**

Original Canadian Cookbook by Helen Gougeon Schull (Montreal, Tundra, 1975) for **American Beef Pot Roast**

"Recipe Exchange" by Mary McGrath, a weekly column in the *Toronto Star*, for **Friendship Cake**

Index

290